BULLETPROOF

THOMAS GRAVES

PAMPAS
PUBLISHING

This is a work of fiction. Certain real locations, events, and persons, are mentioned. All other names, characters, places, events and incidents are products of the author's imagination or are used fictitiously and are not to be construed as real. Any resemblance to actual locations, events, locales, organizations, or persons, living or dead, is entirely coincidental.

Book design by Walsh Associates, Inc.

Printed in the United States of America

ISBN 0-9771269-0-0

To order Bulletproof visit: www.pampaspublishing.com

BULLETPROOF

Latin America

1

23 June

"Damn, it's cold tonight. I'd sure like to get wheels up before my ass freezes off," David Anderson said to his fellow cargo pilot and friend August Payton.

"Stop complaining. We've only been here for two hours," Payton said as he threw his cards on the table in the La Paz, Bolivia airport hangar. "At least it's not that hot humid crap we lived through in Angola. Plus, running dope here is a cakewalk compared to that duty."

"I know, I know," grumbled Anderson as he moved closer to the space heater that warmed his feet in the 13,300 foot *altiplano*, high plain, cold air, "but I wish the civil war had never ended. Running guns for both sides was a dream. The money was great and the Cape Town vacations were awesome."

While the two U.S. military-trained pilots flew arms, money, and contraband for the Angolan government MPLA party and opposition guerrilla leader Jonas Savimbi's UNITA party, they also flew missions for the giant South African diamond concessions. Since the diamond money alone did not support their lifestyles once the Angolan civil war ended in April 2002, they moved to La Paz to fly cocaine throughout Latin America. Anderson and Payton reluctantly gave up the beautiful African coastline for land locked Bolivia, but the money was excellent, the hours were short, and they soon discovered that the *Latinas* were almost as beautiful as the South African women.

It was 8:05 P.M., and both pilots had arrived three hours earlier at the *El Alto* airport from the city of Trinidad in north-central Bolivia. Each of the silver DC-3s carried more than six hundred pounds of refined cocaine and was parked inside the cavernous hangar twenty-five yards from where they sat. Anderson and Payton killed time playing cards while they waited for final delivery instructions to the Fuerzas Armadas Revolucionarias de Colombia (FARC) narco-guerrillas in Colombia and the Sendero Luminoso narco-terrorists in Peru. As he dealt another hand, Payton looked to his left across the hangar at the two FARC and the two Sendero who would accompany each flight. The four guerrillas were visibly nervous, constantly asking when they would take off, fidgeting with their weapons, and chain smoking.

"You know," Anderson said, taking a long drag from his cigarette and slowly exhaling into the cold night air, "it's amazing how flustered these guys get with small changes in plans. One damn hiccup and they get jumpy."

"Yeah," Payton said looking up from his cards, "but I don't blame them. If it goes south, they get a bullet in the head. We just come back and make another run."

While the FARC and Sendero kept to themselves, Anderson and Payton played one last hand and then got some shut-eye. After two hours, Anderson shook Payton out of his cot.

"Dave, we got the call," Anderson said, ripping the alpaca blanket off his buddy. "Time to get moving."

"Man, I just put my head down," Payton said groggily. "What time is it?"

"Quarter past midnight. Plus, we've got a change of plans."

"Say what?" Anderson sat up and rubbed the sleep out of his eyes.

"We're not wheels up at the same time. You leave before I do, and we're supposed to reload the planes before the FARC and Sendero notice anything. They're asleep, so we've gotta hustle."

"What's going on?"

"No clue, but we have to move more than five hundred pounds from your bird to mine. Come on."

"Whatever the boss says," Anderson grumbled as he got to his feet. "We get paid the same either way."

Both aircraft were originally scheduled to depart La Paz at 5:00 A.M. with roughly equal loads. The midnight phone call changed the delivery amounts and instructed the FARC plane to depart first and the Sendero flight to follow several hours later. After transferring the cocaine, Anderson stowed his gear in the cockpit and woke up the FARC handlers who would accompany his flight. He and his Ecuadorian co-pilot walked around the aircraft to check the exterior mechanicals one last time, and Anderson gave the night operations manager a thumbs up that they were ready to go. Payton was waiting for Anderson at the stairs of the DC-3 when he came around the nose of the plane.

"Good luck, bro," Payton said and gave Anderson a high five.

"You too. Be careful and watch the air like a hawk when you cross the border. They're still out there looking for us." Andean region military and law enforcement units had recently shot down drug runners after the U.S. president voiced continued support for Colombia's anti-drug efforts.

"See you at Las Palmas soon," Payton said with a grin, referring to the Las Palmas Resort Hotel in the lowlands of Santa Cruz, Bolivia. "We'll have warm weather, some bucks, and cold beer."

"And babes, don't forget the babes," Anderson shouted as he stepped through the DC-3's door.

Anderson's drug-laden silver bird lumbered down the runway and lifted off at 1:35 A.M., headed north for Colombia. The plane gained altitude slowly, and the dark, desolate early morning altiplano horizon made his 40F cockpit feel even colder than it was. He shook off the chill as he rechecked his instruments, and the first blast of hot air from the heater was almost as welcome as a beautiful woman's soft caress. Almost, but not quite.

The aircraft had no Bolivian markings, and the flight plan showed it originating in Manaus, Brazil. If something went wrong, all paths would dead-end in Brazil. Ten minutes short of the border, Anderson's co-pilot verified his maps for the Colombian landing strip. They had put down here dozens of times before, but it never hurt to check again. The DC-3 would arrive at 7:00 A.M., unload, and return to La Paz. Anderson hoped the FARC would be at the landing strip on time as he hated waiting in a remote location with a hot load. Too many bad things could happen. He scanned the airspace for drug interdiction aircraft, but his mind was on the good time he and Payton would have in Santa Cruz with extra dollars in their pockets and willing women underneath them.

Colonel Arturo Guevara of the Colombian National Police (CNP), Colombia's primary drug fighting force, unfolded a map on the hood of his jeep, seventy yards from the remote jungle airstrip. "Captain Otero, are you and your men ready?"

"We are, sir," Otero answered. "We have positions on all four corners of the strip, and fields of fire covering the entire area. My men are concealed fifty yards down on the access road."

"Remember the rules of engagement. You don't fire unless your life is in danger. We take them alive today. Is that clear?"

"Yes, sir." Otero looked at his officers to be sure they understood.

Guevara had hoped for a break like this, but was still not convinced it was real. He would soon find out. Intelligence information on cocaine trafficking was often inconsistent and unreliable. An anonymous caller tipped the CNP that a cocaine-ferrying DC-3 would land at this remote airstrip forty-five miles inside the border. Authorities considered the call credible. Guevara had forty-eight of his best men with him, and Bogotá sent a Colombian Army Counter Narcotics Brigade (CN) to assist in the take-down. The unit commander, Captain Sebastián Ramírez, had worked with Guevara before. While Guevara's men secured the airstrip, Ramírez's would storm the plane and detain the pilots and passengers. As was customary in foreign countries, the police and army worked together on drug matters.

"Ramírez," Guevara said, "your rules of engagement are the same. Are you ready?"

"We are, colonel." The CN detachment's black fatigues and tactical body armor set them apart from the CNP regulars in green. "We will be twenty yards from the door when the plane comes to a full stop, and my snipers will shoot the pilots if they try to take off. Our intelligence tells us there are only two passengers, both in the middle of the cabin. We'll overwhelm them."

"We now communicate via secure radio, and you move only on my command," Guevara said. "Is that clear?"

"Yes sir." The officers responded in unison.

Successful ambushes meant being ready early, and everyone was in position by 6:05 A.M. As the sun broke above the tree line, vehicles approached two hundred yards away.

"We have two brown jeeps and a green truck approaching from the west," Otero called in. "You should see them within a minute."

"All units, report status," Guevara commanded.

By the time the last unit called in, the FARC reception caravan was in sight. The vehicles bounced slowly along the edge of the dirt airstrip and stopped within earshot of the CNP's concealed positions. The occupants slid out of their seats, still half asleep.

"Colonel, I count nine men, and only six are armed," Otero whispered. "Four with AKs and two with FALs."

"Can you hear what they're saying?"

"They're complaining about the soccer game last night. That's it."

"Anything else?"

"No." Ramírez watched the FARC from behind the thick jungle growth. "They put their weapons in the truck bed and aren't setting up any security. They're just waiting for the plane to get here so they can load up and move out."

"Good. Let's hope it stays that way," Guevara said.

The DC-3 rumbled over the horizon, inbound from the south. Both Colombian units held their concealment. Guevara knew the next several minutes were critical. If the pilot saw movement, he might bolt on a touch-and-go. Even after landing, he might gun the engines and make a run for it. The snipers were insurance, but were no guarantee. The DC-3 bounced and landed at the predicted time, slowed, turned, and came to a full stop less than ten yards from the FARC vehicles.

The pilot shut down the engines and the co-pilot opened the rear door. As the CNP took their weapons off safe, Guevara's squad leaders relayed hand signals to their men. The instant the stairs hit the ground, Guevara barked, "*Go! Go! Go!*" and his men swarmed their targets. Before they could react, the FARC reception team stared down the muzzles of M-4 carbines.

Ramírez and his men sprinted to the aircraft as soon as the co-pilot disappeared back into the plane. From the top step, the lead commando tossed a flash bang into the cabin to his left and turned his head to shield his eyes. He moved through the door immediately after the detonation.

The first live targets were the two FARC sitting on small crates facing each other twelve feet to the left of the door. Both held their ears reacting to the flash bang. The lead commando threw an

M-4 burst to the FARC on the right as the number two commando cut down the man on the left. Ramírez was third through the door, followed in quick succession by the other five. The fourth and fifth men swung to the right to check the rear. The last three commandos dead-checked the FARC with several head shots to make sure they would not fight another day.

Ramírez took the lead to the cockpit, his pistol in his right hand. Two operators flanked him with their carbines trained on the front of the cabin. They saw the co-pilot, on his hands and knees where the flash bang knocked him to the deck just beyond the FARC. Ramírez shot him twice in the side of the head from less than eight feet. He crumpled in a heap, and Ramírez stepped over him on his way to the front of the plane.

Raising his eyes, Ramírez saw the barrel of a pistol bearing down on him. Anderson had been around the world too many times to pilot a flight unarmed, and grabbed his gun the instant he heard the flash bang. His lone round hit Ramírez dead center on his body armor. Ramírez's number two man immediately hit Anderson with multiple M-4 rounds in the upper chest. He slumped back against the instrument panel, and Ramírez tagged him with an insurance shot through the forehead from less than two feet.

All four on the plane were dead in less than ten seconds. Ramírez immediately put a 9mm semi-automatic pistol in the co-pilot's hand. He next rounded up all personal identification while his men stuffed flight plans, logs, and notebooks into their backpacks.

Eager to interrogate the pilots and passengers, Guevara ran to the DC-3 as Ramírez and his men came out. Local drug running mules were of marginal information value, but pilots and crew knew key logistical details about the drug network's operations.

"Unfortunately there are no survivors, colonel," Ramírez said coming down the stairs. He spit on the ground disgusted.

"None? No one survived?"

"Not one. Two guerrillas and both pilots tried to fire on us. I'm sorry, colonel, but my men were in danger. We had no choice."

"I understand," Guevara said, resigning himself to the loss. "Can you help us interrogate the men we captured?"

"I would be glad to."

The CN unit had flawlessly executed an elegant plan. Ramírez knew that none of his men was in mortal danger and no one would prove him a liar. He would help with the colonel's interrogation, but the prisoners knew nothing of the overall drug-running operation. Only the men on the plane had information of substance, and they were permanently unavailable. After twenty-five minutes of interrogation, Ramírez excused himself as he reached into his backpack.

The satellite phone he pulled out was not the normal Colombian military issue. It arrived via courier from La Paz the same day $100,000 was deposited in his Uruguayan bank account. He turned the phone on, rotated the antenna skyward, confirmed a connection, dialed the La Paz number, and was connected within seconds.

"Señor, the operation is complete," Ramírez said quietly. "The crew and passengers are dead. We removed all IDs, and we will destroy everything as you instructed. The CNP believes we acted in self-defense, and I'll make sure there is no internal inquiry. Those in custody won't give any information of value."

"Well done, captain," was the business-like response. "The remaining $100,000 will be in your account within twenty-four hours. I will contact you soon for other projects."

Oscar Dávila put his phone on the living room coffee table and took a long sip of freshly-squeezed *maracujá* juice. He hated to lose sixty pounds of cocaine to the CNP, but had to offer authorities an occasional sacrificial lamb to take pressure off his heavy volume corridors. Today's loss was a cost of doing business. Losing

Anderson and the Ecuadorian co-pilot was the least of his worries. They were easy to replace.

Dávila got paid regardless, and owed the FARC no cocaine. Under their operating agreement, the FARC assumed full responsibility once shipments landed in Colombian territory. Any on-the-ground loss was their problem. Dávila was especially pleased with the Bogotá commando group's performance. The contact with the Counter Narcotics Brigade two weeks earlier produced the expected results, well worth the $450,000 he paid the commanding officer and the $200,000 to Ramírez and his men. They were highly trained, liked money, and were discrete. That made them the ideal tool, and Dávila would use them again at the first opportunity. With the Colombian operation done, he called the hangar at El Alto to send the waiting DC-3 to Peru.

2

30 June

Raúl Orellana stretched to work the sleep and tightness out of his body as the blue-green waters of Lake Michigan came into view. His flight from Miami would arrive at Chicago O'Hare several minutes ahead of schedule. It was only a three hour flight, but at sixty-seven Raúl felt the effects of the six hour flight from La Paz the day before. He sipped a bottle of water and made some mental notes for his meeting at the Phoenix Corporation Tower in the Loop. Phoenix was a private company with annual revenues of twenty-four billion dollars. It had world-wide operations in oil and gas, chemicals, agriculture, telecommunications, construction, infrastructure, high technology, water treatment, power generation, and power trading. Raúl was the senior representative and political advisor for Latin America, and Phoenix's top two executives relied on him to make operations south of the border run smoothly.

One of those two executives, Geoff Whitworth, was the founder and president of Phoenix. A University of Wisconsin math-economics graduate with a reputation for a magic business touch, he bought and merged several nearly bankrupt energy and manufacturing enterprises in the early 1980s and turned them from cash bleeders to cash cows. The cash allowed him to acquire more companies, and the restructured entity became Phoenix Corporation. The other top person, Steven Price, was executive vice president and chief operating officer. He was Raúl's immediate boss. A Stanford Law School graduate and two-term U.S. Representative from Minnesota, Price joined Phoenix ten years earlier, shortly after being named in his mid 40's as a partner in the world's most prestigious international management consulting company. He had grown tired of telling people how to run their businesses and wanted to run his own. Geoff Whitworth gave him that opportunity. Price was known for an exceptionally sharp mind, someone who identified and acted on new business opportunities quickly. He and Whitworth complemented each other well.

The corporation grew rapidly in the late 1990s through further mergers and acquisitions that opened new markets and developed new business lines. Phoenix was soon the envy of corporate America and a darling of the press. It had an outstanding name and history, an excellent record of sustained growth and financial results, and an impeccable reputation with bankers, analysts, and foreign governments. With no outside shareholders, Phoenix was master of its own fate and free to enter virtually any business enterprise.

Because of increased competition and domestic regulation, Phoenix focused its attention on emerging market economies during the mid-1990s and quickly developed strong positions in Europe and the Far East. They saw even greater opportunities to the south. Since their businesses did not depend on close contact with mass consumer markets, it made sense to place an office in a logistically convenient geographic center. Phoenix's visionary senior management believed La Paz was ideal for their Latin American regional headquarters.

Raúl Orellana and Steven Price had known each other for over twenty-five years and had worked closely together at Phoenix for the last eight. Raúl was in Chicago at Price's request to discuss Phoenix's regional strategy, but knew that today was no ordinary meeting. He was the key to Phoenix's success in Latin America, and wanted and expected the acknowledgement his efforts deserved. Raúl told close friends that Phoenix would show its appreciation during this trip. That meant Steven Price would step up to the plate and reward him publicly and formally.

Raúl got into the back seat of the Phoenix corporate limo, buckled his seatbelt, and stretched his legs as the car pulled away from the terminal. He adjusted the leather-bound radio controls in the center console and drank a bottle of mineral water. The car accelerated onto the freeway, and the Chicago cityscape became an indistinct blur as he thought of the long road that brought him to this time and place.

The experience of his family's flight from Bolivia during a repressive political regime in the 1950s was still indelibly seared into him. His father managed a La Paz manufacturing plant owned by the then recently deposed ruling political party. The new government fired all the workers and replaced them with party loyalists. Raúl's entire family was publicly shamed and narrowly escaped with their lives by spending their last *centavo* to flee the country. They eventually made it to the United States, and slowly got back on their financial feet.

Coming to the U.S. as a young man was a tough adjustment, but Raúl's discipline saw him through the University of Miami. He learned a great deal in the U.S., but the most important lesson did not come from the American classroom. It came from Bolivia. He vowed that no one would ever again shame him or his family, and he would never again lose face.

Bolivian political regimes changed frequently, and the family returned to La Paz after a few years. Raúl spent over a decade in the Bolivian army as an intelligence officer and then tried his hand in the private sector. He soon met Maria Catena, a black-haired beauty from Cochabamba. The daughter of one of Bolivia's wealthiest businessmen, her father owned farms, a local airline, and the largest beer bottling plant in the country. Maria fell in love with Raúl, but his family's political past and relatively low financial and social status did not please María's father. He refused Raúl's proposal of marriage. When the father rebuffed a second proposal, Raúl took matters into his own hands.

Raúl and some army friends hijacked Catena's beer bottle shipments, and would not return them until the father agreed to the marriage. The elder Catena consented when he was on the verge of bankruptcy, but after the ceremony Raúl reneged on his pledge and then forced the father to sign a share of the family business over to him. That was the start of Raúl's fortune, and he never looked back. The stress gave Maria's father a massive heart attack, and Raúl laughed at the news of the old man's death.

Maria discovered Raúl's machinations several years later, and a difficult marriage became an impossible one. Neither wanted the public embarrassment of a divorce in a Catholic country, so they lived separately, Raúl in La Paz and Maria 150 miles away in Cochabamba. Raúl kept emotional and financial control of Maria, periodically compelling her to appear with him at high-profile political or business affairs where a wife was a convenient accessory. She complied because he threatened she would never see their two daughters again otherwise.

Raúl straightened his tie and shot his cuffs as the car approached the Phoenix Tower. Even though he dressed down in a blue blazer and khaki trousers, he wore his favorite gold cufflinks. He checked in at the ground floor reception desk, and the security guard verified his company ID.

Once in the elevator, Raúl inserted the card in the lower left side of the control panel to go straight to the executive offices on the 46th and the 47th floors. The 46th housed financial, administrative, and operations senior managers. The 47th was Whitworth's and Price's exclusive domain, with their spacious executive suites, the board room, and Whitworth's private dining room.

Tracey Olsen, Price's secretary, greeted Raúl as the elevator opened onto the 47th floor reception area. "Hello, Mr. Orellana, and welcome back. How was your trip?"

"Long as usual," Raúl said with an uncharacteristic smile, "but I had no delays. At least I got to play golf yesterday in Miami."

"Please, come with me." She led him down the hall to Price's office. "Mr. Price is with Mr. Whitworth and will be back shortly. Can I get you something to drink? Coffee or water?"

"No thanks, I'm fine."

Raúl dropped his briefcase in the chair at Price's conference table. He ran his hands through his thick gray hair and thought about going back to La Paz with good news. It was about time. He had been a wealthy man a long time, but this was not about money. It was about what he deserved.

Tracey Olsen told Price of Raúl's arrival when he came out of Whitworth's office. He smiled as he walked down the hall. Raúl was exceptionally astute, was a good friend, and they shared a vision of how to run a world-class organization. That was why Phoenix had been so successful in Latin America. Though professionally similar, however, Price and Raúl viewed the world in starkly different personal terms.

Price was cold, calculating, and unemotional. Raúl was not only cold and calculating, but was also extremely emotional and given to fits of Latin passion. Those fits often drove Price to distraction. The outbursts had gotten worse in the last couple of years, but Price realized Raúl was just that way and there was nothing he could do about it.

A more fundamental difference had to do with how they looked at people and business. Price saw business as a contest where entities tried to beat their opponents to the next deal and then move on. It was an exercise in profit maximization. People and emotions were important only to the extent they helped or hindered the corporate entity. There was nothing more impersonal than business. Raúl, on the other hand, saw business achievement as the way a man defined himself. It was a question of pride and honor, was about people, and was personal. Raúl never understood Price's failure to grasp that, and Price never understood why Raúl let things "get to him." Despite those two disparities, they clicked.

"*Che*, it's good to see you," Price said as he walked into his office.

Though he had never lived in Buenos Aires, Price affected the Argentine habit of calling good friends "che." He wore an elegant blue suit, a French silk tie, and Italian loafers. His black hair had not one gray streak, and his Caribbean tan was as deep as ever. Raúl knew Price did not merely wear the right clothes. Price had substance, and was the smoothest executive Raúl had ever seen.

"Steven!" Raúl exclaimed as they hugged. "It's been too long since my last trip."

"No kidding," Price said, walking around to sit at his desk. "Grab a chair. Geoff is tied up on the phone for a few minutes, and we'll get started as soon as he's done."

"You look distracted," Raúl observed as he sat opposite Price. "What's up?"

"Nothing in particular." Price swiveled his chair to look out at Lakc Michigan. "I've just been thinking about how far we've come since we met in Lima almost twenty years ago. I never imagined we'd wind up here together."

"I know," Raúl laughed. "I never would have guessed it either."

"I was also thinking about how hiring you was the best decision I ever made."

"Thanks. You're too kind."

"No, seriously," Price said looking straight at Raúl. "You were our first representative in Latin America, you established most of our business lines, and you brought us commercial prominence, financial gain, political influence, and a first rate reputation. You're the real reason for our success there. We're just lucky we got you before someone else snapped you up."

"I'm glad you did, although working with Mark sometimes drives me nuts," Raúl said, referring to his in-name only boss in La Paz, Mark Hansen, president of Phoenix Latin America.

"Look, I know running things from behind the scenes has been a pain in the ass. At least you've been able to work around him."

"Despite him is more like it. I hate having him hanging around but, as I told the President of the Republic last week, that will change when Mark retires soon. Now that he's leaving, I can dedicate all of my efforts to Phoenix. It will be nice to move to the next level."

"It's an exceptionally important step," Price nodded in agreement. "Do you know one of the great things about our relationship over these years?"

"What's that?"

"I respect you completely," Price said, "and I've always trusted your counsel and advice. You've never failed me."

"As you have never failed to listen to me or do the right thing by me. I'm looking forward to this next phase."

"Mr. Price?" Tracey Olsen appeared in Price's doorway. "Mr. Whitworth is heading to the board room."

"Thanks, Tracey." Price stood and picked up his notepad. "Ready, Raúl?"

"*Listo, como siempre.*" Raúl smiled and patted Price on the back as they walked out.

3

10 August

U.S. EMBASSY — LA PAZ, BOLIVIA

"U.S. Embassy, may I help you?"

"Yes, I'd like to speak to your Regional Security Officer, John Denning."

"May I ask who is calling?"

"Max Jenkins."

"Mr. Denning, call for you. It's a Mr. Max Jenkins."

"Max Jenkins? I don't believe it. Put him through."

"John?" the familiar voice asked.

"Hey Max, it's been a long time since I've heard your voice. Where are you?"

"I'm retired and living in Asheville. How are you and Paula doing?"

"We're great. I'm on my second year and already have a one year extension."

"La Paz?" Jenkins asked incredulously. "You can't be serious."

"Yeah, that's what I thought when I got this posting. I wondered who I pissed off to be sent here, but we fell in love with the place after only a few weeks."

"How's the job?"

"The political upheaval in this country is unreal. I've never seen anything like it. Other than that, it's pretty much the normal frustrations of any job. Most of the people here are great, but some just don't have a clue. I spend my time trying to balance the security needs of the embassy and the DEA contingent. We've got a ton of DEA people here, and they chew up a lot of my time."

"Just remember, they're paying you big bucks and you have a great medical plan," Jenkins laughed.

"Look, don't start. If I did this for the money, I would have quit years ago. If you can believe it, this is the second year in a row they're cutting our cost of living allowances. Some things never change. So, tell me, what's going on?"

"There's a new corporate executive headed your way soon. I'd like you to keep an eye on him and give him a hand if he needs it. His name is Richard Blackstone, and he'll be the new top man at Phoenix Corporation."

"I saw the name floating around. Friend of yours?"

"Yeah, he is. His father was President of Overseas Investment Corporation of Brazil and was kidnapped in Rio when I was the RSO there."

"Interesting, but that would have been a local police matter. How are you two connected?"

"A week after the kidnapping, fourteen year old Richard Blackstone came to the embassy and told the Marine Guards he wanted them to teach him to shoot. They didn't know what to do, so they brought him to me."

"You're kidding," Denning chuckled.

"Nope. Said his father was a Marine, and he trusted the Marines to teach him how to protect his family. He rolled his eyes when I said the local authorities would take care of his father's case. He already knew better than that."

"How'd you get rid of him?"

"I didn't. I gave him a Coke, told him an embassy car would take him home, and that the Marines couldn't help him. He didn't buy it and said he wanted to hear 'no' straight from them."

"Damn," Denning laughed, "this gets better and better."

"To make a long story short, I sorted it out so the Marines took him in once a week and taught him how to shoot and drive. They loved working with him. A special police unit rescued his father after two months, but Richard stayed with the Marines until his parents sent him off to boarding school a couple of years later. We've kept up ever since."

"So, after all this time how the hell does he get to La Paz?"

"He did his undergrad at the University of Virginia, got a masters degree at the London School of Economics, and then set up a business consulting practice in Rio. His political and business contacts were pretty extensive, and the State Department retained him for some work. They saw he had access to people they didn't, and increasingly looked to him for information they couldn't gather on their own. He traveled frequently to rough spots, so they made sure he had the skills to protect himself. Blackstone's a low-profile guy, but he knows how to survive in a world of nasty people. After a few years in Rio, he left to get an MBA from Columbia. He's done well in the corporate world, although he was knocked around a bit early in his career."

"What do you mean?"

"He blew the whistle on some corporate corruption deals. He did the right thing, but the senior execs burned him at the stake for it. After that, he kept his head down and hoped being more of a 'corporate player' might make his life a bit easier."

"Some transition from consultant to corporate suit. Why did he do it?"

"He married a Northwestern grad in Rio and didn't want to start a new life living on an airplane. He'll do anything to protect his family, and thought the corporate world was the way to go. Anyway, he e-mailed me this week that he's going to La Paz. I gave him your number and told him to look you up."

"I'll be glad to talk to him, Max. Has he been here before?"

"Just a couple of quick business trips. Oh, he'll ask you for some firearms help."

"What kind of help?"

"After what happened in Rio, he always travels armed. The Bolivian Embassy in D.C. gave him temporary import papers for two pistols and a shotgun. Once he gets settled in, he'll need to get the permanent paperwork. He can do that on his own, but I'd appreciate it if you could grease things so he can carry."

"I'll take care of it. Max, I really have to go. We've got a budget meeting, and I've got to fight for some bucks before we submit our requests to D.C."

"Thanks, John. Good luck."

4

21 August

The rising sun on the tail-end of an overnight flight is always spectacular. To my left, the sun's bright orange-white glow illuminated the horizon. Across the aisle to my right, there was only pitch black. I stretched and tried to get comfortable. My lower back felt like someone had hit me with a baseball bat, and my oxygen deprived thighs cramped. I adjusted my blanket and closed my eyes, hoping somehow I could sleep another hour and wake up magically rested. Instead, I heard the breakfast cart coming down the aisle with glasses and trays clinking. Any chance for sleep was long gone.

I was an hour from landing in La Paz and taking over a new job as president of Phoenix Latin America. Only three months ago, I was the TecnoStar Corporation executive vice president for Latin America, living for the last six years in Buenos Aires, Argentina. TecnoStar decided earlier in the year to move its Latin American headquarters to São Paulo. I declined the transfer as I felt São Paulo was too polluted and dangerous for my family.

Those were merely convenient excuses not to move. I was in my mid forties, and by most people's measures, relatively successful. I had a hard time believing I was successful, however, when I was miserable in my job. The real question was; success in whose eyes and by what standard? I hated working for corporations that treated people like interchangeable pieces and paid bonuses to board members who contributed nothing to the enterprise. It was impossible to sit silently in a meeting with a straight face when a human resources VP said her goal for the year was to ensure that "people know that they're our most valuable assets." I realized I was behind the curve when she could not understand why people resented being compared to inanimate objects that are bought, depreciated, and sold. I was sick of it. I had to opt out, at least for a while, to get my bearings.

I floated the idea of writing a book, but did not have the self-confidence to try it. A 4x4 trip with the family throughout Latin America seemed like fun, but I never followed it through. Having been in senior corporate jobs for so long, I saw few options. I was in limbo, felt desperate, and lacked direction. How on earth did I go from wanting to do great things that made me happy to wearing a coat and tie every day and "doing deals"?

Even though I hated this existence with a passion, I did not have the courage to let it go. I had fallen into the trap of letting my job define who and what I was. Despite my apprehensions, I left TecnoStar with no job. My entire being screamed for something else. Then Phoenix appeared, like the mythical bird rising from the ashes. It was not my salvation, but perhaps it would help me find direction in my life. I hoped this lifeboat would take me somewhere I wanted to go, not down with yet another professional, intellectual, and emotional sinking ship.

TecnoStar was one of the largest corporations in the world and had business lines similar to Phoenix's. Because of that, I knew the senior Phoenix executives in Chicago and La Paz. I met Steven Price at a conference in Buenos Aires, and he seemed to be favorably impressed with me while we did business together over several years. With similar views on Latin America, we got along well. I had worked some with the top man in La Paz, Mark Hansen, but he seemed disconnected. I had also met Raúl Orellana, but had no direct experience with him.

"Mr. Blackstone, would you like breakfast?"

"No thanks, just orange juice."

I drained the juice and did a contortionist's routine over Julie to get to the aisle. She and our children in the two seats in front of us were still asleep. I wanted to get to the bathroom before the inevitable rush fifteen minutes from landing. When I got back, Julie woke up and stretched, pulled herself up in the seat, and looked at me through barely open eyes.

"Good morning, sweetheart, how are you feeling?" She extended her arms above her head.

"I feel pretty good. Do you want anything to eat?"

"No thanks. I know you don't feel as great as you put on. What's bothering you?"

"Nothing really."

"Come on, I know better." She buried her head in my shoulder. "You've been pulling away from me for the last couple of days. I feel it when you touch me, I hear it in your voice, and I can see it on your face. In case you haven't noticed, the bridge of your nose is peeling again, and that means Mr. Stress is paying you a visit."

"Yeah, I know. It's the normal worries about any new job. When I resigned from TecnoStar, I swore I wouldn't take another job like it. I guess I'm angry that my resolve didn't last long. When Steven Price called me to ask if I wanted to interview for the top job in La Paz, I wish I hadn't been so eager to spend two days in Chicago."

"Do you wish you had turned it down?"

"No. I've just got some concerns that seem larger than life right now."

"Such as?"

"I'm worried about Raúl Orellana. It's the same stuff we talked about last week. Steven Price told me that they promised Raúl the top job a few years ago. After I accepted the offer, Price explained to Raúl it would stay with an expatriate. He said Raúl took the news well, but no one takes that sort of thing lying down. After only a few hours at headquarters, I could see that Raúl is strong-willed and influential in the region. He's also powerful inside Phoenix, and it looks like my predecessor was little more than a figurehead. Price said my finance manager in La Paz had a serious run-in with Raúl over some expense account items last year. It got nasty, and Raúl won. Price didn't blame Raúl, but instead told me that my finance guy has an attitude problem. I don't think that bodes well."

"Did you bring this up with Price?"

"No way. I didn't think it was a good idea to squawk about Raúl before I even set foot in the country."

"Anything else, darling?" she beamed at me. "Because quite frankly, I don't think you need to waste your energy worrying about stuff like that."

"That's it," I said and then kissed her. "Now, it's my turn. Have you thought some more about opening an import-export business in La Paz?"

"You bet. It got away from me in Argentina, but I'm finally going to put to good use all those antique shows my mother dragged me to." Julie leaned forward to wake the children. "Rise and shine. We're landing soon, so get your things together and take a bathroom trip if you need to." They moaned, protested, and moved slowly.

I checked our passports, immigration papers, and customs clearance forms as the pilot dropped the landing gear. To our left, the *Cordillera Real* mountain range ran the length of the horizon. The sun's rays barely touched the snow-capped peaks twenty miles away, but they already shone like newly polished diamonds. To our right, the brown, barren high plain extended forever, enveloped by the dark blue-gray cloak of the slowly receding night. Only several hundred feet below was a sprawling city of small brown houses, huts, dirt yards, and asphalt roads.

We landed smoothly and hurtled past the El Alto airport terminal. Taxiing back to the gate, we passed a silver DC-3 parked at a hangar to our right. It stood out from the modern planes nearby, and I admired its elegant lines and wondered where the grand old plane had been and what stories it could tell. We came to a full stop, and when the door opened the cabin temperature dropped from 72F to 45F in seconds.

It was difficult to breathe, and Julie looked shaky. The flight attendant said there would be a slight delay while they brought the stairs. That was welcome news as it meant we did not yet have to walk. We were at the top of the world, and I breathed faster to compensate for the altitude. It would take a while for my red blood cell count to increase enough for me to feel normal. I leaned against the seat, and heard someone retching behind me. A young girl threw up into an air sickness bag, and her father rocked her gently.

"Is she going to be okay?" I asked.

"She'll be fine. It's the altitude. This happens every time."

"Do you live in La Paz?"

"No. We have a one-hour layover here on our way home to Santa Cruz. She always throws up as soon as they open the door. I'm a doctor, and this is something to watch for in children. Are you visiting?"

"We're moving here. It's our first trip to La Paz as a family."

The doctor warned us that children often suffered from the altitude more than adults because of their faster metabolisms. He also said we should drink *mate de coca*, coca tea, for the headaches and nausea associated with high altitude. It was not narcotic and worked wonders. His colleagues swore by it, as did his wife's friends who said it cured menstrual cramps. The stairs finally arrived, and I thanked the doctor for his advice.

A Bolivian MP in an oversized green coat directed us to the

terminal building by holding out his hand and pointing left. He said nothing. We walked inside and lined up to present our passports. Immigration lines are often noisy, but not this one. I suspected everyone was suffering from severe oxygen starvation.

The line moved slowly, but the official stamped our passports quickly the minute I spoke to him in Spanish. He wished us a good day and moved on to the next in line. We walked to the small baggage claim area where dozens of porters swarmed us. We had a lot of luggage, so I chose the man with the biggest cart. As our last two bags came out, a Japanese tourist ten feet from us keeled over face first. Our porter nonchalantly said that the lack of oxygen gets to tourists all the time.

The customs inspector told us to open all our bags and asked what I had to declare. Amazingly, he was not interested in our eight bags or my three firearms. He focused on my laptop computer. Travelers frequently brought electronics in for friends to avoid paying import taxes on local purchases. I told him that it was for work and not resale. He motioned us to move on.

The porter wheeled our bags outside where an intense high plain sun greeted us. I marveled at the majestic cordillera and then realized that there was no car from Phoenix to take us to the hotel. I started to flag some cabs, but our sixteen-year-old, Sean, grabbed my arm and asked if we could watch the DC-3 that had just started its engines. Julie and Kathy, our twelve-year-old, waved us on and sat on their suitcases for a break. Sean and I hurried over to the fence to get a better look. The pilot taxied to the runway and took off, and we wondered out loud where he was going and what he was carrying.

5

"Señor Blackstone?" inquired a stout gentleman in a dark gray suit as Sean and I turned around after the DC-3 took off. "I am Primitivo Grampo. I apologize for being late, but our car broke down and I had to come in a taxi. Unfortunately, Mr. Orellana could not be here to receive you."

Primitivo was Phoenix's "do everything" man, and handled passports, visas, and national identification cards for expatriates. In a culture obsessed with image and protocol, it was noteworthy that Raúl did not meet me at the airport and curious that a company with a fleet of twelve SUVs could spare only one for the arrival of a new CEO. It was hard to misread this one. Raúl sent me and everybody else a clear message that he considered me his equal, if not his inferior. It appeared that an internal struggle had started long before I got to La Paz. I was not angry, but could see that Primitivo was afraid I would take Raúl's absence out on him.

"Don't worry about it," I said. "I'm more concerned right now about getting everyone to the hotel so we can rest."

"Señor Blackstone," Primitivo said eyeing the mountain of luggage, "I think we will need several cars."

The taxis were so small it took all of our planning, logistical, and engineering skills to accommodate the luggage. Twenty minutes later we finally were on our way to the hotel in four taxis, though not entirely sure we or the cars would survive the journey. The taxis were held together with clips and pins. Our driver called them "transformers" because they were built in Japan with the steering wheel and controls on the right hand side, then transformed in La Paz for left hand driving. The gauges were still on the right, but the steering wheel and pedals were on the left. I smiled and was speechless. No one would ever believe this.

We pulled onto the road and headed for the city of El Alto, less than half a mile away. Several hundred feet above La Paz, home to 750,000 people, it is a teeming mass of humanity, cars, trucks, buses, motorcycles, donkey carts, street vendors, tire garages, car repair shops, markets, kiosks, and warehouses. *Cholitas*, the indigenous women, wore bowler hats, billowing skirts, and brightly colored shawls. Men were more subdued in gray slacks and white shirts. We alternated between breakneck speed and panic stopping to avoid donkeys, pedestrians, and other taxis.

After several minutes, we pulled up to a bank of tollbooths on the edge of El Alto and saw La Paz below us. To our left was a two hundred foot-high sheer cliff, and to our right opened the massive three mile-wide bowl that held the city of almost one million. It looked as if someone had poured billions of tons of concrete over the edge from El Alto. Looming behind the city twenty miles away, twenty-one thousand foot snow-capped Mt. Illimani seemed close enough to touch. Wisps of clouds made it appear to float magically above the city.

The driver paid the toll and started down the blacktop to La Paz. A several foot concrete barrier to our left separated us from traffic going up to El Alto. Pedestrians jumped over it continuously, dodging traffic to catch public transport in both directions. A group of men in jogging suits ran up the road. I could hardly breathe, but they were running—and smiling. Incredible.

"Can you believe that?" I grabbed Julie's arm. "Look at those guys!"

"No, I can't." She shook her head. "I'll leave the running to you."

After riding for many years in Argentina, Julie was looking forward to finding a stable in La Paz. A good friend of ours with a ranch outside of Buenos Aires gave her several contacts to look up. I had not ridden since I was a child, because I was not entirely comfortable with a horse's free will. Julie said I was reluctant because a horse was something I could not control. I ran to be alone, to relax, and to clear my mind.

Brown, barren, dusty slopes, devoid of vegetation, surrounded the city. There was nothing green. We passed an abandoned power station, then a crumbling brewery. Time had stood still in La Paz. We drove down the *Paseo del Prado*, the central avenue, where modern ten and twenty story buildings flanked us. A fifty foot central pedestrian walkway with benches and fountains separated traffic going up and down the avenue. Magazine stands, book vendors, musicians, and sellers of every artifact imaginable jammed almost every square inch of it.

Rounding the traffic circle at the end of the Prado, we pulled up to the Plaza Hotel. I opened the car door, and a violent attack on my sense of smell made me wonder if a sewer had burst. As I squinted and pinched my nose, a bus in front of us disgorged dozens of European tourists. A cholita at the bus door held out her hand and asked for money while a small boy urinated on the front tire. Welcome to La Paz.

Clutching our carry-ons and breathing heavily, we walked slowly up the steps and through the revolving doors into an inviting, elegant lobby. In the midst of abject poverty were beautiful carpeted floors, sumptuous leather furniture, and gleaming polished brass. Waiting for the elevators, we saw the Japanese woman who passed out at the airport. Two friends guided her slowly through the lobby, and a hotel employee wheeled an oxygen tank behind her. We were in our rooms within a couple of minutes and the children were out immediately. Neither Julie nor I could sleep.

"Sweetheart," she said, "let's take the doctor at his word. Could you call room service and order some mate de coca?" The room service attendant told us to add sugar liberally. We did as instructed, and sipped the headache and nausea away.

After negotiating faulty Monday morning traffic lights and early morning chaos to get the children to their first day of school and drop Julie off to start house-hunting, the company driver had me back downtown at the office before 9:00 A.M. We pulled into a slot on the third of four parking floors in the building, and I was surprised that no security guard covered the garage entrance. I pressed the buzzer on the outer door of the Phoenix ninth floor offices, and the receptionist politely asked if she could help me. When I told her who I was, the door flew open. She nervously invited me to come with her, motioning urgently to the first secretary we saw.

"Verónica, this is Mr. Blackstone," the receptionist said as she introduced me to the retiring president's secretary. Verónica Milla was in her early thirties, conservatively dressed, and would be my secretary.

"Mr. Blackstone," she said with a pleasant smile and a firm handshake, "it's a pleasure to meet you. I'm sorry we weren't prepared, but we expected you tomorrow. Mr. Hansen is out today packing up at his house, and Mr. Orellana should be here before lunch."

"There's no need to apologize," I answered in Spanish. "I just wanted to say hello and make a few calls."

"Oh, you speak Spanish?"

"I do. You can talk to me in English if you prefer, but I'll generally speak Spanish at work."

"Your office is right next to Mr. Orellana's." Verónica pointed to the office behind her. "It's ready for you to move in."

She ushered me into a large corner office with modern furniture and a small conference table. Walking towards the window, I took in an uninspiring view of downtown La Paz. I turned to speak to Verónica just as a stern-looking woman in her mid fifties appeared behind her in the doorway. It felt as though the Spanish Inquisition had arrived, and Verónica's body language told me I was not the only one who felt that way. "Mr. Blackstone," she said haltingly, "this is Carolina Santos, Mr. Orellana's secretary."

"It is a pleasure to meet you, and welcome to Bolivia." Carolina eyed me carefully, as if she were cataloging the exchange to index, reference, and pass it on. She spoke formally as though she were giving me instructions. "Mr. Orellana will arrive around one o'clock, and he will take you to lunch. I will advise him of your arrival." She turned on a sharp heel and was gone.

Elegant and functional Venetian blinds covered the floor-to-ceiling glass partitions between the Phoenix offices. Large exterior windows made the environment bright. The furniture was a modern Italian black leather design, and the computers were state-of-the art with flat screens. I expected a La Paz office to be considerably darker and more rustic.

As we reached the other side of the floor, I saw an office with an unobstructed view of Mt. Illimani. "Who has this office?"

"Our engineering manager was in here until last week. As you know, he's moving to Lima, and his replacement arrives in a few days."

"Please get some people to move my furniture in here, and take all this furniture to Mark's office. Move your work area to this side of the floor as well."

Looking at the sea of concrete from Mark Hansen's office made me feel like Dilbert imprisoned in his cubicle. My heart and soul sang when I saw that mountain. I ignored the small voice in my head that whispered this was not the best thing to do my first day in the office.

"What?" Verónica asked. "We expected you would take Mr. Hansen's office. Mr. Orellana designed the layout so you would be next to him. I am not sure he'll want you to move."

"Thanks for the warning, but I love this view."

"I'm sorry. I didn't mean it that way."

"I know. Just get some people to move everything over when you get the chance."

"Yes Mr. Blackstone. I will take care of it."

6

"Richard, welcome to La Paz." Raúl found me reading in Mark Hansen's office and gave me a cordial but far from friendly handshake. "I'll put my briefcase away and we'll go to lunch."

Raúl looked older than I remembered. The lines on his face had deepened, and a slight stoop made him look shorter than 5'9". His hair was completely gray, but his blue eyes were as steely and penetrating as ever. We did not speak in the elevator. While he scrolled through his phone messages, I tried to figure out who this man was. Raúl was not an employee, but the company paid him very well and gave him an office, a secretary, a generous expense account, and a driver. He spent two or three mornings a week in the Phoenix offices, and stopped by for thirty minutes around lunch or at the end of each day to check messages, correspondence, and e-mail. He spent the rest of his day on his own affairs. Phoenix obviously considered Raúl special.

International corporations operating overseas retained well-connected nationals to represent them, and to facilitate access to business deals and government officials. Making the local a representative instead of an employee gave the appearance of an arm's length relationship. Employees were subject to scrutiny from corporate conflict of interest oversight and audits, but corporations more easily skirted those rules with representatives. These relationships were mutually beneficial. Phoenix paid Raúl to identify business opportunities, and he used the company to bolster and improve his own reputation. Similar scenarios abounded all over the region.

"Are you settled in at the hotel?" Raúl asked as the elevator opened on the ground floor.

"We are. The children started at the American School this morning and Julie is house hunting. I'm impressed with the school. Who would have thought?" I put my sunglasses on. I rarely wore them in Buenos Aires, but the intense high altitude sun was blindingly bright.

"People come here and expect to find the fifth world of everything," Raúl said as we stepped onto the sidewalk. "This is an incredibly poor country, but the school is a real prize."

We crossed the Prado, entered the Sucre Palace Hotel, and walked up one flight of stairs to the restaurant. The maître d' pulled Raúl from the waiting crowd of executives and took us to our table. He was not among equals here and was treated as though he owned the hotel. I wondered if he did. We sat down, Raúl ordered a whiskey, and I ordered a beer. I was sensitive to the fact that he did not get my job, so today I would listen a lot more than I would talk.

"Raúl," I started slowly, "before I came here I looked at dozens of project files, political risk analyses, and bank reports. You name it, I read it. It seems like everything we touch does well. What's not written up in those reports that I should worry about?"

"Being an American company overseas is a challenge, but especially so in Bolivia because of coca eradication. Bolivians hate the program, but U.S. foreign aid is tied to its success. That makes our position even more delicate."

"Every single report mentions coca or cocaine," I said shaking my head. "It seems like it's the eight hundred pound gorilla that won't go away."

"There are good reasons why the problem is here to stay. After Peru, Bolivia is the second largest producer of coca leaf in the world. The primary use of coca leaf is cocaine production, but there is a long-established legitimate coca industry here. The *Quechua* and *Aymara* who worked the silver mines hundreds of years ago used it. They called it *hoja sagrada*, sacred leaf. It's a cultural issue for Bolivians."

"Legitimate uses for hoja de coca?"

"Miners were fed little during the workday, and they used coca to suppress their hunger. It's a mild stimulant and it protected them against the altitude and the cold. Coca remains a central part of many people's daily lives, and it's ingrained in religious rituals and natural medicine."

"Is there any legitimate coca production in the country?"

"There is. Bolivian law permits legal cultivation of almost 30,000 acres in the Yungas for traditional purposes. Incredibly enough, an official government entity regulates it."

"Unreal. So, back to where we started, what's the specific gripe?" I asked.

"American intervention in a foreign country is the problem. The war on drugs severely disrupted the lives of a lot of people, and it got worse when the U.S. conditioned aid on the success of the eradication program."

"You're saying Bolivia may not want to eradicate, but it does to keep the aid money flowing."

"Exactly," Raúl said, sipping his whiskey. "It's a recipe for a lot of people to be pissed off."

"That's bad if that anger flows to us," I said. "Does it?"

"Not yet. First, it's directed at the U.S. government and not at our company. Second, we have development projects that generate permanent jobs and income for Bolivians. The projects are high profile and good political capital."

"That's great, but is Phoenix's involvement in the eradication effort widely known?"

"Absolutely not." Raúl lowered his voice. "We manufacture some of the eradication chemicals, and my aviation company supplies the aircraft. That's not widely known."

"Can we do anything else to reduce our exposure?"

"You have me. As your political advisor, I make sure the locals don't get in our way. The upper class has manipulated the Bolivian people for generations, and we will continue to do so. Phoenix stays profitable and safe."

Raúl was quick and savvy, and Phoenix had done well to retain him. His last comment, however, disturbed me. He had no respect for his own people and had no sense of community. But then, Bolivians were not really Raúl's people, were they? He saw nothing in common with them. It was obvious that Raúl would step over anything and anyone to get what he wanted.

Verónica had two items waiting for me when I returned from lunch. One was a fax from Bolivia Logistics International (BLI), our customs clearance agent in La Paz, regarding the shipment of our household effects from Argentina. The other was a headquarters letter asking for a recommendation on providing coca leaf to our altiplano project laborers. Sensing that coca leaf would be a headache, I ignored it for the moment.

"Hold these in a folder for me and I'll see about them later," I said handing the messages back to Verónica. "I'm going to school to pick up the children. While I'm out, please call the U.S. Embassy to see if I can meet with the Regional Security Officer and the Commercial Officer this week or next. I'd like to spend an hour or so with each one. While you're at it, see if you can get me thirty minutes with the embassy doctor."

"Are you not feeling well?"

"I'm fine, but I haven't figured out how to breathe. It's not a big deal."

"I will see to it," she said, making notes on her agenda.

"Thanks." I headed out the door.

"Mr. Blackstone," Verónica called out as she got up from her desk, "I have your cell phones. Mr. Hansen still has his, so I ordered a new one for you. Here is one for your wife, and two for your children in case of a security problem."

"Thanks. See you tomorrow."

The woman was efficient, and her concern for my family's safety impressed me. No wonder Mark played golf all the time. She probably ran the office for him.

7

Yet again I woke up with the same dry mouth, cracked lips, and bloody spit that greeted me each morning since we arrived. This seemed to be normal in high altitude, so I better get used to it. Going back to sleep and dreaming of breathing normally seemed like a great idea, but I was already running late. I leaned over and kissed Julie's cheek, her lower lip, and then her neck. She moaned as she curled up in me and put her feet between my legs to warm them. Now I really did not want to get out of bed.

"How did you sleep, sweetheart?" I asked.

"Okay, but not really great. I like the cool weather, but the dry air is killing me. How about you?"

"About the same. I woke up at three again, and I can't figure out why. It takes me forever to get to sleep, and then I wake up gasping for breath. I asked Verónica to make an appointment for me with the embassy doctor. I'd like to know if this is normal or if I'm paranoid."

"Probably paranoid."

My first stop of the day was Roberto Solís, the BLI General Manager. After walking up three flights of spiral stairs, I stood in front of a reinforced steel door, a video camera, and an intercom.

I buzzed and waited. The secretary opened the door and I entered an office packed with desks, people, cigarette smoke, and hundreds of three ring binders piled high on dozens of desks. This was more like the La Paz I imagined. Our household effects would arrive from Buenos Aires soon, and Solís assured me that everything would clear customs without problems. Living in a hotel had its charms, but we would tire of it rapidly. I mentioned that Julie wanted to start an import-export business, and Solís offered that BLI could assist with all logistical issues. That was welcome news as it would save Julie a ton of start-up time.

I returned to the office to meet with my company driver. Mark had released him so he could take care of me and my family full-time. Lucho was in his early forties, lean and strong, and had the rugged look and the rough hands of a man who had worked for years in the altiplano. His face was wrinkled, his eyes sharp and penetrating. He was about 5'7", darkly tanned with a prominent thin nose, and carried himself with the confidence of someone who knew his way around. I offered him a cup of coffee, and we talked about our families, soccer, and the job. Lucho seemed like an honest, decent, and capable man. Even so, I was not entirely comfortable having someone intimately familiar with our habits and schedules. I would do some more work on him. As I walked out of the office, Verónica told me I could see the RSO, the Commercial Officer, and the embassy doctor Friday afternoon.

Lucho had his first run taking the children to school on Friday morning, and they were chatty and got along well. We dropped Julie at our rental house so she could make a list of the things that needed repair. Lucho and I started out talking about sports on the way to the office, but the conversation quickly turned to economics and politics.

"Oh Señor Richard, it's very bad here. Corruption is everywhere. It's in the government, in business, and in the military."

"What would you do about it, Lucho?"

"You need to kill all the politicians, all the police, all the military and many businessmen. Then you start all over again. That's the only way."

Lucho was serious. I laughed quietly as I got out of the car and headed to my office, but feared his candid assessment was based on a life of experience.

My furniture was moved from Mark's office, and I now had a spectacular mountain view. I wanted to thank Verónica for her help, but her desk was clean and she was nowhere in sight. I suspected that Carolina would know where to find her.

"Have you seen Verónica?"

"I am sorry Mr. Blackstone, she's not here," Carolina answered in a business-like tone. "Verónica has been released from employment with Phoenix." She seemed disturbingly pleased to give me the news.

"What do you mean, 'released'?"

"Mr. Blackstone, I really cannot say. All I know is that Mr. Orellana told her to remove her personal effects yesterday."

"Carolina, please call Raúl and tell him I want to meet this afternoon. I should be back from the U.S. Embassy shortly after five. Thank you."

I went to my office, closed the door, and picked up the phone.

"Verónica? This is Mr. Blackstone. Are you okay?"

"I'm fine." Her voice broke as she struggled not to cry. "I hope I haven't caused any problems."

"What happened?"

"Mr. Orellana called me into his office yesterday afternoon and told me I was fired. Carolina watched me clean out my desk, and security walked me out of the building."

"What did Raúl tell you?"

"He said I should not have moved your furniture."

"That's ridiculous. Did you tell him I asked you to do it?"

"I had no chance. He ordered me out," she said, choking back tears. "He said I did not perform my duties as expected and I exceeded my authority."

"You're not fired, you're still my secretary. Come back Monday and report for work."

"But what about Mr. Orellana?"

"I'll take care of him. Get some rest this weekend."

I was pissed, but wanted to get a better read on Raúl. I knew my finance manager Gustavo Domínguez would have some insights, so I poked my head into his office and told him I wanted to take him to lunch. Gustavo was the only Bolivian manager in the La Paz office. A University of Texas MBA, he had worked for Phoenix's U.S.-based accounting firm for almost seven years in Dallas and Miami. Gustavo wanted to return to La Paz to be near his family, so Mark Hansen hired him to replace a manager relocating to Europe.

Gustavo was typical of some Latin Americans educated in the United States who went home only to be disappointed by the way things were run. They might not have noticed the corruption before, but time out of their native country often made them harsh critics. Gustavo seemed to be one of those. The norms of conduct and business ethics he learned in the U.S. did not mesh easily with the Latin American style of conducting business.

Despite outstanding job performance, Gustavo got into hot water early. He caught Raúl and his family making personal trips to the U.S. on a Phoenix corporate aircraft and using company funds for private dinner parties at his home. Raúl could afford the expenses, but liked having the company pay for his lifestyle. Mark Hansen passed the matter on to Steven Price who then flew Gustavo to Chicago for an "attitude talk." Price informed him that Raúl was not an employee and that he was critical to Phoenix's success in Latin America. Senior management would overlook in

Raúl's case what they would not tolerate from anyone else. The message was clear: Raúl is special—lay off. Gustavo had been quiet since that episode.

Steven Price warned me about Gustavo. It appeared that Price had allowed him one politically incorrect corporate transgression, but would not permit another. Gustavo did not know I was aware of his history with Raúl, so I would have to take it slowly. We found an isolated table at a pizza place around the corner from the office. He was receptive but guarded.

Gustavo started apologetically. "I don't want to get myself in trouble. I've seen how much influence Raúl has in the company. Headquarters executives hang on his every word, much more than on Mark's."

"How did Mark react to that?"

"Even today, I'm not sure he's got a clue. He was the head of the company, but Raúl has always had the stroke. Mark probably figured the situation was normal."

"Do people outside Phoenix see that Raúl is the real power in our office?"

"You bet they do. Ask Verónica. She hears it from secretaries at other companies."

"Interesting you should say that," I said, taking a bite of pizza. "Raúl fired her yesterday."

"I'm not surprised."

"Why?"

"Raúl doesn't like her, and Carolina can't control her."

"She doesn't work for Carolina. What are you talking about?"

"Verónica saw how Raúl controlled Mark, and she didn't like it. Raúl and Carolina both know how she feels, and it causes a lot of tension. I think Raúl has been waiting for Mark to leave so he could get rid of Verónica, and moving your office was the perfect excuse."

"There has to be more to it than that. Raúl can't be that petty."

"I'm not so sure. He has a mean streak in him. I know."

"Look, I bet this is nothing more than Raúl getting his nose out of joint, and it will pass quickly enough. I'll take care of it."

We paid the bill and negotiated a tortuous path around the hordes of street vendors on the sidewalks. If I ever needed a nail clipper, flashlight, shoehorn, or trilobite, I could find it on the streets of La Paz seven days a week, twenty hours a day.

We crossed the street and were almost run over by a minivan. There were at least twenty people squeezed in like sardines along with their chickens and dogs. A teenager hung out the front window and shouted something unintelligible. Gustavo said the boy announced the route for those who could not read the sign on the windshield.

8

On our way to the U.S. Embassy, Lucho and I drove by the Universidad Católica where a mass of students held banners and beat drums as they chanted anti-American slogans. I wondered if others saw the irony of Latin American university students protesting the U.S. Capitalist Pigs while they wore Levis and Nikes, ate Big Macs, and drank Coke.

The embassy reflected the "hardening" of U.S. assets overseas after years of terrorist attacks around the world. The building was set back a hundred feet from the street. Protected by high walls and automatic gates, the grounds covered an entire city block. The windows were three feet high by one foot wide strips of bullet and bomb resistant polycarbonate. A long line of Bolivians streamed out of the gated entrance in the middle of the block, probably asking for a visa to visit the U.S. Their faces revealed the defeat and frustration of those who have been told multiple times that there was an irregularity with their paperwork.

Lucho dropped me off across the street from the embassy and parked several blocks away so we would not upset the security group's comfort zone. The guard at the security station checked my passport and gave me a claim receipt for my cell phone and folding knife. I walked through the lobby metal detector and sat in front of the Marine Guard booth to review the notes I made the night before. The Regional Security Officer and the Commercial Officer were good people to meet early in a new assignment, as they could explain local conditions better than anyone.

I had become good friends with a number of RSOs in some of my overseas assignments, and had tremendous respect for them. The RSO is a Diplomatic Security Service Special Agent assigned to diplomatic missions overseas to protect embassy personnel, property, and information against terrorists, foreign intelligence agents, and criminals. They are the ambassador's advisor on all aspects of security and the operational supervisor of the U.S. Marine Security Guard detachment. The RSO is the primary liaison with foreign police and security services overseas, and provides unclassified security briefings and advice to expatriate business executives. They are tied in.

The RSO's assistant appeared before I made much headway with my notes and escorted me past the Marines to the administrative offices. Two left turns and three offices later, the RSO's baritone voice almost knocked me over as he shook my hand solidly.

"Mr. Blackstone, welcome to La Paz. I'm John Denning." He motioned me to sit down.

"It's a pleasure. Thanks for seeing me today. By the way, it's Richard."

Denning was a powerfully built man about fifty years old with short brown hair and forearms that looked like hams. His wire-rimmed glasses gave him a studious look, but he had field man written all over him. At 5'10", he was slightly shorter than me, but outweighed me by at least thirty pounds. His office was similar to any corporate office, except for the locks on the file cabinets, two computers instead of one, and pictures of the American President, Vice President, and Secretary of State on the wall. One computer was for ordinary work, and the other was for a secure State Department system.

"Max Jenkins told me you were in town," Denning said as he poured coffee and a couple of glasses of water. "He and I go way back."

"That's what I understand. If you know Max that well, then you're probably aware of how we know each other."

"I do. Max said you met shortly after your father was kidnapped in Rio."

"Max and the Marines taught me some valuable lessons. I developed some physical skills and learned to trust only those who earned it. My father's own security team was responsible for his kidnapping. That was an eye opener I won't forget."

"You never know when those skills may come in handy, especially in this part of the world."

"I hope it doesn't come to that. Speaking of which, if I throw out the civil unrest, everything I read tells me that La Paz is pretty safe. Is that true or am I missing something?"

"No," Denning laughed, "the reports aren't lying. The popular press would have you believe this is a war zone, but it's generally safe—depending, of course, what part of town you're in. You're not exposed to the same kind of violence and crime as in Colombia, Peru, or Brazil. The biggest worry in La Paz is ordinary street crime, but you should avoid El Alto on weekend nights. It can get rough up there. As a rule of thumb, stay away from the large protest marches and demonstrations. You can get into trouble fast if you get caught up in them."

"I've seen labor protests around Latin America before, but nothing like what's been happening here."

"There are several constants in Bolivia. The first is that presidents are elected and tossed out every few years. The second is that public protests play a key role in that process, especially lately. The third is that the leaders of those protest movements often wield greater power than the president himself, and they are firmly entrenched in the country's political structure. Get this; the leader of the coca growers is a Deputy in the House of Representatives and is the head of the Movement Toward Socialism party. One word from him and his cronies and the masses block the streets leading to El Alto, occupy government buildings, or invade oil field installations. They've done it time and again this year."

"Seemingly without any lasting resolution."

"That's because presidential resignations, protest marches, states of siege, or curfews don't resolve one fundamental conflict in Bolivia."

"Which is?"

"The split between the poor high plain indigenous groups in the west and the oil and gas rich upper classes in the east. La Paz is poor and Santa Cruz is rich. That's a gross oversimplification, but you get the point. No protest march or change in government will ever resolve that problem."

"Speaking of Santa Cruz, any protest marches there?"

"None, but they've got other issues. Drug money runs Santa Cruz, so you have to watch who you associate with."

"Are there any restricted travel areas around the country, any places I should avoid?"

"The Chapare. It's a heavy drug area, and you don't want to be caught there. By the way, Max asked me to help you get a carry permit for your pistols. You have two?"

"Correct. Two 1911s. I know .45 ammo is hard to come by here, but I love them."

"Good man. I've already spoken to the Bolivian National Police colonel who can take care of that for you. He's available late today if you can get your weapons together."

"Thanks. Just tell me where I need to go. One of the things we'll want to do is get out on our own. Are family day trips safe?"

"Absolutely. We do it all the time. You can go almost anywhere, and I'd suggest Yungas, Lake Titicaca, and Copacabana. Make sure you have a spare tire on the back of your truck, and take another one strapped to the roof."

"Bad roads?"

"That's part of it. The real problem is tire theft, so lock up the spare. Street kids and gangs steal tires and sell them on the black market. Also, take a lot of water in the Altiplano. It's dry up there."

"I don't recall significant terrorist or guerrilla activity here. Is that still the case?"

"Pretty much. A government attorney in Santa Cruz investigating some tax evasion and drug issues was blown to hell in a car bomb last year, but that was isolated to the particular case. A group called The Broad Anti-Corruption Front has started bombing foreign oil and gas company offices to force the government to re-nationalize the oil business. So far, they're just a nuisance. There is some recent activity that worries me, though, and I think it could get worse. A well-armed militant indigenous movement opposed to foreign investment and multinationals has sprung up. The local security forces have had several armed confrontations with them, and authorities confiscated a large cache of weapons, ammunition, and explosives."

"What's the problem?"

"Anything and everything. One of their gripes is that they want Bolivia's gas kept in country rather than sold to foreigners. I guess it's a small detail that there is no internal gas market. They also want the U.S. to drop the eradication program."

"Are they on their own, or is someone helping them?"

"The local umbrella labor organization, the Central Obrera Boliviana (COB), and the *cocaleros*, the coca growers, coordinate most militant activity. They've targeted the security forces and have blocked the major roads in and out of La Paz several times. It's possible they'll go after specific multinationals, so make sure your security guys are up to speed."

"The COB and the cocaleros must be getting help."

"We suspect that Chavez," referring to the Venezuelan president, "has his hand in some of this, but we don't have any proof. We also think that the FARC has been training them for the last three years. It shows."

"Does the FARC fight or just sit and watch?"

"We think they stick to training. They haven't yet launched any cross-border raids. That's good news, but not much comfort."

"Damn. If the FARC's in Bolivia, it's more serious than just some pissed off locals."

"It is," Denning said. "The indigenous groups never had the money or the training to do anything significant. They're not much of a threat on their own. It's a different story with FARC help."

"Does the FARC provide the money too?"

"We think so, but the COB and cocaleros also finance themselves. It's all tied to the cocaine trade."

I shook my head and made a few more notes. "Anything else I should watch for?"

"Be careful taking buses around La Paz. That's where you're most likely to be separated from your wallet. You also need to know there are two kinds of taxis. One takes you, and only you, to your destination. The second is like a bus. It picks up as many people and farm animals as possible and drops them off in turn. They're not dangerous, but you'll probably need a shower after the ride. Beyond that, there's not much else. Do you have a house yet?"

"We've found one in Achumani relatively close to school. The compound has an outer wall with a gate, and each of the houses inside has ten foot walls topped with broken glass and barbed wire."

"Great. How about a full-time driver?"

"Mark Hansen's, Lucho. Do you know him?"

"I do. He's a good guy. Lucho was with the presidential detail a number of years ago, and he drove for us on some DEA field work. He'll take good care of you."

"I'll remember that. Thanks."

Denning walked me to my next appointment. The Commercial Officer is the embassy's liaison to the business and financial community and an excellent source for information on the local economy. Jennifer DiAngelo was in her mid thirties and stunning. She had shoulder length black hair, not a wrinkle on a classic face, and legs that went all the way to the ground. She wore no ring, and I wondered what she did for dates in La Paz. We spent an hour discussing the general commercial and financial affairs of Bolivia, and she had complete command of the regional scene as well. The topics were a laundry list of issues in all Latin American countries: privatizations, opposition to privatizations, labor problems, debt problems, tax evasion, lack of budget to pursue tax evaders, no money for development plans, lack of transparency and insecurity in the law enforcement and judicial system, corruption, and money laundering. I knew her advice would be top notch.

After we wrapped up, she took me to the physician. I told him of my headaches and waking up in the middle of the night gasping for air. His smile told me I was not the first to have this problem. He said that headaches, dizziness, nausea, and difficulty sleeping were not unusual above 8,000 feet. The problem was more severe at our present 12,000 feet. My nighttime problem was called high altitude sleep apnea, and my body was trying to adjust to the lack of oxygen. It would go away within a couple of weeks. Small comfort. His parting suggestion was to drink mate de coca frequently.

The doctor showed me to the lobby and wished me well. I started to call Lucho, but put my phone away when I saw him on the corner to my right flashing the car lights. I sprinted across the street and got in the front passenger seat before other drivers could honk at us for blocking traffic. We drove back to the office, and I was upstairs before five o'clock.

9

I was on my third phone call and second cup of coffee when Raúl finally appeared in my office doorway. He strutted in with the self-assured air of a man about to bless an inferior with his presence. His aura of self-satisfaction preceded him like overdone musky cologne you can smell a block away. I liked neither. I wanted to avoid a confrontation with him so early in my assignment, but my pre-game pep talk to myself did not do much good. Whatever good will and desire I had to soft pedal his firing of Verónica dissipated faster than I could reel it in.

"Richard, apologies for not getting here more quickly," he said casually, taking a chair and making himself at home. "I was on a conference call with Steven."

"I know. I'll get to that in a minute. I came in this morning and heard that you fired Verónica. What's going on?"

"She's been a performance problem, and I thought it would be good for you to get a fresh start," he said matter-of-factly, as though my agreement with his assessment was a foregone conclusion. "Her insolent and disruptive attitude was not good in a small office like ours. I could recommend some first rate secretaries, or we could share Carolina. She's excellent, knows the business, and can keep track of both of us."

"Thanks, but I need administrative support, not someone to keep track of me. I told Verónica that she's not fired."

"What? It makes me look bad if she comes back."

"I'm sorry you feel that way, but she's my secretary, and I decide whether she goes or not. Having her return to work is not a plot to hurt you."

I started the conversation irritated, but was now angry. As Raúl talked, any remaining patience oozed from my body and I wanted to slug him. He was equally pissed at me. His crossed arms and legs showed it. It was a pride and face issue for him. It was principle for me. My hope for a smooth arrival in Bolivia had hit a serious speed bump, but I could not let Raúl get away with this. Despite my anger, I bit my tongue. He was tight lipped and waited for me to speak.

"There are some other things that we need to discuss," I said slowly.

"And those are, Richard?"

"Verónica said you kept Mark's schedule of government meetings and you went with him to most of them?"

"That's correct."

"Raúl, your time and expertise are too valuable for you to be bogged down in that sort of administrative crap. I'll draw up my own meeting schedule, and will normally attend alone unless there is a particularly sensitive issue. We need you to concentrate on the new legislation. Does that make sense?"

"Yes," came the terse reply.

"Great. Now, one other thing. You've covered financial and operating items with Chicago recently while we transitioned. That's been a great help, but I can take those over now. Oh, Mark also said you discussed political issues as they came up."

"Correct. We had nothing formal."

"I'd like to structure that discussion a bit more."

"And just how do you propose to do that?"

"I want you to prepare a weekly memo to me highlighting relevant political developments. Make it a one-paragraph summary of each piece of legislation or issue, how it affects us, who the players are, and what your action plan is. I'd like to see the report every Monday morning by nine so we can review it at eleven. I don't need to see anything if there are no changes from the previous report."

I sipped my coffee and thumbed my note pad. I had one more thing to discuss, but it escaped me. Seeing the break in my train of thought, Raúl started to get out of his chair. His movement jogged my memory.

"Oh, forgot one. I'll handle all the contacts with the embassy from now on. That includes the U.S. Ambassador, Deputy Chief of Mission, RSO, Commercial and Political Sections, MILGROUP, Defense Attaché, and the DEA Attaché. I know you'll be glad to get that load off your shoulders. I think that's it." I put my notepad down and looked directly at him.

Few things make a foreign rep feel more important than playing around at the American Embassy. This one hit hard, and Raúl was steamed. He got up and left without saying a word. His anger at being passed over for my job was tangible, and this discussion made it worse. I decided to get everything out on the table with Steven Price, but thought better of it once I started the e-mail. I told Price the facts, but omitted the personal antagonism. He responded within five minutes: "I'm glad you've hit the ground running." Headquarters was happy. Lovely.

Back in his office, Raúl closed the door and speed dialed the third number on his cell phone directory. *There is more than one way to address this problem,* he thought. He tapped the desk impatiently while the phone rang four times before being picked up.

"*Nacho*, Blackstone's car needs some tire work tonight before Hansen's going-away party. Watch him and his family closely," Raúl barked into his cell phone. "We need to teach this new gringo a lesson about Bolivia."

"I will welcome Sr. Blackstone appropriately, Don Raúl."

Raúl rang off and toggled the screen saver to bring up his e-mail. It was time to send a note to Chicago.

The conversation with Raúl irritated me, and I decided to call it a day. While we sparred, John Denning left a message that I had a 7:00 P.M. appointment with the La Paz police to get my pistol permit. As I passed Raúl's office on the way out, he typed furiously on his laptop. It was curious Raúl was the only one in the office who did not have a desktop system. Perhaps he was doing something productive, but I doubted it. I was angry, but was not sure if I was irritated with myself for stirring the pot so early or with Raúl for being such a jerk. Probably both. I was also pissed because I rose to his bait. Raúl knew which buttons to push to get me to react, but at least I had found some of his.

I asked for Col. Gerónimo Ortiz at the police station reception desk and found his office on the second floor. He explained that he rarely approved firearms permits for foreigners, but John Denning asked him to make an exception for me. A sergeant verified the import paperwork and explained that the permit was valid for any pistol. He liked guns, and wanted to look more closely at my 1911s. His sidearm was a 9mm, and said he would like to try an American .45 some day. I told him that all he had to do was ask. When the sergeant appeared with the permit, Ortiz advised me to travel armed in El Alto, Santa Cruz, and anywhere we went on day trips.

I walked down the steps to the Prado and headed back to the hotel with a smile as the Colonel's instructions were precisely what I had already decided to do.

10

Lucho picked us up for Mark Hansen's going away party in his own van, and explained that he found our Mitsubishi SUV jacked up on bricks in the Phoenix garage with all the tires gone. The thieves even took the spare and left the folded tire cover on the hood. It seemed absurd for that to happen in our own garage, and I made a note to discuss it with our security company. That meant talking to Raúl, since his company had the contract. They had a good reputation, but that smelled like a conflict of interest.

Broken glass and razor wire covered the eight-foot wall surrounding Raúl's home, similar to the house I would rent and many others throughout Latin America. The structure was a two story cream stucco with a red tile roof, tall ground floor windows, and several first floor balconies. The expansive garden was thick with eucalyptus trees, and an oval swimming pool bordered the far side of the property. The grounds were well lit. This would be a tough place to move around undetected at night. Once in the house, Julie and I noticed that the heavy, dark furniture did not match the pleasant exterior. I suspected the interior reflected Raúl's natural disposition.

We started to mingle, and Raúl introduced us to his wife María. She was beautiful, elegant, and charming. She warmed to our arrival, but seemed cold to Raúl's presence. Raúl appeared surprised to see us on time, and my gut told me he was aware of our tire trouble. I suspected he had his finger on everything that happened in La Paz. María took Julie to meet some of her friends, and Raúl took me around to his. We were social tools tonight.

I finally broke free of small talk and found Julie near the edge of the dining room, talking with an Australian couple who had lived in La Paz for several years. Lee Jordan headed up LatAm Mining Company Ltd., and his wife Chlöe, Dutch by birth, moved to Australia in her late twenties to escape European winters.

When dinner was served, we faced the challenge of where to sit. Raúl's wife did not have a formal seating arrangement, which meant we could eat with our new Aussie friends. Dinner was pleasant, but Julie and I were exhausted, so we called it an evening as soon as we finished dessert.

I was up early Sunday morning to see how a short run in La Paz felt. I got an A for effort and an F for judgment. I felt better than when we had arrived, but a regular five or six mile run would not happen soon. At forty-six, the lack of oxygen in La Paz erased any illusions of ever-lasting youth. I gave up after two slow miles and decided that breakfast would be more enjoyable.

I watched television news over coffee, a story about "renewed" violence in Colombia. I was not sure why they said renewed, since it never stopped. Colombian government and FARC clashes had left five "leftist" guerrillas dead. Car bombs blew up stores, warehouses, and at least one police station. I grunted and threw a piece of bread at the screen.

"Exercising your right to talk back to the television again?" Julie asked. "Still a juvenile, I see, talking to an inanimate object."

"This is absurd," I said, already exasperated. "It's another story calling the FARC 'left' and the paramilitaries 'right.' Those words have meant nothing in Colombia for years. They're just labels people use for their own agendas. The other thing is that . . ."

"Honey it's not even eight o'clock yet."

"It pisses me off when they call them guerrillas or rebels. The connotation is that they're some sort of legitimate insurgent opposition force. They aren't. They're a bunch of thugs who threaten to kill people if they don't hand over their land or help the FARC. Just because they control a large portion of the country doesn't mean they're legitimate. They're a bunch of goons who run a multi-million dollar drug, kidnapping, and extortion business. It's about power and money. At least Carlos Castaño was straight up when he led the paramilitaries. He didn't deal drugs, and was honest about killing guerrillas. The guy made headway where the Colombian government didn't. Too bad the drug-dealing component of the paramilitaries killed him. Anyway, there are always two sides to every story. I just wish the media would be honest enough to admit that."

"You're preaching to the choir, darling," Julie said, looking at me over her newspaper. "The fact is that most everyone has an agenda. Now, are you done?"

"Almost. I think it gets worse."

"And how's that, dear?" She went back to the paper.

"What's frightening is that they're just a small part of something much bigger."

"What are you thinking of?"

"Terror and insurgent groups are developing a world-wide network. People seem shocked to find out that European terror groups train with the FARC, or that Islamic extremist groups that hate each other train together in Indonesia or the Philippines. This isn't hard to figure out. They're just like any other business and will join forces when it's convenient. That's bad news for civilized people. The only thing these creeps respect is the muzzle of a gun."

"You and I know that," she said. "The best we can hope for is that the rest of the world wakes up before it's too late. Now, my love, are you done?"

"Finally."

"You should call Chris today. When you get in a mood like this, you need to blow off steam with him."

Chris Hendricks had been my best friend since our senior year in boarding school. Julie was right. I needed to call him soon.

By 10:00 A.M. in Chicago, Steven Price had put down his Sunday Chicago Tribune to read Raúl's Friday e-mail. He was not surprised that Raúl said Blackstone talked to him "like a child" or that Raúl felt he had "lost face." He had accused Price of the same thing over the years. Price thought Raúl's emotional response was a pointless distraction. It was not the first time he had seen this movie. Price then re-read Blackstone's e-mail describing the same meeting, and wrote off Raúl's strident tone to his volatile Latin temperament. He deleted both e-mails. This would all blow over in a few days. It always had.

11

After a month in La Paz, the American Chamber of Commerce meeting in Santa Cruz would be a nice break. As we gained altitude, I saw that the streets leading from El Alto were choked with hundreds of vehicles ferrying people to La Paz. Everything moved inexorably down the hill like molten lava, slowly but surely, regardless of impediment or obstruction. The plane turned to Santa Cruz, and the early morning sun revealed subtle details on Mt. Illimani's face. The ever-present wispy clouds gave the peak an ethereal aspect. I wondered what part of the mountain swallowed the Eastern Airlines flight from Peru years ago. It was rumored to have ferried drugs and was blown out of the air in a "settling of accounts." This part of the world seemed to be one continuous settling of accounts.

We cleared Illimani, and the landscape revealed dozens of emerald green high mountain lakes and a few small villages. Near the end of the one-hour flight, the sharp, snow-capped peaks, the mountain lakes, and the high plain gave way to soft rolling hills and a sea of dense green growth interrupted only occasionally by cultivated fields.

The Boeing 727 braked rapidly after we touched down, and I tossed my newspaper into my briefcase. As we turned and bounced to the terminal, I saw that the Viru Viru airport was more modern than El Alto. New money. Drug money.

I stepped out of the plane under a bright blue sky, huge white cumulus clouds, warm air, and ninety-nine percent humidity. It was hot, but I could breathe. I walked to the taxi stand, and the first driver in line started his engine, presuming I would take his car. He was wrong. The drivers' faces, eyes, and demeanor told me who I would take. The first looked like a hustler and the second was asleep. The third was alert and ready to work. He threw the car into gear and we raced toward town on a two-lane asphalt road. To our left were open green fields, and to our right was a never-ending parade of auto repair shops, warehouses, and bars. The wind blew continuously, and I asked the driver to raise his window so I would not be consumed by the sand and dust enveloping the car. How could a place so green be so dusty?

Sunlight streamed through floor-to-ceiling glass windows to illuminate the Las Palmas Hotel lobby. The receptionist told me the meeting was in the third salon at the rear of the hotel. As I walked by the pool and open-air restaurant, I saw why people from La Paz flocked here. The hotel was a series of two story white stucco cottages with red orange tile roofs. The rooms surrounded the pool on three sides, each set back eighty feet or so from the pool. I picked up my name tag at the check-in desk and got an earful of Aussie before I turned around.

"Richard, how the hell are you, mate?" Lee bawled as he slapped me on the back.

"Great, Lee. I thought you were coming, but didn't see you on the plane this morning."

"I came in last night so I wouldn't have to get up at the crack of dawn. I took a dip in the pool this morning. The only thing missing was a beer."

The man knew what he wanted. I preferred waking up with Julie. I put my name tag in my pocket, poured some coffee, and we took seats at the back of the room close to the exit. The first several presentations were boring, but the president of a U.S. oil and gas company had a decent handle on the current environment and made some good points. He was followed by the best speaker of the morning. Paul Trasky owned newspapers in La Paz and Santa Cruz, and his topic was the interplay of politics, drugs, and economics.

"The U.S. government," he started, "has established a dangerous cycle of dependency in the Andean region. This cycle results from the interaction of economic conditions and the drug trade. Bolivia, Colombia, Ecuador, and Peru don't like the U.S. intrusion into their internal affairs, but they desperately need the development money and the military assistance."

Trasky's assessment was to the point. The Andean countries did not have the economic fundamentals to handle the influx of money the U.S. gave them with the eradication program. The aid money became a fix, and the Andean countries needed constant injections to keep themselves going. It was a vicious cycle.

"The basic problem," Trasky continued, "is that regional political regimes are unstable, and civilian power is weak. A few examples are instructive. Massive public protests forced two Bolivian presidents to resign in the last two years. As current civil unrest shows, our institutions continue to be shaky. Ecuador's president resigned and fled to Brazil under public pressure. Peru has been stuck in neutral since Fujimori left, and the Colombians still have trouble fighting the FARC. Unbelievably, the Colombian government publicly offered foreign bounty hunters million dollar rewards to hunt the FARC. We have a delusional president in Venezuela who has publicly stated that the U.S. hates him because he refused the sexual advances of their female Secretary of State. As if that were not enough, he picks a fight with Colombia whenever he can.

"We don't have visionary leaders or strong institutions to

move countries forward. Not a day goes by without an allegation or rumor that some Latin American president, minister, or governor is involved in the drug trade or some other criminal activity. That's so common it's no longer news. Our regional economies are fragile, and they may not strengthen soon. The region will remain mired in the drug trade until Latin America resolves these issues."

Although Trasky did not say it outright, the United States had established a master and servant relationship with many countries in Latin America which co-opted and corrupted systems out of their normal development cycles. The "reward" money caused funds to flow to countries unready to assimilate them. The money raised expectations, countries got hooked on it, and then became convinced they could not live without it.

"It's critical for you to understand," Trasky said, "that Latin America's problems were generations in the making, and they will not be solved overnight. Even the best leaders cannot remedy all of a country's challenges with one five-year plan, but must instead address the most pressing ones first. The problem is that there are so many. It's important to recognize that corruption will continue to affect politicians, businessmen, and the military for years to come. Presidential decrees and IMF edicts are not the solution. Neither the U.S. nor the IMF is to blame for Latin America's troubles, although it's convenient for our politicians to claim otherwise. We will trail much of the world until we learn to value hard work and develop a strong sense of collective responsibility. Quite simply, Latin America is responsible for many of its own problems and will have to work hard to overcome its self-inflicted wounds."

After Trasky wound up, Lee and I headed poolside for lunch rather than eat the conference leather steak. I had not yet taken a sip of my beer when a Brazilian Varig Airlines flight crew walked by. Lee said they would be poolside within fifteen minutes, and he beamed when his prediction came true. These beautiful, lithe, tan women looked as though they and their *tangas* had just walked off the Rio beaches. As a light breeze dried the perspiration on my forehead, another beauty walked by the pool. She was tall with olive skin, had long light brown hair, and her short white linen skirt and high heel slip-ons left little to the imagination.

"Not what you expected?" Lee observed my reaction.

"No, not after what I've seen in La Paz," I said, thinking of the portly cholitas in bowler hats.

"She's a *cruceña*, from Santa Cruz. Her father is German, a local government official. Her mother is Brazilian."

"Tell me how you came by this information?"

"Just wait. You'll see."

Within a couple of minutes, a fellow in his late fifties put his arm around the young woman, gave her a kiss, and led her toward the back of the hotel. Her escort was the oil and gas company president who spoke at the morning session.

"Correct you are, mate," Lee said when he saw my reaction. "A little Santa Cruz nooky. He comes here once a week, bones the babe, and is back to La Paz in a flash. Chlöe knows his wife pretty well. She adores him and doesn't have a clue. Everyone around here knows."

"Lee, they should sell tickets to watch this."

"Sometimes it gets even better," Lee said as he pointed discreetly to the other side of the pool. "Look to the right of the pool near the back. See the guy with the beard smoking the cigar, between the two women?"

"Got it," I said.

"That's Oscar Dávila, the former mayor of Santa Cruz. He's a wealthy businessman, said to be part owner of the hotel and one of Bolivia's top drug lords."

"By that, I take it there's no proof against him?"

"None. Not a shred."

"That's the fascinating thing about Latin America," I observed. "Everyone knows he's a drug lord, and they talk about it openly.

People also know he kills his enemies and has the politicians in his pocket. Money, drugs, corruption, politics, power, and impunity. They all go together."

"Not quite like the first world is it?"

"Oh, hell, Lee, it's the same everywhere. It's about power and control. Do you really think the average U.S. politician is any different? They're just a bit smoother, that's all. At least here it's out in the open, and people know these guys are all corrupt. In that sense, it's more honest than in the U.S."

"Here's another one for you," Lee continued as he eyed a curvaceous Varig stewardess applying lotion to her tanned thighs ten feet from him. "The DEA loves this place for rest and relaxation. Sometimes Dávila and the DEA agents are poolside at the same time. It's ironic as hell. I know some of the DEA guys in La Paz, and they have a tough job. They chase slippery people, and getting proof on these jerks is nearly impossible. That's why he can sit over there with his high-priced pussy and not have a care in the world."

We realized the afternoon session was about to start, looked at the scenery around the pool, and decided to order another round of beers. Lee told the waiter to bring three when he saw Paul Trasky walking over. Lee knew Trasky and introduced us. I told Paul I enjoyed his talk and would like to see him in La Paz if we got the chance. His first question for me was what I considered my most reliable source of information.

"Taxi drivers," I answered.

"No kidding. Why?"

"They read all the papers, listen to the radio, work like dogs to make ends meet, and talk to more people in a day than we do in a week. If you take it with a grain of salt, they're the best source. Give me two days of taxi rides in any country, and I'll have a better grip on social, political, and economic conditions than I could get from any consultant or banker."

"Damn, Richard," Trasky laughed, "now I'm afraid you might

steal some of my sources."

I was beat when I got back to La Paz, so Julie and I had a quiet dinner after we put the children to bed. She drew a bath and I shot off an e-mail to Steven Price to give him my impressions of the conference. Despite the problems in the region, there were a number of attractive new projects. Even though it was not a discussion topic today, I was concerned about security. The FARC and Sendero were reasonably quiet, though the COB and the indigenous Bolivians were becoming more violent. The bad guys were smart and flexible, and they never went out of business. Just as I always looked for new opportunities, so did they.

12

Jeremy Goodnature, Stan Jacobs, and Bob Martin of the Green Earth Movement (GEM) arrived in Santa Cruz after three days of meetings outside Bogotá. They were in Bolivia to meet with other militant environmentalists to coordinate their eco-terror activity. GEM was formed six years earlier by members of mainstream environmental groups. Most of the U.S.-based organization's 530 members were college educated and overwhelmingly upper-middle class. Goodnature founded GEM because the mainstream groups were unwilling to engage the enemy. The enemy was generally anyone who thought differently than GEM.

Their first attack was a letter bomb that killed a Houston energy executive and his secretary. A car bomb two years later killed a Los Angeles chemical company VP and his three Environmental Legal Fund car pool companions. A faulty timer caused the bomb to detonate prematurely, so it also killed the toll booth attendant and a driver in the next lane. GEM recently sank an oil and gas company yacht with its entire board of directors and senior executives while they were on a corporate retreat. Goodnature lamented that only six people died. GEM expressed no remorse for their acts, and referred to their victims as "necessary casualties" or "collateral damage."

GEM never claimed responsibility for their actions, but law enforcement and intelligence agencies suspected them. There was, however, no proof. GEM succeeded because they were aggressive and were not on anyone's radar screen. The string of successes, however, brought them increased notoriety. That required them to forge alliances to lower their profile and mask their activity.

Goodnature knew the best places to stay in any city, and in Santa Cruz that meant Las Palmas. It was there that GEM would meet with Grupo Eco Verde de Bolivia, one of the country's more vocal environmental organizations. The discussion with Eco Verde founder Alejandro Pacheco was likely to be contentious. GEM wanted local support for Bolivian subversive operations, but Eco Verde wanted to avoid violence. Goodnature and his associates ordered beers and discussed strategy while they waited for their potential partners. Within minutes, a heavy-set Bolivian sporting a Hawaiian shirt sauntered into the pool area with two colleagues in tow. Pacheco dropped himself into a chair directly across from Goodnature.

"Jeremy," Pacheco said as he stroked his three day facial growth almost defiantly, "I know what you've come to talk about, but there is something else I want to cover first."

"Well, it's good to see you too, Alejandro. What's pressing on your mind?" Goodnature asked.

"Spike 20. It's back. The Colombians are secretly using it for eradication, and I'm afraid the Bolivian government will do the same here."

Spike 20 was a powerful DOW Chemical Company herbicide and was high on Pacheco's hit list. It destroyed large areas of land and made the eradicated areas virtually unusable for prolonged periods of time. Eco Verde wanted GEM support to get rid of Spike 20. GEM said no. Goodnature would support some programs in exchange for subversive operations, but Spike 20 was not one of them.

"We know you don't like the stuff, but the Special Drug Police and the UMOPAR eradication units haven't confirmed they'll use it in Bolivia," Goodnature said.

"Since when have you trusted the government, Jeremy?"

"We want to protect the Andean environment as much as you do, Alejandro. The fact is that Spike 20 is not nearly as bad as coca. If you and Eco Verde were really concerned about the environment, that's what you would go after."

"That's absurd, and you know it."

"Do you know how bad coca cultivation really is?"

"I'm sure you and your gringo friends are about to educate us."

"More than two million acres of rain forest in the Amazon basin have been destroyed to clear land for coca," Goodnature said, ignoring the sarcasm. "The natural habitat and bio-diversity both take a beating. Slash and burn clearing is a huge jungle air pollution problem. The growers plant their crops on hillsides to make them harder to see and harder to reach. You've seen how growers operate with no terracing along the land contours. Heavy rains and strong winds almost instantly erode the soil. It may never come back."

"You sound like a U.S. government agronomist," Pacheco muttered. "You wanted to fix the problem when we covered this last year."

"We still do, but we've done our homework. Have you?"

"We have," Pacheco shot back. "Even the label says not to use Spike 20 near good trees and warns that exposing the root system can kill the tree. They can drop the stuff from higher altitudes than the current herbicides, it lasts longer, and eventually leaches into the ground water. DOW designed it to kill weeds under railroads, not to eradicate crops. We have to stop it."

"Look," Goodnature said, leaning across the table, "this is one battle you're not going to win. The cocaine business is so big that governments will use everything at their disposal to fight it—and that includes Spike 20. Deforestation is just one part of the problem. The environmental effects of the processing are even worse."

"So what? I don't buy it."

"So what? Listen, Andean region cocaine processors pour four million gallons of ethyl ether, three million gallons of sulfuric acid, two million gallons of acetone, and—get this—180 million gallons of kerosene into the ground every single year. Plus, you can add to that the fertilizers and the pesticides they use to grow coca. At some point, all that runs off into streams and ground water. That's what I mean when I tell you that Eco Verde should be a lot more concerned about processing than about Spike 20."

"Does that mean that you're going after coca processors?"

"No way. I'm not going after either one."

"It sounds to me like you're not willing to do anything. Spike 20 is bad, Jeremy. I won't move unless you help us on this."

"Alejandro, here's the deal. Spike 20 is a dead issue, and there's nothing we can do about it. Let it go. I want your commitment to act against the government and local companies. We'll give you money, training, and logistical assistance. If you join us, then I'll support you locally, but Spike 20 is not on my list. I'm leaving it and the drug business alone. My dog's not in that fight because there's nothing we can change. I advise you to do the same."

Goodnature sat back and polished off the last of his Amstel. He knew Pacheco was a coward, but hoped the promise of money and training would sway him. It was the last overture Goodnature would make. He would never tell Pacheco the real reason for his reluctance to take on Spike 20: the DOW patent had expired. Eco-terrorism was a for-profit business, and there was no profit without deep pockets. DOW was no longer a profitable target, and that made Spike 20 irrelevant, regardless of the environmental damage.

"Screw you, Jeremy. We're not going to help you blow people up here. You can do all you want in your own country, but we actually want to improve the environment in Bolivia. I often wonder if you really do."

"Why don't you come out and say what you're thinking?"

"You're not serious about your commitments. We had a verbal agreement a year ago, and now you're abandoning us."

"Things change. The world is a dynamic place."

"Spare me, Jeremy. It sounds like your word is dynamic. You shouldn't do this to your friends, especially those who know about letter bombs to energy company executives. Unless you consider Oscar Dávila an environmentally sensitive kind of guy, your local operating money doesn't come from eco-sensitive Bolivian contributors."

"Tell me," Goodnature said as he folded his napkin, "did you just commit a verbal indiscretion, or did you threaten me?"

"Take it however you want, but let's just say you don't want someone spreading such news around," Pacheco smirked. He lit a cigar and leaned back in his chair, believing he had bested Goodnature at his own game.

Goodnature did not look up as he ran his right index finger around the rim of the empty beer glass. He took an imperceptibly short breath, looked up to smile at Pacheco, and spoke to him in a measured voice. "Don't get exercised about this. We'll have dinner, drink some beer, and I'll treat you to a night at the Concha de Oro." Goodnature meant the finest cathouse in Santa Cruz. "We can get our thoughts in order, and we'll figure out something that makes everyone happy. We need to work together. How does that sound?"

"I'm all for it, but you need to convince me. See you tonight."

Goodnature knew Pacheco could not resist a paid night out. As he watched the Bolivians leave the hotel, he realized he did not need this pissant Andean outfit. Eco Verde had no money, marginal influence and credibility, and now they were being difficult. They had a loud bark, but always backed down at fight time.

Pacheco and Eco Verde were an unnecessary distraction. Goodnature picked up his cell phone to make dinner plans, but first he called Oscar Dávila.

13

I looked forward to lunch with the embassy RSO, John Denning, at La Venenciana so I could finally get some expert advice on a few nagging issues. The restaurant was near the end of a dead-end residential street lined with houses and four-story apartment buildings. The street was so narrow that cars had to park half on the sidewalk to allow traffic through, and an SUV would need several attempts to turn around. It had ambush site written all over it. Lucho and I would back in next time.

La Venenciana was in a two story white art deco house with large windows on both sides facing the street and two first floor balconies with flowers. The restaurant was on the ground floor and the owners lived above it. The interior was bright, the sunlight reflecting pleasantly off cream-colored walls and white table linens. I sat at the back next to a set of French doors opening onto a terrace. The waiter brought me a beer and John Denning soon arrived with a khaki-suited Latin man in his mid 40s.

"Richard," Denning's voice boomed from ten feet away as he extended his hand, "it's good to see you. This is Felipe Torres. He's the DEA Attaché at the embassy. I thought you should meet."

"It's a pleasure," I said and offered Torres my hand.

"The pleasure is mine, and welcome to Bolivia," Torres replied pleasantly.

"I hear you've already gotten a taste of Las Palmas," Denning said with a smile. "Lee Jordan mentioned that you were there together several weeks ago. Good meeting?"

"Most of it was a bore, but the scenery was great. The one guy who made the trip worthwhile was Paul Trasky."

"Paul founded the Andean Times years ago, and he's plugged in," Denning observed.

"You're not alone on boring conferences," Torres said. "We've had some snoozers this year. At least there's more to Las Palmas than conferences."

"I'll say," Denning laughed. "Every time we go there, my wife spends more time watching my eyes than the kids."

"I can see why," I said, remembering the Varig stewardesses. "Guys, I need some help on something. Did Lee tell you about my hoja de coca problem?"

"He did," Denning said. "That's why I brought Felipe."

"Thanks. The laborers working on our infrastructure projects want us to provide coca leaf and two chewing breaks a day. This is a brave new world for me, and I'd appreciate a bit of insight."

"I'll tell you what the U.S. Embassy position is," Torres started slowly, as if his comments had a "buyer beware" provision attached, "and I'll tell you what people actually do. It's obviously your call."

"Fair enough. I'm just looking for some background so I can make a decision."

"The embassy takes a dim view of anything related to coca," Torres said. "At the Sheraton inauguration many years ago, the hotel covered a lobby table with small Bolivian statues and coca leaves. The deputy chief of mission at the time went ballistic and demanded that the hotel remove the display. He said the coca was a slap in the face of the U.S. eradication effort. The hotel was pissed, but they removed it. Anyway, if it spells 'coca' we're against it. Period."

"How common is coca leaf?"

"It's part of daily life," Torres answered. "Eighty percent of rural Bolivians chew coca, ten percent use it some other way, and only ten percent never use it. Because of its widespread use in the countryside, many European companies regularly provide it to their altiplano laborers."

"How about U.S. companies?" I asked.

"Almost never," Torres said, "and they strongly object to its use. European companies see it in a cultural context, and U.S. companies see it as a legal matter."

"Does the embassy have a formal position, or do you stay out of it?"

"We don't tell companies what to do because we really don't have to. Everyone knows about eradication, so they generally stay away from coca. I hope that helps."

"It does, and thanks. My headquarters punted on this one, and I think they hoped I would turn it down for them. This is a no-brainer. We'll provide it. Senior management will squirm but so be it."

As I listened to Torres, it seemed I spent more time talking to people about coca than running Phoenix. Coca and cocaine were always in the news and the government talked about them continuously. In this dirt-poor country of nine million, over 300,000 people actively worked in the coca-cocaine production chain. It generated over a billion dollars a year and dominated people's daily lives.

Beyond the cocaine business, Denning and Torres could tell me more about Raúl than anyone else in La Paz. I wanted to discuss Raúl with Steven Price during my interviews, but worried that I would not be seen as part of the "team." What happened to people in a corporate existence when being a "team player" meant not asking relevant questions? I was tired of worrying about this sort of crap, and had to dangle one out there.

"Raúl and I talked about eradication at length the other day," I said. "There doesn't seem to be anything in this country he's not intimately associated with."

"You've got that one right," Denning said. "He's connected to the highest Bolivian political, business, and military circles. All of his companies are successful and you'll see his fingerprints everywhere."

"What does he have?"

"Anything and everything that's profitable," Denning said matter-of-factly. "He's got a telecommunications enterprise, a chemicals manufacturer and distributor, an engineering and construction company, a development concern, a private security group, and a large aviation company with both fixed wing and rotary aircraft. The embassy commercial officer could tell you much more than I can, but you get the idea."

"He hasn't missed anything has he?"

"Not really," Denning said, "but there is something you need to understand. With hindsight, it's easy to say that Raúl made all the right moves. But it wasn't so obvious at the time. Raúl put his own money into local agricultural projects years before the U.S. Agency for International Development or any other international development organizations were seriously interested in Bolivia. He started peanut farms, hearts of palm plantations, and ice factories in the poorest regions of the country. His projects employ the locals and alleviate the harm coca farmers suffer from eradication."

"So he takes some of the heat off the embassy and gives you wiggle room?"

"Exactly," Denning replied. "We figured it made political, financial, and operational sense to take Raúl on as a partner. He could shoulder some of the financial and operating risk. With tight budgets, a well-heeled local partner is extremely attractive to the U.S. government. He can also deflect a huge amount of our political risk. That's a priceless asset."

"But how did he get in so tight with eradication in the first place?"

"That's another story," Torres answered. "We got to know Raúl when he was Bolivia's senior representative at the Cartagena I drug summit in 1990. The U.S., Bolivia, Colombia, and Peru were the only participants. Without him, Bolivia would not have been there. Raúl understands and communicates our policy goals and objectives to the Bolivian government. He influences perceptions, actions, and attitudes. The man is rock solid for us in a region full of people we can't trust."

Torres had good reason for being Raúl's cheerleader. Corporations and governments need insiders to get things done. The conversation confirmed that people thought Raúl was wonderful. I still did not like him.

"We use his security company," I continued, "and I know you guys do too. This part of the world is famous for lousy security services, so how did he put together such a well-trained group?"

"Contacts, like every thing else," Denning responded. "He started in the early 1990s, recruiting from the elite anti-drug troops. U.S. Special Forces and our government agencies trained a lot of them. He provides security to the embassy, several other foreign diplomatic missions, and a bunch of foreign corporations."

"And that doesn't include his aviation company," Torres interjected. "His air fleet provides services we can't afford on our own. We use his crop dusters and turboprops for eradication, and his jets move U.S. government personnel around the region and back stateside. He's even got a Boeing BBJ2 business jet we fly when the Bolivian government doesn't have it tied up for some political junket."

"That reminds me," I said, "I've been warned not to take any free rides on Bolivian military flights."

"Not unless you want to die," Denning said. "The things are

death traps. One of the reasons we use Raúl's company is that he has an impeccable safety record and provides service cheaper than anyone else."

"A lot of it just comes down to budgets, doesn't it?"

"Speaking of which," Denning said with a pained expression, "we need to get back to the embassy pronto for a damned budget meeting. It seems like it never ends."

"Understood. I've been there more times than I can count."

Lucho and I were back at the office by 3:00 P.M. to learn that the Bolivian Minister of Defense cancelled my meeting with him that afternoon. So much for my second attempt to discuss our radar projects. I suspected Raúl knew it before I did, so I walked over to his office to find out what happened.

"Raúl, any idea why the defense minister cancelled?"

"I don't know." Raúl shrugged and quickly brought up his screensaver. "Ministerial whim I suspect. The minister's secretary called with apologies. No matter how much money you invest in the country, you're just another target for a cancellation. You're on his schedule Thursday at 11:15 A.M."

Raúl was pumped. He told the minister that Blackstone had a conflict and could not attend today. It would take only a few more no-shows and the insulted ministers would permanently shut him out. Once that happened, he would be unable to conduct any business with senior government officials on his own. *Blackstone will soon have to beg for help*, Raúl thought.

"I hope so," I said. "I'm going out to the house to help Julie unpack and move in. Today is our first night out of the hotel, so we'll celebrate. By the way, what are you doing Wednesday night?"

"I have dinner plans with a business partner coming in from Quito. Why do you ask?"

"Julie and I wanted to get together with you for dinner."

"Thanks for the invitation. Perhaps another night."

"Sounds good to me."

I had visibly shocked him. Good job, Richard; keep the guy off guard. Verónica told me he was tied up Wednesday night and could not cancel the commitment. There was nothing like disarming the jerk.

14

"Come on guys!" Goodnature shouted to his GEM companions as he knocked on their doors at Las Palmas. "Time to hit the road. The plane's waiting."

"I thought we were leaving tomorrow," Stan Jacobs complained.

"Nope, the charter crew called and said we have to leave now. There's some sort of scheduling foul-up."

The only call was from Goodnature telling the crew they would leave a day early. The sooner the better. Goodnature cleaned his room meticulously and told the others to do the same. When dealing with subversive groups, a scribbled telephone number or note could unravel an entire operation. If they hurried, they would be in Santiago, Chile, by noon. Then the Pacific breezes of the Viña del Mar coastline and their next round of meetings were only a few hours northwest by car.

Goodnature settled into his seat on the jet and closed his eyes. It was a long night, and he was beat. He schmoozed Pacheco at the Brazilian *rodizio* restaurant and won him over by agreeing to support the fight against Spike 20. He soothed Pacheco's nerves further by agreeing that Grupo Eco Verde could remain an environmental "political activist" organization. There was no need for them to get involved in violent subversive activity. Not yet.

Goodnature then treated everyone to a night at the Concha de Oro, less than a mile from Las Palmas and its rival in elegance and luxury. The Concha's twenty suites had bars, bedrooms, sitting areas, Jacuzzis and high-end audio and video equipment. The attentive staff served any food or drink twenty-four hours a day. If a guest's companion was not sufficiently exciting, the Concha had a large selection of erotic videos. The cathouse of choice for men of means and the favorite of expatriate businessmen, it was safe and discrete with no romantic entanglements. Pacheco liked tall blondes, and Goodnature ensured that several were available. The GEM members took advantage of the Concha's favors as well. Goodnature particularly enjoyed the two short brunettes whose darkly tanned skin excited him in ways that his San Francisco girlfriend never could.

The rest of the evening was set in motion earlier in the day. Pacheco made one mistake when he speculated about the letter bomb and another when he wondered about GEM's financial backers. That error caused Oscar Dávila to dispatch Ilidio Quevedo from La Paz to solve the problem in Santa Cruz. This would be routine for Quevedo, but he would enjoy it. He was very good and he loved his work.

Quevedo and his assistant arrived at the Concha de Oro thirty minutes after GEM left, about 1:00 A.M. Eco Verde were easy prey after their sexual escapades and heavy drinking. Quevedo bound, gagged, and took all three to a house less than half a mile from Las Palmas. Once there, Quevedo gave them an hour to get their wits about them. If they were too drunk, they would not know enough to be scared. Fear was the key to extracting information, and people talked when they were scared. Eco Verde might have been scared sooner had they noticed that Quevedo put them in a soundproof room.

Pacheco was first in the batter's box. His companions were tied to chairs less than ten feet away. Quevedo made them watch to heighten their anxiety. He was so excited, he could hardly stand it. Pacheco was completely naked so Quevedo had access to his entire body to inflict pain. Pacheco was defiant, which made it even more exhilarating.

Pacheco reared back, swore, and spat. Quevedo didn't know if he was brave, stupid, or still drunk. Time would tell. A burning cigarette was the first treat Pacheco enjoyed, and Quevedo found his favorite spots—eyelids, armpits, nipples, and genitals. Pacheco screamed in agony and stopped spitting. He said he knew nothing. Quevedo went to the fingernails and pulled out two with pliers. Pacheco nearly passed out. Still, he admitted nothing. Quevedo finally wired up his genitals and anus. Pacheco seemed almost to enjoy it before he screamed for mercy. After twenty-five minutes, he mumbled that he knew nothing. He was bluffing, and had tried to intimidate Goodnature with a rumor.

Quevedo had heard enough. He pumped several 9mm bullets into Pacheco's and his two associates' heads, threw the bodies into the back of a truck, and took them to Oscar Dávila's meat processing plant. Once inside, he fed them through the industrial meat grinder. Pacheco was so fat it took two people to push him through. The grinder ensured that Pacheco and his colleagues were crushed, cut, torn, and mixed into a soggy, pulpy mush. The Santa Cruz Zoo tigers would notice a slight taste difference at breakfast the next morning.

Although Goodnature did not know the details, he knew Pacheco was no longer on the planet. He ran his hand over the leather seat, sampled the caviar, and sipped the champagne. This was the way he was meant to live, and other people paid for it. It was like being a politician, only better because he did not have to pretend to answer to anyone.

15

"Don Raúl, I just met with Blackstone," the Bolivian Minister of Defense whispered into his telephone. "I told him you have the radar project. The bank confirms the deposit in my account exactly as you promised."

"Jorge, as long as you help us, you know we'll help you. Bring the family to the house Saturday for lunch. It's important you know that his arrival does not change how we do business."

"Thank you, Don Raúl. We'll see you Saturday."

Raúl removed his laptop from a locked briefcase and booted it up. As the display flickered and icons appeared, he wondered why he had so many security features to lock his hard drive and encrypt data, e-mails, and financial transactions. There was virtually no risk in a country that was largely illiterate. *What a waste of time.* He dialed up the Internet instead of using the office cable connection. The cable had been acting up, and he was in a hurry.

Raúl's eyes flashed across his Merrill Lynch, Citibank, and Hong Kong Shanghai Bank accounts. The latest wire transfers were on their way to his U.S., Colombian, and Peruvian partners to ensure that business continued normally. The money would flow through various financial institutions around the world, legitimate manufacturing companies in the Far East, and would come back through the Caymans as dividends and foreign exchange transactions. Funds would then move into offshore financial instruments and finally to the end accounts of several front organizations. Raúl logged off and left for a drink with friends at the Mallasa Golf Club.

As I walked to lunch, I dodged police barricades that cordoned off the Prado and diverted downtown traffic to side streets. I looked up the avenue and saw several thousand people massed near the San Francisco church a few hundred yards away. Traffic was a mess and was about to get worse.

"G'day, Richard," Lee said as I walked up to our table at the Sucre Hotel. "We have a front row seat for the show."

"What's up? The police are everywhere."

"It's a protest march, and it's routine in La Paz. You'll get used to them. I invited Paul Trasky to join us so we can finish the discussion we started at Las Palmas. He'll be here in a few minutes."

The marchers came down the street fifteen abreast, a sea of humanity beating drums and waving flags and banners. They chanted angrily about social injustice and American imperialism. Paul Trasky joined us as a firecracker mortar exploded sixty feet away. He said La Paz protest marches were carefully scripted and orchestrated. The central labor union filed an application with the city government, and a designated official approved the request expeditiously and assigned a time and location. The events invariably took place on the Prado at lunch time to inconvenience the greatest number of people possible. Paul called it a racket and said people on both sides made money. As the cocaleros appeared with large bushels of coca leaf, I told Lee and Paul we would provide coca to our altiplano laborers.

"Will your headquarters accept that?" Lee asked.

"Not sure, but they really don't have a choice. They said it was my decision, and I made it. How they deal with it depends on whether or not they put things in perspective. The fact is, they don't want to touch this."

"Of course they don't," Lee said. "Since it's controversial, they want you to handle it. I've been there before."

"They're scared of it, but it's all pretty stupid. It's contentious for them, but it's a non-issue for us. For all their talk about 'think global, act local,' they don't have a clue."

Coca was everywhere in Bolivia, and to survive I had to learn more. Paul knew the business from every angle, and I figured a journalist would give me a different twist than the DEA. He said an estimated sixty thousand peasant families worked in the coca and cocaine processing business and it contributed from half a billion to a billion dollars per year to the Bolivian economy. Bolivia's poor economy, weak institutions, and rampant corruption made the coca trade an attractive avenue for political and economic enrichment. Washington ignored Bolivia for years, but that ended when cocaine was deemed a national security threat. Paul said people would be shocked to learn how extensively the U.S. was involved in drug eradication and interdiction overseas. I asked him to try me.

The first significant American military involvement occured in 1986 with Operation Blast Furnace. During Operation Snowcap a year later, the U.S. Border Patrol sealed off the Yungas and the Chapare, SEALs trained Bolivian troops in riverine and interdiction operations, and U.S. Special Forces trained the counter-narcotics police in other interdiction and seizure procedures. U.S. Air Force advisors assisted with air interdiction in the Beni area, and additional personnel participated in airport civic action projects around the country.

"So, where does Raúl fit in?" I asked warily.

"He's connected to everything and everyone. The U.S. Embassy has worked closely with him since he was the liaison on the first U.S. military involvement."

"Is there ever any talk about him and drugs?"

"Zip," Paul said concisely. "Most people are tainted by something to some extent. It's just a question of how much. Raúl's an exception and everyone knows he's clean. The embassy wouldn't touch him if there were ever a hint otherwise. Too risky."

"How about kickbacks and payoffs on normal business operations?" I wondered.

"Who knows, but that sort of thing is so common no one cares," Paul laughed. "Business corruption is normal. It's a way of life. You have to remember that governments around here keep their eye on the big picture."

"And that is?"

"A lot of people are grateful for what Raúl and Phoenix have done. Raúl helped Bolivia become one of the biggest recipients of U.S. aid in Latin America. It started with agricultural assistance, but went on to include infrastructure—roads, bridges, airports, power plants, schools—and then things like health programs. At the same time, U.S. military aid shot way up when Washington figured out that Bolivia is strategically located to fight drugs. Raúl and Phoenix were here from the beginning, and people remember that. Needless to say, both have profited handsomely."

"You're saying that Raúl was in the right place at the right time?"

"In spades. I'll give you an example. During Operation Safe Haven in 1991, the DEA supervised six hundred UMOPAR troops in the Beni Department that looked for a local drug lord. He had ties to the Medellín cartel and operated out of Santa Ana del Yacuma. The government found nothing during house-to-house searches and they made no arrests. They did, however, confiscate a lot of aircraft. Any guess who bought the planes at fire sale prices?"

"Hmm. Let me think hard on this one," I said. "Not . . . ?"

"You got it," Paul smiled. "Raúl started an air transport company. He routinely picks up confiscated aircraft at big discounts from market values and uses them for DEA eradication work."

"How very convenient," I said, "and how incestuous."

"Perhaps," Trasky rejoined, "but remember that the Americans and Bolivians had to sell the planes, and Raúl was one of the few legitimate businessmen who could afford them. He stepped in for good business and political reasons. It might look like an inside deal, but it was the only option available."

"Point well taken," I conceded. "They didn't have much choice, so subsidizing a familiar face wasn't a bad idea."

"Exactly."

"Does his involvement with the U.S. Embassy or eradication hurt Phoenix?"

"Not really, because Phoenix's and Raúl's direct participation isn't widely known. Plus, your development projects generate good will, so people see you positively."

"How about Americans? Do we have any fans, or do people despise us?"

"Bolivians don't hate Americans," Trasky said, "but they don't trust the U.S. government. They dislike the DEA and think the U.S. is hypocritical."

"Paul," Lee interrupted, "tell Richard about the DEA agent in Santa Cruz."

"In 1992," Trasky said, lowering his voice, "a DEA agent shot a Bolivian in a bar fight. The police arrested the agent and detained him in a local jail. A Santa Cruz judge dropped the charges several hours later, and an embassy employee spirited the agent out of the country on a late night U.S. government flight. He disappeared and that was the end of it. The Bolivian foreign minister asked for an explanation but got none."

"How about the guy he shot?"

"The official version was that he lived, but I never found him. I finally tracked down the nurse who treated him at the hospital. She said he died and asked that I never talk to her again. The woman was terrified."

"Did the guy have any relatives?"

"None I could find. It seems the father was dead, and there was no trace of the mother. Anyway, the point is that Bolivians see Americans getting away with anything, including murder."

"I can't blame them."

"Now," said Trasky slowly, "it's my turn."

"Okay, but is it Paul Trasky journalist or Paul Trasky lunch partner—or are they inseparable?"

"Lunch partner."

"Shoot."

"At some point, the Bolivian government and the press will ask for your opinion on coca and eradication. I'm not asking for an answer, but suggest you sort out your thoughts on it."

"Reporters ask me about coca at least once a month," Lee said. "Get ready."

"I don't like what it does to the Bolivians. In many ways, I don't think it's any of our business. I also know that it's a complex issue. By that, I guess I mean that the company that cuts my paycheck is heavily involved in eradication."

"Here's the problem," Trasky said. "Latin Americans and most of the world see drug use as a demand-side problem. American politicians see it as supply-side because that lets them shift the blame. No one forces Americans to buy drugs. They buy them because they want to. Free will bothers U.S. politicians more than anything else, because it's behavior they can't control. Ignoring the fact that free will is the real issue makes drug control much harder in the long run because they never get to the root cause. It also makes the U.S. look more hypocritical than ever.

"There's an analogy here. American financial institutions and politicians complain that Latin American countries take out loans they can't repay. But notice that banks keep lending money, even when they know it's unlikely to come back. Then everybody gets into a public pissing contest about who to blame for third world debt problems. It's just as irresponsible to take drugs as it is for a government to borrow money it can't pay back. The only difference is that authorities consider one illicit and the other legitimate."

I looked out the window at the protest march and realized that Bolivians felt the U.S. treated them like trash. They believed the U.S. chased drug lords harder in Bolivia than they did in Los Angeles. The agency guys were good people who did an outstanding job, but bureaucrats interested in their next promotion or the next election ran the show. How would I feel if someone invaded the U.S. to eradicate the evils of violent movies corrupting their youth? We were spending billions of dollars to protect ourselves from drugs. Who would protect us from the politicians and bureaucrats?

16

After a relaxing Saturday at home, we had dinner with Lee and Chlöe and Henry and Jessica O'Connor. Henry was the oil and gas executive with the mistress in Santa Cruz. I wondered if he would bring his wife or his mistress. We got to the restaurant before Lee and Chlöe, and I knew when we sat down that I would regret arriving without reinforcements. Jessica was there, but Henry was not. Julie and I sat down on either side of her and ordered drinks. Jessica already had a few in her, and she ordered another one.

"What do you know? Henry's not here yet," she said with mock surprise. "He played golf all day and then went to the office. He said he had to catch up on work. I don't believe it."

"What do you mean, Jessica?" I asked.

"You know exactly what I mean. Who's he screwing?"

I almost choked and sipped water to buy time. Everything stood still on me as I remembered seeing Henry with his babe in Santa Cruz. Jessica was a babe in her own right, but I guess Henry needed something more. In any case, this was not my fight.

"I can't tell you anything about that Jessica," I said slowly. "This is news to me."

Lee and Chlöe walked toward our table. "Richard won't tell me who Henry's sleeping with," Jessica announced as they sat down.

"Come on, Jessica," Julie said. "You don't know he's having an affair."

"Bullshit. Men think they have this wired. But you know what? When men's instincts tell them their wives are having affairs, they get it right ten percent of the time. When women's instincts tell them their husbands are fooling around, they get it right ninety percent of the time. I know he's got someone else. Either that or he's gone fag on me, which I doubt. I don't think a boyfriend would wear the gold earrings I found in the front seat of his car last weekend. Oh, and I talked to my mother about it. You know what she said? 'First, you have a house full of servants. Second you travel First Class to Miami twice a year to go shopping. And, third, your father did it for thirty-five years. Accept it, stop complaining, and realize how lucky you are. At least he takes care of you and the children and you're not out on the street.' How's that for a mother? Now I don't feel guilty about screwing his brother for the last three years. He's a lot better equipped than Henry anyway."

That bomb dropped, and you could hear the paint dry. Henry appeared fifteen minutes later and Jessica gave him a hug and kiss as if nothing were wrong. She looked like she had always been by his side—and like a woman whose husband abandoned her years before. We went through a couple of bottles of wine, and I waited for something to happen every time Jessica opened her mouth. It never did, and dinner was great. We rolled out of the restaurant at 1:20 A.M. and were not sure there was enough oxygen to digest our dinner. I wondered if Henry would live to see another day or whether Jessica would remember tonight.

It was a joy to sleep in on Saturday and take a break from the weekday schedule. Julie's internal clock rang at 5:30 A.M. on weekdays, but she disconnected it on weekends. I woke up just short of nine. Normally I would do anything to stay curled up in bed with her, but today was different. I rolled out of bed and stole quietly downstairs. Before she stirred, I was back with coffee and a tray of scrambled eggs, bacon, sausage, toast, coffee, and orange juice. The smile on her face and the twinkle in her eye as I came into the bedroom made my day.

Later in the day, we prepared an afternoon barbecue and invited some of the children's schoolmates and a few of our friends. We cooked sausages, sweetbreads, ribs, and steak over open charcoal. One guest was our attorney and the other had a small automotive parts manufacturing plant. Lee and Chlöe were on their way, but were delayed because of the all-important beer run.

The party was typical of Latin America, with the men on one side and the women on the other. I mentioned that we had dinner out the night before, and they asked with whom. When I answered, they wondered if I had seen Henry's mistress yet. It seemed everyone knew about her. Jessica had to know I was lying.

Justo, our attorney, already had his mind made up. "She's a *monumento de mujer*, a monument of a woman. We should be so lucky."

"Wouldn't your wife object?" I asked half in jest.

"That's not the issue," he responded indignantly. "As a Bolivian man, I have not only the right, but also the obligation to have a mistress. If not just one, then several. My associates would think less of me if I did not."

"I don't think Julie would accept that."

"Pity. I guess she has no sense of humor?"

"On the contrary, she has a fabulous sense of humor. It just doesn't apply to my jumping in bed with other women."

17

"Excelsior Palace Hotel, por favor," Jeremy Goodnature told the driver as the GEM team climbed into a taxi at the Lima airport. Goodnature looked out the window at a typically overcast, cool, humid Lima day. Less than half an hour in Lima, he already missed the Viña del Mar coastline, the Chilean wine, and the women. The drab Lima cityscape reminded him that they came for business and not for scenery. They checked into the hotel, and Goodnature sent Jacobs and Martin to meet with GreenForest Action while he visited Professor Julio Arraya at the Universidad de Lima.

Goodnature first met Arraya through a mutual friend during his Georgetown junior year abroad in Lima. Arraya was a political philosophy graduate student at the Pontifícia Universidad Católica del Perú, and he introduced Goodnature to Sendero Luminoso leader Abimael Guzmán. The Sendero launched ten thousand armed guerillas against the government in 1980 after almost a decade of planning. They assassinated political figures in the countryside and conducted extensive car bombing campaigns in Lima. Thirty thousand Peruvians died in the conflict, but Goodnature considered them "necessary casualties." Goodnature's upper middle class prep school background qualified him uniquely to understand Sendero's suffering at the hands of the Great Imperialist. He was ashamed that the United States was a country of self-serving cretins who oppressed the third world. After several late-night discussions with Guzmán and his followers, Goodnature visited a Sendero jungle camp.

The trip convinced him he would never join Sendero as a guerilla, since living in the jungle or in an urban rat house was a needless hardship for a pointless struggle. Sendero was, however, a guide for achieving his goals and objectives. Goodnature decided to form a "green earth" group in the United States, but he had neither people nor money. Environmentalists and gun banners seemed natural targets for support. The tree huggers had some environmental objectives but no money. The gun grabbers were well heeled but would never get their hands dirty. The two complemented each other perfectly, and eco-terror would have deep pocket funding. That would in turn finance Jeremy Goodnature. It was elegant, efficient, and extremely profitable.

Goodnature talked a good game and he loved to fleece his contributors. Clean air was the least of his concerns, and he drove a low mileage SUV. Guns were his constant companions, regardless of local laws, customs, or gun free zones. He knew the money would pour in, and it did. GEM's cash accounts stood at six million dollars, and he answered to no one. Sucker punching was fun, especially when the victims felt good about it.

GEM was Goodnature's vehicle to reel in the true believers who wanted to ensure world environmental purity. He combined the best Latin American models to create a new guerrilla organization under the umbrella of an environmental group. He drew almost exclusively from the Sendero's jungle tactics, the Uruguayan Tupamaros' urban tactics, and the Brazilian Carlos Marighella's all-inclusive philosophy.

The Tupamaros National Liberation Movement was the ultimate urban guerrilla group in Montevideo in the 1960s and early 1970s. Named for the Inca revolutionary leader Tupac Amaru, their first formal action was a 1963 raid on the Swiss Gun Club in Montevideo. At first they distributed stolen food to the poor in and around Montevideo but soon engaged in murder, kidnapping, and urban terrorism. The 1970s military dictatorship eliminated the Tupamaros as a fighting force, leaving the remnants to form a minor Uruguayan political party. Before Brazilian security forces killed him in 1969, Marighella wrote *The Minimanual of the Urban Guerrilla*, a staple in the reference library of every urban subversive around the world.

Goodnature brought it all together by creating the ultimate guerilla network in the context of the ecological struggle. Environmental or political goals, however, were not his objectives. Money and power were, and he would do anything to get them. Goodnature also loved to blow things up. For the moment, he was content to be Oscar Dávila's bought conduit to Sendero and other guerilla groups in Latin America. Dávila was a convenient and necessary partner. Although Sendero could not be brought to heel, they would do just about anything for cash. For the last decade, they were more concerned about their bank accounts than anything else. Even revolutionaries had to retire, and old warriors wanted nothing less than first-class capitalist luxury.

"Julio, you look great, old friend," Goodnature said as he embraced Arraya in the doorway of his university office. Arraya joined Sendero as a college student and was their logistics coordinator. The university environment gave him excellent cover, both then and now. The government looked for terrorists in the jungle, when most of them were right down the street in classrooms, law offices, and retail shops. Some of Sendero's best bombers were attractive women.

Fujimori hurt Sendero badly in the late 1990s, but they kept enough key players to maintain operations. Fujimori was tough, honest, and predictable. His head of state security, Vladimiro Montesinos, however, was a double-crosser. Montesinos switched sides, depending on who had the bigger bank account. He cheated GEM and Dávila when he sold ten thousand assault rifles to the FARC and kept the money. Montesinos was in a Lima jail on corruption charges and would not be easy to replace, but there was always another Montesinos out there. Perhaps Goodnature would find a more trustworthy crook next time.

Goodnature stepped into Arraya's office, cramped with overflowing bookshelves and a large wooden desk buried with paper. The desk lamp flickered intermittently, the paint peeling off the walls was more gray than white, and the lone window was caked with dirt and cracked down the middle. Cigarette smoke filled the room, and Goodnature immediately saw that Arraya was not the only one smoking.

Goodnature's eyes locked on the man in the back right corner of the office. He was slightly over six feet tall and apparently fit, judging from the way his upper body filled out his polo shirt and sleeveless vest. With his black hair, dark complexion, and several days of facial growth, he looked Middle Eastern. He took a slow drag on his cigarette, the exhaled smoke surrounded his head, and he eyed Goodnature. He did not speak. Goodnature's body language signaled fright, and Arraya stepped in.

"We were just finishing, Jeremy," Arraya said as the stranger emerged from the corner with a cat's slow grace. "I'd like you to meet Mr. Mansour. I asked him to stay so you could meet."

"A pleasure," Jamil Mansour said in impeccable English as he approached.

"Equally," said Goodnature, wincing from the vice-like crush that enveloped his hand.

"Mr. Mansour is visiting from Ciudad del Este, Paraguay. He's been our exclusive supplier for over a year, and we were discussing my latest purchase. He can get you grenades, carbines, mines, plastic explosives, anti-tank weapons and surface to air missiles—anything. He handles only the highest quality goods, delivers discreetly and on time, and has the best prices. We've never been disappointed."

"Glad to hear it," Goodnature said.

"This man can help you, Jeremy. He's not limited to Latin America, and can deliver items to the U.S."

"I'll remember that, Julio. Thanks."

Mansour gave Goodnature a rundown of the merchandise he handled, general purchase terms, and delivery options. Despite his initially menacing appearance, he was the ultimate salesman and quickly put Goodnature at ease. Mansour shook hands with Arraya and told him he would be in contact shortly. He shook Goodnature's hand again and said he looked forward to working with him.

"I got your message," Arraya said once Mansour left. "The money men want us to pick up the tempo of the game?"

"Julio, it's not a game. You've become terribly cynical."

"Just like you, Jeremy, but let's not confuse the issue. The power to the people crap is gone. Do you remember that woman, the exchange student from New York, who was appalled by my attitude toward money?" He lit another cigarette.

"I sure do," laughed Goodnature, "and I'll bet she's a contributor today."

"Well, my conscience is still in the same place it was then. It's in my pocketbook. The only difference today is that the average Peruvian has figured out that Sendero screwed them. Our campaigns pushed so many people out of the countryside and into Lima that the place is virtually unlivable. There are a lot of unhappy people, many of them pissed at us. We're working hard to regain popular support, but it's slow."

"Well, at least I have something that will make you happy; a wire transfer."

"How much?" Arraya flicked ash on the floor.

"Nine million dollars for now, possibly more to follow later this year."

"And the purpose of such a large sum is . . . ?"

"Some high profile attacks," Goodnature said, as if the answer were self-evident. "Significant enough to make the authorities dedicate time and resources to chasing Sendero. We want the government off guard and destabilized."

"We want that as well. What are you looking for?"

"Just make sure it has your signature on it. If you make it look like Al-Qaeda, you'll have the Americans all over you."

"We can do that. Plus, the money will help train the recruits we're getting."

"Recruits?" Goodnature asked, surprised. "You're getting new recruits?"

"You bet we are, more than we can handle."

"Where on earth from?"

"All over. Last year we had almost a hundred from Central America. Drug gangs. Surprisingly violent bastards. This year we have a lot from Argentina and Brazil, and they are well educated. Many are in their twenties, and some have college degrees in law, accounting, medicine, and engineering. We've put in a formal three month training program for them."

"You can't be serious, Julio. How did this come up so fast?"

"It's been years in the making, but it's finally coming to a head. The Central American drug gangs are going regional and they need new skills. It's a bit more complicated with the others. In the 90s, Argentina and especially Brazil bet their future that prosperity was right around the corner. They expected to become economic powers by attracting manufacturing and service businesses away from the U.S. and Mexico. All that has gone to China and India, and competing with those two is impossible. Young professionals understand that they're caught in a permanent cycle of poverty, so it's fashionable to be a revolutionary again. We train them and they go home and start their own guerrilla movements."

"What's the quid pro quo?"

"Ah, always thinking about the money. We stay out of their way, but we get twenty percent of the extortion and drug money the first five years, fifteen percent the next three and then ten percent the last two years. After ten years, they're completely on their own with no ties to us. It's a great business, Jeremy."

"Who would have thought?" Goodnature had not seen it coming.

"That's not all. The huge volume of Muslims is the biggest surprise."

"You can't be serious."

"Dead serious, and they're coming from all over—Western Europe, Iran, Iraq, Syria, Pakistan, Malaysia, Indonesia, and the Philippines. We've even cut a joint venture with Abu Sayyaf to train their people. The Americans squeezed everyone so hard in Afghanistan and Iraq that they started looking for training outlets several years ago. What started as a trickle has turned into a steady pipeline."

"What kind of deal have you cut with them?"

"None, and I don't want one. They are a different breed, my friend. They are not like us. They are, however, good clients. They pay cash, they listen, they train hard, and they disappear. That's as close to them as I want to get."

"Anyway, back to the topic: can you execute some serious attacks?"

"We can. What's your timetable?"

"The choice of dates is yours, but I want you active as of yesterday. Understand?"

"Jeremy, for that kind of money we can do just about anything. Trust me, you'll be pleased. Stay tuned to CNN."

18

The Mercedes truck pulled up to the TransWorld Moving storage yard in Chicago at 7:40 P.M., and the driver keyed in a five-digit security code on the pad by the gate. The pad beeped, the green light flickered, and the electric gate shuddered open. The security guards waved casually, since the truck had been there three times in as many weeks. The TransWorld facility stored shipping containers for senior corporate executives moving to the U.S. from overseas, and some of the moving crews worked late at night.

The threat of terrorist attacks against the United States caused U.S. Customs and Border Protection (CBP) to shift their priority from drug interdiction to keeping terrorists and their weapons out of the country. One concern was that terrorists would use cargo containers to deliver matériel. Early in 2002, CBP launched the Container Security Initiative (CSI) to pre-screen foreign cargo before it reached American shores. Since they could not inspect every single container, the National Targeting Center was established to determine which containers were high risk and inspect or possibly stop them before they reached the United States.

CBP knew that not all container cargo was dangerous. TransWorld specialized in moving and storing the personal effects of senior executives, and their 160 corporate clients were the elite of American industry. CBP determined that Transworld's containers represented no risk and issued a blanket waiver for all of their clients. The fast track entry status meant that those containers flew through the system unchecked.

The truck pulled through the gate, and the team noticed that TransWorld had not yet installed video cameras. Active surveillance would not make their task impossible, but would increase their cost of doing business. The driver backed the truck to a stop twelve feet from container AH115. The team piled out, speaking English to avoid drawing attention to themselves.

They examined the seal on the container, broke it, and unwired the lock. The door swung open to reveal a container crammed with personal effects. The team removed furniture and boxes to reach what they came for, tucked away in the right rear corner as usual.

"Hey, guys," a guard making rounds called out, "need any help?"

"No, thanks," the team leader replied. "This one's easy. Just an exec coming back from overseas who needs a few things for work before he moves in."

"I guess that's why they make the big bucks. See ya."

"Must be," the leader answered. "Screw this," he muttered under his breath. "I wish they wouldn't try to be so helpful."

The crew emptied the container and arranged the personal effects alongside their truck. After almost an hour, they came to several stacks of watertight, crush-proof boxes at the back of the container. They made sure the boxes were not damaged or leaking. The team then removed and packed them in the secure false bottom of their truck, specially insulated to thwart police drug-sniffing dogs. No dogs had ever found a stash.

They filled the empty spot in the container with ballast to compensate for the weight loss, and put the furniture and personal effects back. Each team member walked around the container with a flashlight and vacuum cleaner, making sure there was no residue. There was never a problem with the triple-sealing process, but they were always thorough.

Within three hours of arriving, they had emptied, repacked and resealed the container. Even a trained eye would not know it had been opened. The guards did not log them out, and the team hoped TransWorld would never catch the oversight. Porous security procedures kept their work hours short. They would return in a month to take the same container to Mark Hansen's retirement home in Montana—relieved of 830 pounds of cocaine.

"When does the next shipment come in?"

"Van der Bors is relocating from London in five or six weeks. We'll confirm soon, but I think we're looking at over a thousand pounds," the team leader said.

"Ah, life is good. Bonuses will be up this year."

Life was indeed good. The team waved to the guards on the way through the gate and made a slow right turn, congratulating themselves on another successful operation. Some of the best cocaine in the world would soon be on the streets and in homes all over America.

19

Oscar Dávila read the encrypted e-mail confirming the successful removal of 830 pounds of cocaine from Mark Hansen's container the night before. Downstream delivery was made by midnight, and final payments were wired, received, and confirmed shortly thereafter. Bankers and lawyers kept the systems up and running for clients twenty-four hours a day when large sums were involved, especially when it meant large commissions for those same bankers and lawyers. At the right price, everyone played.

Dávila had transported thousands of pounds of cocaine in executives' shipping containers for over three years without a hitch. The next large shipment was Van der Bors' transfer from London to Chicago. Dávila normally alternated shipping methods to avoid establishing patterns, and he was apprehensive about this first back-to-back delivery using the same mechanism to the same location. He had no choice. The shipment was in the pipeline, and his Far East customers would be furious if it arrived late. Being late meant customers went elsewhere, and that required cultivating new ones. Dávila hated that.

Van der Bors was the Phoenix Corporation fiber optic project manager in Bogotá, but had moved to London for a two year assignment. Once in London, the job morphed into a three month temporary to be followed by permanent relocation to the U.S. The company knew the move was temporary months before his arrival in London. They did not tell him because they feared he would quit and take a job with another company in Colombia if he knew he was ultimately headed for the U.S. His short-term status meant UK Customs did not inspect his container, which remained sealed at the British port of entry. U.S. Customs would never suspect a Phoenix executive coming from London.

Regardless of its origin, the container would fast track through TransWorld's Chicago facility. Even so, Dávila did not want a shipment coming from Colombia, so brightly illuminated on the U.S. government's radar screen. Scrutiny got bad years ago when the wife of the U.S. Army colonel who headed the anti-narcotics mission in Colombia was discovered running drugs through the diplomatic pouch. It got even worse within the last year when five American soldiers assigned to a Colombian counter-narcotics base were arrested upon arrival in the U.S. with thirty-five pounds of cocaine. Dávila's formidable network of contacts identified Van der Bors' relocation as an opportunity to move a large volume of drugs. Corporations protected their executives' private information, but how much a packing company clerk knew was amazing.

Next on Dávila's shipment schedule was the repatriation of construction equipment to the U.S. from Latin American projects. Phoenix had a construction equipment subsidiary in Latin America that leased equipment worldwide to its own projects and those of other companies. The fleet included off-highway trucks, backhoe loaders, scrapers, hydraulic excavators, paving equipment, front shovels, pipelayers, multi-terrain loaders, and 100 to 300 ton cranes. Phoenix housed the fleet in port facility tax-free zones where Dávila's collaborators had unfettered access. Much of the equipment went to government sponsored projects with preferential processing through host country customs in Latin America, Europe, the Far East, and the U.S. Once past customs, loading or unloading large quantities of product was easy. The mechanism was one hundred percent successful with no losses. Dávila planned to move 13,700 pounds of cocaine around the world in the next eight months, much of it hidden in construction equipment.

Dávila turned his computer off and walked out of his study through French doors to the garden patio to read the Sunday paper and eat breakfast. He was in an excellent mood as he eased himself into a chair and took a sip of coffee, but that disposition changed instantly when he saw an uninvited guest walking across the lawn.

"Do you frequently invite yourself to other people's houses for breakfast, Payton?" Dávila asked his American cargo pilot.

"Only when I think that advance notice will result in orders to keep me out." Payton took a chair opposite Dávila.

"It's a good thing that my people recognize you. Otherwise you might be a bloody pulp by now."

"Yeah, and it's a good thing that I'm a great pilot or your finances might be in the shitter now," Payton said as he signaled Dávila's maid to bring him an orange juice.

"You're already trying my patience. What do you want?"

"What I want is more money, Oscar."

"Excuse me?" Dávila said putting his coffee down and staring at Payton.

"We've lost three pilots from shootdowns or interdictions in the last six months. I didn't see that many American pilots go down in Angola in twelve years! Losing Anderson was the last straw."

"What are you saying?"

"I'm saying that Dave was way too smart to let a bunch of CNP regulars take him down, and that tells me that your intel is not nearly as good as you think it is. This is getting to be a health hazard, and I want an extra ten thousand dollars per flight, or I'm out."

"Let me explain this to you, and I want you to listen very carefully. First, my intelligence network is working just fine. Second, I decide which pilot lives or dies, and you should thank me that I chose Anderson instead of you. Third, you're already extremely well compensated, and you won't get a penny more. Now, you have a choice, and you don't have much time to make it. Either you work under our current terms and conditions, or I'll see to it that you never fly for anyone again."

"Up yours, Oscar. We'll talk about this again." Payton threw his napkin on the table and stalked off through the garden with one of Dávila's bodyguards close on his heels.

"I'm sure we will, you cocky American prick. I'm sure we will."

20

The senate committee hearing room was full but not overflowing. Drug war budget reviews no longer captured the attention they once did, even though the government spent more on the war than ever. What started as a minor item of less than $100 million in the 1970s, the budget now ran to $14 billion a year, distributed to dozens of agencies directly and indirectly related to the effort. Virtually everyone on the committee was an ally in the war on drugs, and it made for a friendly environment when agencies came forward for funding.

As the lawmakers took their seats, adjusted their microphones, and conferred briefly in hushed tones, the Director of the White House Office of National Drug Control Policy sat at the speaker's table and opened a folder. First up for the morning, the director was point man for the annual budget request. He opened his remarks with the casual, measured cadence of a man in complete command of his material.

"Thank you, Mr. Chairman and members of the committee, for your time today and your strong support of the administration's war on drugs. You have the full text and backup data for the budget requests in front of you.

"Our National Drug Control Strategy has three priorities.

First, stopping use before it starts through education and community action; Second, healing America's drug users by getting them the treatment resources needed; Third, disrupting the market by attacking the economic basis of the drug trade. At the committee's request, I will concentrate today on the third priority.

"In terms of foreign sources of drugs, Colombia supplies over ninety percent of the cocaine to the U.S. market. That reflects major shifts from Bolivia and Peru to narco-terrorist controlled territory in Colombia and is a danger to U.S. national security interests. This is not an issue of academic interest in a far-off land. The illicit drug trade causes twenty thousand American deaths each year, and the lost productivity, law enforcement, and health care costs approach $120 billion annually.

"If we don't continue to pursue illicit drugs, greater volumes will enter the United States. We combat drugs through both eradication and interdiction, and please remember that those programs work together. As eradication has been successful, interdiction has taken on increasing importance. We interdict in all three critical zones—source, transit, and arrival. Coca production is labor intensive. It requires infrastructure to grow coca, transportation to deliver it to processing labs, and shipment of the refined product to an exit point. Those activities can take place only where there is no law enforcement, and that's why Colombian cultivation and production have increased.

"The guerrillas control so much Colombian territory that coca growers have free rein. We can't get to that territory to eradicate, so we interdict to keep coca out of the processing and supply chain. Our primary transit zone interdiction takes place in the Caribbean, the Gulf of Mexico, Central America, Mexico, and the eastern Pacific Ocean. Almost two-thirds of the cocaine arriving in the U.S. comes through Mexico and Central America, and the remainder through the Caribbean. The foreign drug control programs provided through the Department of State's Bureau for

International Narcotics and Law Enforcement Affairs are critical to safeguard our citizens from the ravages of drugs. Of the total INL world-wide budget request of $1 billion dollars, fully $735 million are destined to the Andean Counter-Drug Initiative countries of Bolivia, Colombia, Ecuador, Peru, Brazil, Venezuela, and Panama."

The director highlighted the need to continue supporting the Colombian Army Counterdrug Mobile Brigades and Colombian National Police operations against high-value narco-terrorist targets. The Colombian component of the budget request included aircraft upgrades, additional ground-based radar, improvements to existing airports in drug growing regions, and more aerial spraying. He noted that a Phoenix Corporation subsidiary was the lead player in the radar and infrastructure upgrades. The budget also included funds for programs in Bolivia and Peru for increased eradication and interdiction, alternative development, institution building, and training of local police forces. A separate budget item of $20 million for the Air Bridge Denial Program and Forward Operating Locations was critical. The FOLs allowed the U.S. to conduct integrated air interdiction operations since the bases in the Panama Canal region had been closed.

"Combating illicit drugs is a regional effort, and that means we must help countries other than Colombia," the director continued. "As counter-narcotics efforts are launched and executed in Colombia, there is a danger that producers and traffickers will shift their operations to other countries. A plan to counteract drug trafficking in the Andean region will not work without continuing support for Bolivia and Peru, as well as Ecuador and Brazil. I would point out that Brazil is the second largest consumer of cocaine after the United States, and they increasingly understand the threat of illicit drugs."

The DEA Assistant Administrator for Intelligence was up next and explained how organized crime networks in Colombia ran the illicit drug trade. They had top notch financial management, marketing, logistics, and telecommunications. They had private armies, fleets of radar-equipped aircraft, and close relationships with guerrilla groups. Organized crime was a powerful foe. The assistant administrator then followed up on the White House concern about Plan Colombia's spillover to other countries, and briefly reviewed several programs. Bolivia introduced a border control initiative, and Brazil developed a Brazil-Colombia cross-border intelligence collection project. He added that Ecuador recently started to monitor the movement of drugs, chemicals, and people from southern Colombia into northern Ecuador.

"Both the FARC and the paramilitaries, the AUC, are involved in drug trafficking, even to the point of controlling local cocaine base markets," he said, highlighting FARC and paramilitary operations with a laser pointer on an overhead projection map of Colombia. "The paramilitaries deny taking part in drug dealing, but we know otherwise. Colombian authorities recently confiscated twelve tons of cocaine, worth $300 million, that belonged to the AUC. The police and the navy found it hidden in the banks of a river in southern Colombia. This is the biggest seizure in five years and is a direct result of our interdiction efforts.

"The AUC is a growing threat to Colombian stability, perhaps even more so than the FARC. They have 10,000 active troops, thousands of civilian collaborators, recruit actively, and control up to 25% of the Congress. They operate freely along the northern coast and export drugs at will to the Caribbean. We are at risk if we don't focus more resources on this group.

"The DEA firmly believes that increases in Colombian Source Zone funding will result in a considerable reduction in cocaine HCL shipments to the United States." The assistant administrator transitioned to a map of Latin America. "Recall that the CSZ is southeast of the Andes." He flashed a photograph of dense, impenetrable jungle. "There are few roads, virtually no commercial air traffic, dozens of clandestine airstrips, no rail network, and a river system that links Brazil, Peru, and Venezuela with Colombia. It's a tough region, and we need more money to get serious. I would also like to point out that the government authorities and law enforcement agencies in each country have recently undertaken successful searches and investigations of local chemical and transportation companies, customs agents, warehouses, and clandestine lab facilities. They're doing a great job, but they need more of our help. The administration has recently recognized this need in its public statements that, even though the formal five year Plan Colombia is about to expire, our support of Colombia's counter-terror and counter-narcotics efforts will continue."

"Senators, if I may," the White House Director began once the DEA Assistant Administrator finished, "before presenting summary comments, I would like to invite Mr. Steven Price, executive vice president of Phoenix Corporation, to make a few brief remarks."

The mood of the reasonably somber proceedings changed as Price took a seat and tested the microphone. Comatose press representatives sprang to life, juggling notebooks, tape recorders, and cameras. The frenzy was worthy of a rock star.

"Well, Steven," Chairman Carlson said, "looks like it took you to wake everyone up this morning."

"Thank you, Mr. Chairman," Price smiled. "I only hope I live up to their expectations. I'm glad to be here and hope to shed some light on the private sector's contribution to this very important cause."

Price reviewed Phoenix's Latin American infrastructure and development projects, as well as the radar upgrades directly related to U.S. and foreign military efforts. He summed up with a brief description of eradication partnerships with the U.S. and foreign governments, careful to avoid details that might compromise local Phoenix operations in host countries. The senators, cordial and solicitous, asked him few questions. Each thanked Price for his support. He turned off his microphone and took a seat behind the two principal speakers. Price knew that he had performed well, likely had some new supporters, even allies. If image was not everything, it was certainly close to it.

"The total budget request for the upcoming fiscal year," the director concluded, "is detailed in the Appendices to the report in front of you. This budget request provides a good balance between fiscal responsibility and our duty to combat a national security threat. Thank you for your time and consideration today. I look forward to your continued strong support."

The systems administrator at the U.S. Embassy in La Paz punched Felipe Torres's phone extension as a stream of report information filled her flat-panel display. "Felipe," she said as her eyes flew across the screen and her fingers routed reports to users, "they've just released next year's budget data. You should have it by now."

"Thanks, Gail." Torres swiveled his chair and toggled his computer. His heart raced as he scrolled through the report, looking for the Bolivia numbers. The report determined which programs and administrators survived the fiscal year to fight another budget battle. By the time Torres found his budgets, John Denning walked in holding his own department's information. "How does it look, Felipe?"

"We're not getting all we asked for, but we'll be ok. Brazil's not getting much. Crap, they cut the million I wanted for some cross-border work. Holy shit! Colombia just keeps marching on. Someone up there must be getting some serious raises!"

The war on drugs was alive and well.

21

Dario Jaramillo logged onto the Internet from his Lima apartment and clicked through several screens to access the Sendero bank accounts. Jaramillo, an economics graduate from the Universidad de Lima with considerable Sendero field experience, could type. That made him the man to keep track of the money. His newest wrinkle was the Citibank CD to encrypt his on-line transactions. The authorities were getting better at monitoring financial activity, and he had to be more careful than ever.

The U.S. Treasury Department established the Office of Terrorism and Financial Intelligence to try to cut the lines of financial support to international terrorists. They hoped that targeted intelligence analysis, aggressive enforcement, and comprehensive international cooperation would enable them to shut down the flow of money. Latin American governments might not always cooperate, but the Americans were tightening the noose.

Jeremy Goodnature met with Julio Arraya two weeks earlier, and that meant the Sendero money was on its way. Jaramillo saw deposits of almost seven million dollars at Citibank, BankAmerica, and HSBC, and notations that two million more would be confirmed in twenty-four hours. Sendero could train more foreign recruits, new revolutionaries and fanatics to provide Sendero with long-term cash flow. They could also stage several high-profile operations in Lima, and pick up activity in remote areas. High on the Sendero tactical planner's list was an attack on the multi-billion dollar Camisea gas development and pipeline project. Jaramillo also had his eye on surface-to-air rockets to take out oil company fixed wing aircraft. Perhaps they could hit a commercial airliner as well. Jaramillo sent Jamil Mansour an encrypted e-mail to confirm the delivery of eighty-five RPGs, fourteen anti-tank tank rockets, and three surface-to-air missiles.

Mansour replied that he would deliver a day early to a location more convenient and safer for Sendero. He asked if Jaramillo needed anything else short-term, especially any exotic items. Jaramillo said no, but that they would need to talk again in a month. Mansour was disappointed, but it never hurt to ask. Exotics took more time to secure, but were considerably more profitable. Money was the name of the game.

After creating chaos with the new funding, Jaramillo could take a vacation in Búzios on the Brazilian coast a hundred miles north of Rio. White sand and warm blue-green water would be a pleasant break from the dump he lived in. That was the reward. For now, he had to work. Sendero could easily pull off the attacks, especially after the Servicio de Inteligencia Nacional (SIN) fell apart when Fujimori fled to Japan. As the SIN deteriorated and was eventually shut down by the Peruvian government, they set up their own private spy operations for anyone who paid cash. Ironically, Sendero became one of their best customers. Everyone had enemies. Under Fujimori, the SIN went to extraordinary lengths to obtain information on government opponents. One of their favorites was to videotape businessmen and politicians road-testing Lima's lovelies in the high-end cathouses. It was one of Sendero's favorites as well. Jaramillo called Arraya and told him the money was in the bank. Arraya in turn dialed a number few people in Lima had.

"Deputy commissioner Tejeda's office, may I help you?" answered the young assistant who took cell phone calls twenty-four hours a day for the Lima deputy police commissioner.

"I wish to speak to deputy commissioner Tejeda," Arraya requested politely. "It's urgent."

"One minute please."

"Tejeda here."

"Ernesto, it's Arraya. I need to see Chairman Gonzalo as soon as possible, and it needs to be quiet. No phones, no people, no nothing."

Sendero knew its leader, Abimael Guzmán, as Chairman Gonzalo. Despite his capture in September 1992, Guzmán was still the force behind Sendero. He was an even greater influence from jail when security forces captured his deputy Oscar Ramírez Durand in 1999. The authorities believed Guzmán had mellowed and that Sendero was out of the narco-terror game. How wrong they were.

"Not now," Tejeda said nervously. "With all the news about Montesinos, they're watching us closer than ever. There was another article in the paper today about the arms sales and the drug money. We need to lie low for a while."

"This can't wait," Arraya insisted. "It has to be in the next day or two."

"You're not listening to me. Not now."

"Ernesto, let me help you out with this. If I don't see Abimael today or tomorrow, I'll send the video of you at the Black Velvet to the television stations. Got that?"

"Give me an hour. I'll call you back." Tejeda rang off.

Sendero's trap for Tejeda would bear fruit for years. They caught him on video *in flagrante* with a Brazilian hooker. Womanizing was widely accepted in Lima, but having it on tape was not. Even worse, Tejeda asked her to bring a farm animal along. The one hour tape disgusted even the most hardened

Sendero. Tejeda called fifty minutes later to confirm the meeting with Guzmán.

Arraya entered the maximum security prison shortly after the 2:00 A.M. shift change. The key security staff were on Tejeda's payroll, which made late-night access easy. Sendero could have sprung Guzmán any time they wanted, but that would surely lead to Tejeda's dismissal. Sendero could not afford to lose him in a housecleaning exercise. Ironically, Guzmán was more effective inside prison than he was outside.

The meeting room was ample and comfortable with two sofas, several chairs, and a coffee table. It was more like a living room than a prison, a room suited to a man of Guzmán's stature.

"Abimael!" Arraya hugged Guzmán. "We're in business!"

"It sounds like you've been fund raising, my friend," Guzmán said with a broad smile.

"I didn't have to do anything. They came to us. Our American friends sent almost nine million dollars."

"How I love to take their money," Guzmán said, picking up a sandwich from the coffee table. "Have you made deposits in my offshore accounts?"

"Of course."

"And yours?"

"As well."

"Good. Don't forget, Julio, we take care of ourselves first." Guzmán sat back, adjusted his shirt, stroked his beard, and looked at the ceiling.

"What do you think?" Arraya asked. "There are lots of targets."

"Make sure it's high profile, but don't kill too many people. That pisses everyone off. Remember what happened to me after Miraflores." Guzmán referred to a two car bomb attack in the Miraflores section of Lima in July 1992 that killed twenty and wounded 250. It angered not only the police but also ordinary citizens. The National Directorate Against Terrorism police captured Guzmán at a Sendero safe house two months later.

"How can I forget?"

"Good. Remember it. Kill no more than fifty, maybe sixty. No kidnappings, no taking over residences. That turns on us fast. Keep it simple. Make it bombs in densely packed places."

"Anything specific?"

"Hit an international hotel first. That will scare them and tie up the security forces. Then go for bridges and power plants outside Lima. Who was the contact this time?"

"Goodnature, same as usual," Arraya replied.

"What a character!" Guzmán laughed. "It's incredible how much money he brings in. Has Mansour sent everything we need?"

"He's filling an order as we speak, including three SAMs."

"Outstanding," Guzmán said, slapping his thigh. "I know what you're thinking Julio. Don't take out a plane yet. That's too high profile right now. Understand?"

"Yes, chairman."

"Good. Be careful and good luck."

Tejeda led Arraya out. He had the money and his instructions. All that remained was to plan and execute the attacks. If he did well, there would be more money, more operations, and more vacations in warm climates. Life in the urban guerrilla jungle was good and was about to get much better.

22

"Steven, it's Richard," I said as I lowered my eyes from Mt. Illimani to the fax in my lap. "Got a minute?"

"Sure, what's up?" Price replied from his downtown Chicago office.

"I'm looking at your travel plans to La Paz next week and then on to Lima and Bogotá. Did you schedule this visit since we talked the other day?"

"Nope. I'm swinging through to pick you and Raúl up for the Government of Peru Economic Summit. Are you not going?"

"The first I heard of the trip was when I got your fax just now. It must have slipped Raúl's mind."

"You're attending with us," Price said with mild displeasure. He knew Raúl had not missed this one. The small things were getting to Raúl, and Price was tired of it. "It'll be good for the new ministers to see that you're on board. It's your call whether or not you go to Colombia."

"I'll pass on Bogotá since I'm going in a few months. You're arriving on the Falcon Tuesday morning?"

"I am. Don't meet me at the airport. I'll make Raúl get out of bed."

"Sounds good to me. See you next week, and have a safe

flight."

I wanted to choke Raúl and throw him out a window. Julie would say I was having an anger management moment. I thought I had worked with some pricks, but Raúl had a Ph.D. in assholology compared to the rest.

"Verónica," I said when I regained enough composure to speak and not scream, "please make my Lima hotel arrangements and put me on a flight from Lima to Miami. I'll stay with friends for a couple of days before I come back."

"Yes, Mr. Blackstone."

The Peruvian government had changed since I was last in Lima, and most of the ministers were new. Business was personal in Latin America, and I needed to meet the key government players to develop a working relationship. While Price and Raúl went on to Colombia, I would spend a couple of days in Miami with my friend Chris Hendricks.

I called Julie to tell her that I was headed home, and signaled to Lucho that it was time to go. On the way out, I poked my head in Raúl's door and told him I looked forward to the Lima trip. His face said it all. I smiled and wished him a good weekend. I headed out and heard the door slam behind me.

Raúl was furious. He could not let this pass. Although he wanted to, there was no need yet to inflict physical harm on Blackstone. Emotional and mental stress were, however, something else entirely. Raúl knew that wives were a pressure point for expatriate managers. Blackstone might leave Phoenix if his wife feared for her safety—or her children's. It would not be the first time a terrified wife convinced an expat manager to quit his job.

"Nacho, can you hear me?"

"Yes, Don Raúl. It's very noisy. We are finishing up. What do you need, *jefe*?"

"Make an impression on Blackstone this weekend. Something to scare his wife and children."

"Done, Don Raúl."

Raúl sat back in his chair and smiled. He could go home knowing that Blackstone was about to have an experience to remember.

"Mr. Blackstone," Verónica called as she caught up to me at the elevator, "could you please sign this letter before you leave?"

"Oops, sorry," I said apologetically. "That was in my stack, and I blew right past it."

I signed the letter on the reception area coffee table and gave it back to Verónica. Standing up, I saw Raúl through the glass partitions, putting his cell phone away, and grinning as though he had won the lottery. The guy cycled even more than I did.

The children agitated for Chinese food, so we decided to eat at a place Julie recently found. A green Jeep Cherokee kept up with us from the house and turned off a block from the office. I was curious, but thought nothing of it. Since the restaurant was downtown, we would park at the office garage and walk to dinner. I sent Lucho home to get some rest and told the security guard we would be back in a couple of hours.

The restaurant was in an old, gray two story city house, with tall, dirty windows and eight foot wooden doors opening directly onto the street. We came through the front door into a large room with dusty, unpolished wood floors and no furniture. We ventured cautiously to the next room and took a table when we saw another family eating. An elderly woman immediately appeared and explained the menu, then disappeared to bring our drinks. Before she returned, a mangy German Shepherd appeared in the doorway looking for scraps. He seemed to know his way around, so we suspected he was a regular. The other patrons did not seem to mind, but our waiter gently ushered the dog out.

We ordered and devoured several delicious dishes of beef, chicken, and noodles and talked about the children's day at school. They were adjusting well and had new friends. I paid the bill, and we stepped out into a dark, cool night that made us zip our coats and turn up our collars. There were few vehicles on the streets, so we expected a quiet walk back to the car. Two blocks from the restaurant, we heard the loud crack of several protest march mortars. Even in La Paz, 10:20 P.M. seemed late for this sort of thing.

I kept my head up and looked around as I checked the chamber on my pistol with my right index finger. I grabbed Kathy's hand and told Sean to hold his mother's arm. We turned right and saw a crowd moving rapidly toward us, forty or fifty people less than forty yards away. They had covered their faces with scarves, carried banners, and were loud and angry. I told everyone to turn around and move fast.

We started to run, turned left at the first corner, and a Molotov cocktail exploded fifteen feet behind us. I felt the heat wave and smelled the tell-tale gasoline signature when another one crashed and exploded in flames even closer. We ran faster and reached the other side of the street as we heard shots. Patches of soft concrete splashed our faces as the rounds hit the wall of the house in front of us. The report reverberated off the buildings and it was impossible to tell which direction the shots came from. I wanted to get my family to safety, and hoped we were running away from the shooter and not towards him.

We piled into the first cab we saw. I closed the door and noticed that the crowd noise had stopped. There was no shouting, no stampeding, no shooting. Nothing. They vanished as quickly as they appeared. I checked to make sure no one was hurt. Kathy was scared, and Sean was angry because something was in his eye. Julie was shaky and wanted to get to our car and go home.

As I pulled out of the company garage, the green Cherokee from earlier in the evening sped past us. I recognized the gouge on the front fender and got a glimpse of the driver; a thin-faced guy talking on a cell phone. I kicked myself for not getting the license plate. Julie put drops in Sean's eye, and Kathy was asleep by the time we got home.

Speeding back to El Alto in his Cherokee, Raúl's man pressed the phone to his ear.

"Miguel, we're done for the night. Give them ten *bolivianos* each, put them back on the bus, and give them a bottle of *chicha* when they get to El Alto. Well done."

He knew he had scared the wife and children, maybe even rattled Blackstone. Some pocket money and firewater was cheap payment for this sort of fun. The simplest things scared gringos. It was a shame he wasted five .308 rifle rounds and still did not carve up any meat. Maybe next time.

23

The landing gear dropped on final approach to Rio, and Jeremy Goodnature pushed himself closer to the window for a better view. Below him was *a cidade maravilhosa*, the marvelous city. The scalloped beaches, dense green growth, and mountains came into view slowly as the plane descended into paradise. That vision got a reality check when Goodnature drove past the *favelas* on his way to the Copacabana Palace Hotel. Rio's shantytowns dotted the city's landscape; the largest of them had 100,000 inhabitants living in absolute squalor.

There was no single excuse for Rio's decline. The 1970s oil crisis hit hard, and the Brazilian economic miracle crashed and burned. The government moved foreign embassies from Rio to Brasília, companies moved offices to São Paulo, crime exploded, drugs flowed, and police and political corruption went from bad to worse. As embassies and companies left Rio, their transparent support structures—security, people, infrastructure—went with them. The unseen safety nets disappeared. As if that were not enough, the urban guerrilla groups that sprang up in the 60s and 70s were replaced by crime and drug gangs in the 80s and 90s. Random street violence was rampant, and the ordinary punk stole for dope. Politically motivated violence was out, the drug fix was in. Drugs blew Rio apart.

As the taxi turned right onto Avenida Atlântica at Copacabana Beach, Goodnature smelled the ocean and felt the humidity even though the windows were closed. To his left, the beach ran for two-and-a-half miles, one end to the other. To his right was a solid wall of high-rise hotels and apartment buildings. No other city in the world could boast the combination of white beaches, aquamarine water, rocky mountains, and people.

The people of Rio, *cariocas*, relaxed and enjoyed their surroundings. They ran, biked, and walked along the beach in droves every morning. Many did their "daily Cooper", hooked on Dr. Kenneth Cooper's circuit training methods years before people in the U.S. heard of him. The jogging path was normally busy and there were usually lines at the workout stations. People of every body shape participated. Cariocas understood that everyone qualified, not just those on the glossy magazine covers.

Joggers and walkers jammed the running path along the beach, not yet full, but alive with sun worshippers playing soccer and volleyball. Then Goodnature saw them, the women of Rio. Scant cloth covered their lithe, brown bodies, their skin glistening in the sunlight, long legs gliding along gently and invitingly. Two hundred feet beyond the tanned goddesses, waves crashed evenly, methodically, and rhythmically up and down Copacabana. Goodnature rolled the window down to let the breeze caress him. Millions of brilliant flecks of light danced and darted across the waves. Forget the favelas. This was paradise.

Following an afternoon at the hotel pool, Goodnature was changed and ready for dinner by 8:30 P.M. The Sobre as Ondas restaurant was only minutes from the hotel and had one of the best views in Rio from its first floor balcony. Diners could see north to Leme beach and south to where Copacabana turned to Ipanema beach. The real spectacle, however, was the ritual dance of foreign businessmen and Rio prostitutes on the sidewalk below. One side spoke English and the other Portuguese, but that did not impede efficient negotiations. Unlike other cities, the dance to negotiate pleasures of the flesh went on openly in Rio's best neighborhoods.

Two of the faces waiting for Goodnature at the table were familiar, and one was not. Gerson Almeida and Ronaldo Nascimento were long-time friends, older than the new generation of activists. They were two of a handful left who fought with Carlos Marighella. The third was Antonio Teixeira, the head of the political action wing of the Movimento dos Sem Terra, the "landless" group that demanded land from the government, *gratis*. Goodnature thought they were ridiculous, but they had political power. They could be useful.

"Welcome back to Rio, Jeremy," Almeida called out as Goodnature hugged his two friends and extended a hand to Teixeira.

"Glad to be back, Gerson. Damn, I miss this view!"

After greetings, they got down to the serious business of eating. With appetizers of sausage and fried cheese pastries, they worked their way through the latest soccer results, Formula 1, and the lamentable state of Brazilian economics and politics.

With the important preliminaries covered, Teixeira stepped up to the plate. "MST wants to join you to fight those destroying the environment and oppressing the people. We have lived for too long under regimes that don't right their wrongs. Our attempts to deal with the government peacefully have yielded nothing. Even President Lula has turned his back on us. We need more direct measures." The Brazilian president had made campaign promises to the MST which he quickly ignored once elected.

Teixeira's intensity immediately told Goodnature he had a recruit. The man was a classic with his "oppressed peoples' struggle for justice" line, and Goodnature wondered what time warp he came through. It was music to his ears, nonetheless, since nobody was easier to manipulate than a fanatic with a cause. "This is serious business," Goodnature said gravely. "How far are you prepared to go?"

"There are no limits," Teixeira responded. "We don't have money or training. You give us that, and we'll give you warm bodies."

"I'll help you," Goodnature said matter-of-factly. "You have to be aggressive and take the fight straight to the government. Are you up to it?"

"We are. This is our destiny."

GEM would fund and train the MST to hit key targets and challenge the Brazilian security forces. Urban targets were best, since they drew attention away from the Bolivia-Brazil border. Goodnature knew Dávila would be pleased. These were new recruits to do the dirty work, new pawns on the board.

After dinner, Goodnature was ready to sample the local talent. Barbarella was the location of choice in Rio, and was at the top of his list. He saw nothing worth hitting on at the pool, so he would spend some cash on first rate women. The challenge was getting the lady back to his room, since Copacabana Palace security screened all young women entering the hotel after dark. They knew who was registered, and were serious about protecting the hotel's reputation. Regardless of her host, a woman known or perceived to be working by the hour did not enter. *Perhaps,* Goodnature thought, *I should get a room at the Meridien tonight.* The French were so much more practical.

24

Fausto Suárez loaded refined cocaine onto the plane and turned his head so the dusty wind would not fill his eyes with grit. It was another hot day in north-central Bolvia, and he was soaked through. Suárez was a happy man, even on these days of hard manual labor when the sweat ran off him in torrents. As soon as he finished with this load, he would go back to work at the dairy plant.

Suárez came to the milk factory as a day laborer when the Swedish government provided start-up funding in the 1990s. It was one of the first Bolivian alternative development projects. The idea was a good one, but the execution was not. The United Nations took over after the Swedes, then turned it over to the Bolivians. Originally well-intentioned, the endeavor was poorly thought out, horribly run, and incredibly corrupt.

The milk project originated when a group of cattle producers proposed that international organizations build a milk plant to market and distribute their milk. The quantity was small, 660 gallons a day, and the project cost half a million dollars. The original project could have succeeded on a modest scale. A small success in Bolivia would have been a huge leap forward. Then people got greedy. The Swedes took over and suddenly needed six million dollars to import a used milk plant with a capacity of eleven thousand gallons per day. The South African used equipment dealer who imported the machinery convinced the Bolivian and Swedish governments that the project would be a shining star of alternative development.

The increase in volume never came. The climate was wrong, technical and road infrastructure was insufficient, and there were not enough cows. The shortage of raw material had somehow eluded their analysis. From 1993 on, the factory lost nearly three quarters of a million dollars a year. The U.N. and USAID masked the failure and kept it afloat with interim funding. The project went into free-fall when the agencies pulled out. The coca eradication program had already eliminated hundreds of families' incomes and destroyed the local economy. The failure of the milk plant was the death blow. A Cochabamba judge ordered the equipment auctioned to pay off debts.

Oscar Dávila was a personal friend of the judge, had him rescind the order, and proposed to buy the plant and turn it around. By the time Dávila made his offer, Phoenix Corporation had made its own. They wanted the factory for their first development project and pushed hard. The federal government committed to Phoenix, the local government committed to Dávila, but the two governments reached an agreement. They approved the sale to Phoenix, but only if the corporation took a fifty-one percent Bolivian partner. Phoenix bought in with Dávila as the majority shareholder.

The deal worked for both sides. Phoenix provided financial backing and new equipment, and got a notch on their development handle. Dávila in turn got to run his own operation with a deep-pocket partner. As the project got up and running, he took control of coca production in the region. Because of Phoenix's involvement in eradication, Dávila knew the authorities would never suspect drugs near one of its development projects. Even better, Phoenix trusted Dávila and his organization so completely that no corporate executive ever inspected the facility. With no counter-drug activity in the area, Dávila worked unimpeded and soon had coca production back to pre-eradication levels. His next step was to produce coca paste and set up refining operations. Dávila then negotiated a contract to fly cocaine out on Altiplano Air, the private air company Phoenix used in the eradication program. The infrastructure was there, and Dávila had only to pull the pieces together.

The town revered Oscar Dávila. He put in an airstrip, cleared and repaired roads, built a small school and a hospital, and ran electricity to every house in town. As far as Fausto was concerned, Dávila understood the local community and had righted a tremendous wrong. Dávila's involvement with coca and cocaine was all for the better. The gringos were the only ones who thought it was wrong. *What did they know?*

Fausto took a long sip of water as he watched the Cessna take off with two hundred pounds of refined cocaine. He lost sight of the plane, then got on his bicycle to return to the milk plant. He did not want to work too late, since the DirecTV installation team was coming that afternoon. That too was because of Oscar Dávila. Life was good, and thanks to Don Oscar it was getting better.

25

I called John Denning Monday morning so he could include our Molotov cocktail incident in his weekly security report. We were at the wrong place at the wrong time, but at least the embassy could let others know what happened. When I met Raúl for our 11:00 A.M. political issues review, he seemed surprised that we had a pleasant dinner Friday night.

The rest of the day flew by as I spent the afternoon fighting fires on the telephone. The sun was setting on La Paz, and the street lights were starting to come on. I took a long look at the red-orange glow around Illimani, packed my briefcase, and called Julie to tell her that I would be home soon.

"Richard, do you have a minute? Richard?" Gustavo Domínguez, my finance manager, stood in my doorway.

"Oh, sorry Gustavo," I said turning from the window.

"There's something I'd like to talk about if you've got a few minutes. I wanted to catch you before you left town."

"Gustavo, you bet I've got time," I said. His demeanor telegraphed that something was wrong. "Talk to me."

"Well," he started slowly, "a month ago I started looking at our cash management procedures and how we fund certain operations. I picked the chemicals business because it has the most international subsidiaries and is pretty complex."

"Were you looking for a specific problem?"

"No. It's just that the corporate treasurer's group handles most of our cash management and there are some local things we can handle better."

"I don't doubt that," I said. "As far as they're concerned, Latin America is no different from any other part of the world."

"I know, and that's why I wanted to work this. I pulled a year of wire transfers, payment data, and some sample invoices. Because of Bolivian import-export regulations, BLI keeps more detailed records of the imports than we do, so I got a few invoices from their files to match up to ours."

"Okay."

"I've looked at a lot of information, and three things don't add up. The first is that Phoenix Corporation has dozens of chemical subsidiaries around the world, and Phoenix Latin America holds the share ownership in most of them. It makes sense for Chicago to do that at the corporate level, but I see no reason why we should hold those investments out of La Paz."

"That's unusual," I said, ticking off the first item mentally, "but it doesn't necessarily mean anything. What else do you have?"

"Some of the invoices show imports and exports for those subsidiaries, but the financial and accounting records show nothing. That seems strange."

"There could be lots of reasons for that—accounting mistakes, swap outs, inter-company trades, you name it."

"I know, but I still want to get to the bottom of it," he insisted. "That's not nearly as important as the last thing."

"And that is?"

"As you know, BLI is our clearing agent for all our imports into the region. We pay them a three and a half percent handling fee on the total value of every import."

"Just for chemicals?"

"No, it's for most of what we bring in—chemicals, power plant equipment, telecommunications gear, you name it."

"I suspect that adds up to a lot of money at some point."

"It does. Several million in fees last year. When they gave me their detailed invoices, Solís's secretary included some of their proprietary accounting information by mistake. I couldn't resist looking at it."

"I would have too," I laughed. "Something interesting always pops up."

"Well, something did. The accounting records were confusing, but I figured them out. The first thing I looked for was the handling fee. Richard, they book only two percent of the fee."

"What about the rest?"

"They pay it to Raúl!"

"What?"

"Based on what we paid BLI last year, Raúl's share was almost eight hundred thousand dollars."

"But we audit both of them every year. I can't believe we'd miss that."

"The last audit was done before I got here. The work papers showed that BLI booked three and a half percent. The only explanation is that BLI and Raúl keep two sets of books."

"Wonderful, Gustavo. Do you have any other good news?"

"Unfortunately, there's more. Company regulations require that we bid out work valued for as much as the BLI contract, but Raúl awarded it on a sole-source basis. Now I think I know why."

"But Mark was the president and Raúl's only an advisor. He doesn't have contract award or signature authority. He couldn't have done it."

"He does and he did. Mark had headquarters create an exception in the Delegation of Authority Guide, and he explicitly gave Raúl that authority. Here's a copy of the Guide and the signed contract."

"Well, I sure as hell didn't expect this," I said, disgusted.

"Sorry, Richard, but I've gone far enough that I had to tell you."

"Don't apologize. Keep working on it, and we'll talk again when I get back. Can I take some information with me to look at?"

"You bet," Gustavo said as he pushed a stack of papers across my desk. "Those are some invoices and backup. I can give you the rest when you come back."

"Thanks. Now, I'm not sure I should ask, but is there anything else we need to cover before I get out of here?"

"Nothing about Raúl, but what should I do if I get another e-mail from headquarters on signing the infrastructure deals?"

"Tell them I postponed the decision because we don't have enough information."

"Great. Oh, one thing just so you know. Chicago is doing some systems maintenance the next couple of days that will affect remote connections. You might have some trouble logging on while you're in Lima. I'll mention it to Raúl as well."

"Speaking of which, I've noticed that Raúl is the only one around here who doesn't have a desktop computer. Why is that?"

"Mostly because he doesn't want one. He's got a state-of-the-art laptop. That thing goes with him everywhere, and he keeps it locked in his briefcase when he's not using it."

"So I noticed. He doesn't strike me as the kind of person who would be so self-sufficient. I would expect Carolina to do all his computer work for him."

"I would too, but apparently not. Anyway, if you have a problem connecting, try web mail and you should be fine."

"Thanks."

"When do you fly out?"

"Tomorrow afternoon. I'll be there for a few days, and then a couple in Miami. Verónica has my itinerary. Shoot me a note or call if something comes up. I may be in tomorrow morning for a few hours, but I doubt it."

"Okay, see you when you get back."

26

The flight attendant opened the door to the Phoenix Corporation Falcon 900, and Steven Price took a deep breath to fill his lungs before he walked down the stairs to the El Alto tarmac. At least they would fly to Lima later in the day, so he would not have to sleep in the thin La Paz air. Raúl waited at the foot of the stairs with a Bolivian immigrations official who stamped Price's passport and welcomed him to the country. Raúl's contacts let Price avoid the normal immigration and customs lines. In the car, Price pulled out an e-mail the Phoenix security group sent him over the weekend.

"Raúl, what's this I see about an attack on Blackstone and his family?"

"I know. Can you believe that?" Raúl said, avoiding eye contact. "Very odd."

"This never happened to Hansen in five years," Price said. "Either Blackstone is jinxed, or we're not taking good enough care of him. Is this place getting that dangerous?"

"I don't think so. Maybe it's just bad luck. I'll see if we can tighten things up."

"Please do. The last thing we need is an incident with a senior expat executive."

Raúl was not Blackstone's babysitter, but was responsible for his safety. He seethed silently as the car wound its way down from El Alto. Blackstone had upset his comfort zone and made him lose face. Now Price questioned his judgment, authority, and ability.

Former President Fujimori's legacy of investment and economic development were evident everywhere in Lima. There was a road repair, a lane extension, and a high rise apartment or office building going up in every neighborhood. The stench of La Paz was absent. Every single building was brown or light yellow. That and the overcast skies made it seem dreary. Still, I liked Lima.

Traffic was chaotic. A mass of small cars honked their horns non-stop and cut each other off at every opportunity. HBO had imported the international finger, and some Lima drivers made it an art form. After forty minutes of finger waving and honking, we arrived at the Los Delfines in the San Isidro neighborhood, a modern hotel near the Lima Golf Club.

I called home before the cocktail party, and Kathy reminded me to see the dolphins. The hotel owner put dolphins in the lobby as a tourist attraction, but ran into trouble when an environmental group called GEM filed a lawsuit to remove them. The owner had better lawyers, so the issue went away.

After a shower and breakfast the next morning, I got my conference credentials and grabbed a chair near the back of the hall. Raúl and Price sat near the front on the inside aisle. Four coffee breaks, a rubber chicken lunch, and ten speakers later, it was almost 6:30 P.M. when the last speaker approached the podium. His presentation was mercifully short, and Steven Price caught up with me outside for a drink just as I saw Raúl walking down to the lobby. The bar was full of Peruvian government officials, and Price asked me to accompany him.

"It's good to see you again, señores," Price said as he extended his hand to the ministers of economy and defense. "I would like to introduce our new president for the region, Mr. Richard Blackstone. He is based in La Paz."

We exchanged handshakes, business cards, and introductory formalities for several minutes. As I sipped my gin and tonic, I marveled at how international businessmen in Latin America operated in a world of power and influence unknown to our U.S. counterparts. We chatted with two of the most powerful decision-makers in Peru, strictly and only because we invested money in their country.

The minister of economy thanked us for Phoenix's efforts, said our infrastructure and power generation projects were important for the country's progress, but he had reservations about the value of the alternative development programs. Over seven hundred communities and farmer's organizations had signed agreements to reduce coca cultivation over a five year period, but severe economic difficulties forced them back to growing coca. "Gentlemen," the minister said, "surely that points to the failure of alternative development."

"But, Mr. Minister," Price responded, "they need those programs to survive."

"That's just the point, Steven. The programs don't let them survive. Alternative development barely makes it in good times. When the economy sours, it's a synonym for poverty."

"Sir," Price reassured him, "Phoenix is a long-term player, and we are here to stay. Alternative development is the best we have right now."

"The other challenge we face," the minister of defense interjected, "is that the alternative development and interdiction programs have forced the drug cartels to seek new markets."

"That's good," Price rejoined. "It means you've won."

"Yes and no. It's like squeezing toothpaste. You move it around in the tube, but nothing really changes. The cartels are still looking for new foreign markets, but they have developed an internal market for the first time. They accept internal prices that are lower than export prices because they get a steady low-risk cash flow. They've been extremely successful, and first-time drug use in Peru is increasing fifty percent a year. Our own people are suffering, but we can't do everything at once."

"Are you afraid you can't fight Sendero and drugs at the same time?" I inquired.

"Precisely," the minister of defense responded. "We don't have enough men. Just when we thought the guerillas were done, we had the problem with the Japanese ambassador. Terrorists have kept a low profile in the last decade, but they are working hard to come back strong. It's only a matter of time."

During a December 1996 diplomatic function, Tupac Amaru guerrillas seized the Japanese ambassador's Lima residence. Among the 450 hostages were President Fujimori's brother, mother, sister, the foreign minister, and the agriculture minister. After months of negotiations, the guerillas still held seventy-two hostages. A Peruvian commando assault force raided the residence in April 1997, and all fourteen guerrillas died in the take-down. Two soldiers died, and one hostage, a supreme court justice, had a heart attack. The Peruvian commandos showed the guerrillas that Alberto Fujimori was not a man to trifle with.

"Sir," the U.S. Defense Attaché broke in, "you know my government will provide the necessary support to fight this war without draining your own ranks. We are funding significant counter-drug operations in the major coca-growing areas, and the air bridge denial program is active."

"If I may also note, Mr. Minister," Price said, "Phoenix is upgrading your airport infrastructure, and we're installing radar at forward operating locations. You're getting the most advanced technology in the world."

"Gentlemen, please," the minister of defense said, raising a hand. "We are extremely grateful for all those things, but I know my resources will be drained. It's inevitable."

Price and I broke off from the conversation, since we did not want to be drawn into a discussion that might commit Phoenix to a course of action. It was easy to be misinterpreted through the fog of a whiskey or two. Anything you told a government minister could easily appear in the next morning's papers. We walked out to the lobby and I asked Price where Raúl was.

"He's visiting some friends, but he'll join us for dinner at ten. Sound good?"

"That works for me. See you then."

I burned off some calories in the gym, took a quick swim, and called home. I still had two hours to kill before dinner and the Internet seemed more interesting than television. The news services ran the standard war on terror drivel, so I decided to do some quick research on cocaine. I ran a couple of Google searches and found a RAND report describing the effects of drug abuse and drug treatment in America. The study examined the use of federal funds to reduce cocaine consumption and found that mandatory minimum sentences, because of the high cost of incarceration, were not cost effective. Vigorous enforcement, the trend in the U.S. for two decades, merely increased dealer expenses, which they passed on to consumers. Dealers got rich.

The report concluded that each incremental treatment dollar generated a social benefit to America of almost eight dollars from reduced cocaine consumption, reduced drug-related crime, and increased economic productivity. The researchers calculated that each additional dollar spent on overseas eradication, however, generated a net loss of almost a full dollar. There was a nine dollar swing in benefits per dollar spent. Unbelievable. I saved the report and a couple of others to my hard drive.

I pulled the reading folder from my briefcase and made a note to print the report when I returned to La Paz. I started to close the folder and the top document caught my eye. It was the package Gustavo gave me. I thumbed through the sheets and felt my neck tighten when I saw the BLI contract Raúl authorized and signed. The attached BLI invoice showed a fee of almost ninety-five thousand dollars. Raúl's share was enough for a new luxury sedan. I disliked him more by the minute.

I turned my attention back to my laptop when it beeped that I had a new e-mail. It was Chris Hendricks saying he would pick me up at the Miami airport and that I would overnight at his house. I wrote a note giving a quick update on the family and telling him to have plenty of cold beer ready. I hit Send and shut the computer down. With an hour to shower and change for dinner, I grabbed a beer from the minibar and put up my feet to relax.

27

Within fifteen minutes of leaving the hotel, Raúl was behind the closed doors of a residence in the Miraflores section of Lima. José Ortiz poured himself a whiskey when Raúl arrived and one for his old friend as well. Raúl was not in a good mood as he sat down in the rattan chair opposite Ortiz.

"José, we don't need any more prosecutors or judges dismissed on corruption charges. They're the hardest people to replace. You need to make sure it doesn't happen again. Is that clear?"

"It is Don Raúl, but we can't control everything. These things happen."

"But Estero? He was one of our best federal judges."

"It's not my fault he bought that stolen Mercedes from an undercover cop. We can't account for stupidity."

José Ortiz was the director of the Peruvian National Police Directorate of Counternarcotics (DINANDRO), and was the primary contact for U.S. law enforcement and intelligence agencies. He was perfectly placed to manage drugs in Peru through his control of the intelligence apparatus and Peruvian military assets. He mingled freely with national and international politicians, law enforcement officials, businessmen, and drug lords. After Montesinos was caught, Ortiz became Raúl's key man for intelligence operations in Peru. He controlled the machine, and he knew how to exploit the gaps in the system.

Peru had no significant laws to track drug-related cash, and authorities were not overly preoccupied with money laundering. DINANDRO's financial investigative unit, DINFI, was the only entity equipped to detect laundering. With Ortiz on the payroll, Raúl could move millions through the Peruvian economy unseen. DINFI had recently confiscated over two hundred houses, cars, and boats associated with drug trafficking, which Ortiz sold for cash and stashed in his offshore accounts. He knew better than to take possession of physical assets.

"José, your e-mail last week said the government thinks coca isn't being eradicated quickly enough. Explain."

"They believe that thirty percent of the abandoned areas in the Apurimac Valley have been regenerated for growing coca. That's too high. The president asked me to send eradicators and Special Forces to lower it."

"And just how are you supposed to do that?"

"You won't like the answer. We have new tools that pull the plants up by the roots."

"Does that mean those areas will never regenerate?"

"That's correct, Don Raúl." Ortiz winced.

"This wasn't supposed to happen!" Raúl shouted as he pushed himself out of his chair and lit a cigarette.

"Listen, it's not that bad."

"And why exactly is that?'

"The Apurimac Valley is sixty-five percent regenerated, but the authorities believe it's thirty. I manipulated the data to make it look lower than it really is. In other areas where it's twenty-five percent, they believe it's ten. We're in good shape."

"What about the overflights and satellite photos? Won't those give it away?"

"The air bridge denial program has been so successful that the

Americans trust me to do all the overflights," Ortiz beamed, "and they suspended satellite recon because they need it for counter terror purposes elsewhere."

"But we're just buying time. They'll notice eventually."

"Of course they will. No shell game can go on forever. We'll go on eradicating near the known targets, and the government will believe we've eliminated more than we have. We'll always be ahead of the curve, but our advantage will decrease over time."

"I don't see any other options," Raúl said, stubbing out his smoke.

"Not unless you want to partner with Sendero."

"Not on your life," Raúl shot back. "I'll use them, but never partner with them. On to other things. What are you doing about my chemicals shipments?"

"The new laws that control precursors put certain countries and companies on a watch list. I made sure that neither Phoenix nor its subsidiaries are on it. My people still check all containers, so you're safe there as well."

When we left the hotel for dinner, I put Raúl in the front seat while Price and I sat in the back. I knew he would see that as demeaning, and he slammed the door petulantly. I was getting to him. When we arrived at the Costa Verde restaurant, I was glad I had not snacked during the conference. An enormous buffet table groaned under an array of salads, meats, and fish, and two chefs prepared a dozen hot dishes.

We sat down and my mind drifted as soon as Raúl opened his mouth. His lips moved, but I heard nothing. I wondered how much he was skimming from Phoenix. I wanted to tell Price, but decided not to rush things. Raúl's phone rang, and he excused himself for a minute. I must have seemed distracted.

"You okay, Richard?" Price asked.

"Oh, yeah, I'm fine, Steven. Just amazed by how much is on this menu."

28

As the American Airlines flight to Miami climbed through the Lima skies, I could not get Raúl off my mind. I stewed on him for an hour after dinner the night before and made a few phone calls as soon as I got up. I asked Donovan & Mason, the Houston law firm, to review Phoenix's and Raúl's corporate structures, and retained the corporate security firm Grant & Co. to investigate his background. I asked Gustavo to keep looking at the payment and wire transfer information. The money always leads to answers.

After I organized my notes, I booted up my laptop to read some of the drug trade information I saved the night before. The more I read, the more fascinated I became. The first article said organized crime controlled the illicit drug business for years. The mafia moved over ninety percent of the heroin entering the U.S. and had no serious competitors. The French Connection New York crime family network bought heroin from Corsican families' Marseilles operations and distributed it in the United States. American and French drug agents broke the French Connection in 1972, and that ended the mafia's stranglehold on the heroin trade. Law enforcement success, however, created opportunities for new players.

The new players were crime syndicates with global reach. The

Colombian Medellín and Cali cartels were the most significant and dealt in cocaine, heroin, and marijuana. They put together immense fortunes and were ruthless. Heavy losses eventually diminished their dominance, but other Colombians still ran the drug trade. It was another opportunity for new players to step into the void.

The Colombians controlled the entire chain of the cocaine business—acquisition, refining, transportation, and distribution. Almost everyone, regardless of where they operated, worked with them. There was one obvious reason why Colombia was the epicenter: its institutions did not work, evidenced by the high level of violence at all levels of society.

The period from the 1940s to the 1960s was known as *La Violencia*, when political parties on both sides either supported guerilla movements or funded their own. Slowly, Colombians became desensitized to violence. As guerrilla groups gained strength, the government lost control of a large portion of the country. That lack of control enabled the drug cartels and the FARC to do as they pleased. Law and order broke down.

Colombians developed world-class money laundering capabilities, moving drug profits around the world beyond the reach of the authorities. They also learned that no narco-trafficking or terrorist organization operated effectively without a network of overseas collaborators. Many terrorist groups around the world watched and learned from the Colombians.

Chris was waiting for me at the curb when I cleared U.S. Customs. We had so much in common we could have been brothers. Chris's American father was killed when the Tupamaros blew up a Montevideo restaurant one summer night. His father was not the target, but the bomb killed him just as dead as the two police chiefs it was intended for. His Uruguayan mother feared for his life and sent him to a U.S. boarding school, the same one my parents sent me to for 12th grade when they moved to Europe. Chris and I were roommates, we became fast friends, and we attended the University of Virginia together.

Chris married straight out of college and went on to international affairs graduate school, then joined the Army to see the world. After several tours, he became part of the U.S. intelligence community and lived in some real pits for another ten years. With a Ph.D., he currently taught international relations at the University of Miami and consulted part-time.

"Dr. Hendricks, how goes it?" I shouted as Chris got out of the car.

"Still with the doctor crap. When are you going to get over that?"

"Never. You opened yourself to abuse the minute you got that degree."

"Up yours. Let's eat."

The Little Havana Café was a place to eat, not a place to see and be seen. We took a table at the back. For less than ten dollars, I got a plate of meat, white rice, black beans, a beer, flan, and two expresos. Over coffee Chris told me he was beat. He had just finished writing a white paper about the drug trade and would bring me up to speed later.

My cell phone vibrated as we walked into Chris's house. I answered hoping it was Julie. "Richard, it's Gustavo. I got your note last night, and I've already worked on it. Do you have a minute?"

"You bet, but give me a second to get settled." I told Chris I needed a spot to spread out for a couple of minutes. He showed me into the study, gave me a pen and a pad, and pulled the door. "Okay, Gustavo, shoot."

"Well, I dug a little more. There are a couple of things. First, I found no more BLI payments to Raúl. I know they exist, but I need to get into their systems or some of Raúl's personal accounts to prove it."

"Too bad, but what you have may be enough," I said. "We can sort that out later."

"Next, I chased down that invoice I gave you. A Phoenix joint venture in the Far East manufactured the chemicals, shipped them to a subsidiary in Houston and then re-routed them to a chemical company Raúl controls here."

"Could you see where they ended up?"

"Some disappeared in Bolivia, and it looks like the rest was re-exported to Colombia."

"Did any money move for this?"

"It did, and that's where it gets interesting. The payments at the corporate level went through inter-company accounts, and they all wash out, but at our level they disappear. I even looked at some of Raúl's companies, but they're not there either."

"You have access to Raúl's corporate accounts?" I asked.

"Only his joint ventures with Phoenix. We use the same banks, and since we're joined at the hip, they gave me access last year when I was looking at some internal control issues. They never revoked it. I can tell you more about that when you get back."

"Does this have to do with Raúl's use of the corporate aircraft and his dinner parties?" I asked.

"Yes. I had a feeling someone in Chicago probably told you."

"Look, no worries here, okay? You did the right thing."

"Thanks," he said, relieved. "Richard, I want to help every way I can to get Raúl."

"Even after what happened to you last time?"

"I do. Headquarters beat me up, but I was right. I'm not going to stop doing what I'm supposed to do. Unless you tell me to drop it."

"Don't stop, but be very discrete. By the way, where are you calling from?"

"Home. I didn't want to use the office phone. I don't trust Raúl."

"Good. Be careful, and keep your eyes open. We'll talk as soon as I get back."

"Thanks."

Gustavo was a good hand, and was showing me what he was made of. Management had clipped his wings, but he was not afraid of anyone.

29

Chris and I started to help with the dishes, but his wife ran us out and told us to get on with our business since we had only one night together. We grabbed a couple of beers and watched the news in the study. There was a special report about the "three frontier" terrorist safe-haven area in Latin America. The common border area of Argentina, Brazil, and Paraguay was a hotbed of subversive activity and Ciudad del Este was its urban center.

Located in the far northeast corner of Paraguay, Ciudad del Este with its 240,000 inhabitants was the Southern Cone hub of illicit drug trading, gun running, migration fraud, money laundering, counterfeiting, theft, extortion, terror planning, and virtually every other form of crime imaginable. According to authorities, over fifty percent of the vehicles on the road were from illicit origins. Everyone was involved. An insurance investigator once found that the President of Paraguay's BMW was stolen from a Brazilian businessman. The correspondent spoke in hushed tones, as if Ciudad del Este's reputation were a state secret. It was no secret to anyone in Latin America.

"I swear, Chris, it's a treat to watch the news and not see a single story about coca or cocaine."

"Missing home, are we?"

"Yes and no. I miss Julie and the children, but I'm already wondering what the hell I'm doing in this job." I extended the chair's leg rest and sipped my beer.

"For the life of me, I'll never understand why you and Julie left Rio."

"You know why."

"I've heard you explain it before, but that doesn't mean I understand it. You got to do a lot of fun stuff, were your own boss, and loved it. It wasn't 'all or nothing'. You could have stayed with it."

"I know, but what's done is done. Right now I've got bigger problems to worry about."

"So I gather. Your e-mail said you wanted to talk about somebody."

"Do you know a guy named Raúl Orellana?"

"Sure do. I met him years ago at a drug conference in Cartagena while I was on a temporary assignment for the State Department. Why?"

I described Raúl's role at Phoenix and told Chris what I had picked up from Denning, Torres, and Paul Trasky. He showed no surprise that I suspected Raúl was behind the truck tire mess and the Molotov cocktails. He shook his head when I mentioned Raúl was taking kickbacks on sole-source contracts.

"You're in some serious shit now, friend," Chris said as he walked to the kitchen to get another round of beers. "This is bad."

"Tell me about it," I shouted after him. "I'm just trying to keep my head down and figure out what's going on."

"You and I know," he said coming back with the beers, "that people like Raúl are always corrupt in one way or another. That's the way it is in Latin America. A lot of people play the game, and everyone looks the other way. Getting caught and taken to task in public is something else entirely, especially when you're the U.S. government's point guy for the war on drugs."

"You're not saying he's pristine, are you?"

"Not at all," he rejoined, shaking his head and drinking his beer. "That was the point of my white paper. There are a couple of dozen high ranking people throughout Latin America I call the 'untouchables'. They're all up to their eyeballs in illicit activity of some sort—drugs, arms, money laundering, prostitution, guerrilla activity, or outright theft and extortion. They're immune because there's no hard proof against them, and they have tremendous political, economic, and military influence. Two are heads of state, and the rest are high public officials or prominent businessmen. Don't forget, many are 'friends' of the U.S. government."

"Did you name any of them in your paper?"

"No way. I'd never get another State Department contract if I did. Naming them would cause 'diplomatic complications', so to speak."

"Would you put Raúl on that list?"

"You bet I would, but the U.S. government wouldn't."

"Why not?"

"He works with us on eradication, is incredibly well connected and respected, and D.C. doesn't believe he's involved in anything illicit. You'll be at the top of his enemies list if you go after him, and that's not a good place to be. Remember: there hasn't even been a rumor about Raúl."

"Granted, but no rumors doesn't mean he's not crooked."

"That's my point," Chris said. "Even if there were a hint, though, it has never been in anyone's interest to stir that water. Of the untouchables, he may well be the farthest out of reach."

"Why the kid gloves?"

"Raúl was the Bolivian government's point man on Operation Condor. That, my friend, is the real rub."

"No wonder. Any U.S. complicity in Condor might come out if Raúl got hit with a scandal. That would ruin some careers."

"You got it. Self-preservation rules. We had no interest in

Raúl's personal business, but we made it a point to stay away from Condor. That's a sovereign issue we didn't want to touch. Blowback can be a real bitch." He drained his beer.

Operation Condor was a 1970s secret network of the Argentine, Bolivian, Chilean, Paraguayan, and Uruguayan intelligence services that pursued suspected leftists, Marxists, and Communists through extra-legal means around the world. The group collected and exchanged information on presumed subversives. It moved at will against suspects within the member countries, kidnapping, torturing, and assassinating. The network also pursued and killed targets in non-member countries. They used several methods; kidnapping and torture until death, a bullet to the head, or their favorite—car bombs. The teams had official government papers under fictitious names. After a hit, the team disappeared until needed again.

"Did you ever see anything about Raúl's involvement in Condor?" I asked.

"No, but several people did. That's not the point anyway. Raúl was the number two man overall behind the Chilean general who ran it. He's a mean, tough, nasty guy. He smiles at you one minute and cuts your throat the next. Trust me, he'll try to make sure you never talk if he even suspects you're after him. Do you carry your 1911s?"

"Always."

"Good. Put Raúl's name on a couple of rounds. He's probably already got several with your name on it."

"I didn't tell Julie I suspect Raúl of the Molotov cocktails, but I know she's worried."

"She should be. So, are you going after him on the kickbacks?"

"A big piece of me wants to look the other way and let this float right on by. I've got a decent job, the pay is good, my family likes La Paz, and I could take the path of least resistance. This will go away, I'll move on, and everyone stays happy. There's no reason to stick my nose into it."

"Oh, yes there is. You and I are hard-wired to take on things like this."

"I know, but you're not putting your job on the line."

"Excuse me? When was the last time you let job security override your sense of what's right?"

"Touché."

"So, what are you going to do?"

"I have to go after him. I hate the prick, and I'd love to get something on him."

"Yeah, I bet you would. I would too. When I wrote the white paper, I had only open source data and rumors. If you have some hard data, I might find something on him."

"I'd love that. I hired Grant to do a security and background check, but there's only so much they can do. There's no way I can turn this over to Phoenix internal audit. They'd ignore it or bury it, so I have to do this on my own. I need to get into a few corporate computer systems to find out what Raúl's up to."

"You have a dilemma, don't you?"

"No shit. Grant could do it, but they can be tied to me—not to mention that I can't ask them to commit a crime by hacking into secure corporate computer systems."

"So, you need someone who can't be connected to you, can hack any system in the world, and loves the challenge more than he fears the consequences. And, would do it for free."

"You have someone in mind?"

"I do," Chris said with a smile. "The guy who helped me research the white paper is our man. He's got a hard-on for people like Raúl. I'll call him after I say goodnight to the boys."

I gathered my thoughts while Chris put his sons to bed and made his call. Even though I knew nothing more than when I left Lima, talking to Chris convinced me to send Steven Price an e-mail. I told him that I was concerned about some conflict of interest issues with Raúl and that we needed to talk. I gave no details and asked him to call me.

Chris gave me a thumbs up when he came back. His systems jock was on board. We kicked back and watched a cable TV shoot'em up double feature. The good guys shot pistols that never had to be reloaded, defeated body armor, and exploded bad guys through walls, doors, and windows. Great fiction. We ordered a double cheese, pepperoni, beef pizza, and grabbed more beers from the fridge. We would pay for this on our morning run tomorrow.

30

Raúl was thrown against the Land Rover door as it bounced over the rutted road in the Colombian countryside. His stomach hurt, he had a headache, and he told himself he was getting too old for this. He unwound from his thoughts as the vehicle rolled to a stop at the back of the Los Condes Hotel ninety minutes outside Bogotá. The dust from Col. Pérez's jeep had not yet settled when Raúl's driver pulled up next to him. Raúl got out of the car, stretched, and was inside before the driver turned off the engine.

Col. Martín Pérez was the Colombian Army's top-level military contact with the Colombian National Police. The CNP's counter-narcotics unit ran Colombia's crop eradication, interdiction, investigation, and enforcement programs. It was largely corruption free. The army was more corrupt, and that made Pérez an easy target at a Bolivian embassy reception three years earlier. Raúl had once considered working with the Autodefensas Unidas de Colombia (AUC), the paramilitaries, but dropped the idea after one meeting with Carlos Castaño. The AUC leader made it clear he would never deal drugs and said his only objective in life was to kill guerrillas. Most groups had a soft spot to exploit, but not Castaño. The point was moot, since Castaño was rumored killed by his own people who wanted to deal cocaine. Raúl still would not work with them as he believed they were unstable.

"Raúl, it's good you made it," Pérez said. "Grab a coffee. I don't have much time. We're in a training cycle with the Americans, and I need to get back soon."

"Screw the coffee. I've had diarrhea all the way from Lima, and I'm out of Imodium. Let's get started."

"Before anything, we need to talk about these latest arrests. I never thought this would be a problem, but it will blow us to shit if it continues. This puts everyone under even more scrutiny." Pérez referred to two separate incidents. In one, American soldiers were caught smuggling cocaine when they returned to the U.S. In the other, a couple of U.S. soldiers were discovered selling assault rifles and ammunition to the Colombian paramilitaries. "I don't care that they deal in cocaine or sell arms, but they need to be smarter."

"It pisses me off and worries me as well, but it's beyond our control."

"Maybe yes, maybe no. I hear an American civilian is behind this. With your reach, you should be able to find out who it is and take care of him."

"Something I can look into," Raúl said coldly. "On to other things."

"The aid and training package includes the army, the air force, and the CNP. I was surprised at how comprehensive it is."

"We expected that," Raúl shot back. "All you had to do was see how much the U.S. was willing to commit. How do we stay ahead of them?"

As head of the Army Counter Drug Mobile Brigades, Pérez knew the details of the counter-drug and counter-insurgency goals, objectives, tactics, and plans. He was astute and capable, and he liked cash. Because of the enormous sums of money flowing to Plan Colombia, corruption in the security forces attracted more attention than ever. Pérez had an impeccable service record without a hint of human rights violations. He was a star in Raúl's stable.

Pérez had recently been named commander of the military-police Joint Intelligence Center (COJIC) at Tres Esquinas in southern Colombia. Three battalions of nine hundred men each received helicopters, intelligence, and U.S. advisory logistical support as part of the U.S. financial package. U.S. Special Forces trained the new battalions in counter-narcotics and counter-insurgency to improve their tactical skills. U.S.-sponsored no-cost leases of UH-1 helicopters enhanced their airborne options. COJIC shared intelligence with other military branches and international counter-narcotics groups in Ecuador, Peru, and Bolivia. As chief of operations, Pérez was essential to all counter-insurgency and counter-drug activity in Colombia.

"We can stay ahead," Pérez said, "but not as easily as before. Our biggest problem is that Plan Colombia gives the security forces new air capability. That hurts us. It's out of our control, so we need to focus on what we can control."

"Be specific, Pérez," Raúl demanded impatiently.

"The new OV-10 and A-37 aircraft dramatically improve the air force's interdiction capability. Plus, they've modified the OV-10s to include armor, night vision equipment, and satellite guided spray systems. The planes are here to stay, and we can't do anything about it. They're also planning radar upgrades and infrastructure improvements at the Tres Esquinas, Marandua, and Larandia airports. Their eyes and ears will be better than ever. The key, however, is that you control those assets."

"I do indeed," Raúl replied. One of his joint ventures would perform most of the radar upgrades and the airfield construction work. He could control when and how the systems worked.

"Even though you've got the aces," Pérez said, "the helicopters still make me lose sleep."

"What exactly are the Americans giving you?"

"Fourteen UH-60 Blackhawks, thirty-two UH-1Ns, and twenty-five UH-1 Super-Huey IIs. That's on top of what we got last year and the year before. I've been ordered to guarantee secure operating conditions for the CNP. They will accept no excuses."

"We knew this was coming," Raúl said flicking his cigarette onto the floor, "but I didn't think it would be so soon."

"We also didn't think the Americans would double their military trainers from 400 to 800 or would raise the cap on civilian security contractors from 400 to 600. In many respects, I'm more worried about the civilians than I am the military—they have more freedom and are more dangerous."

"As the Americans say, shit happens."

"Raúl, we can't win by brute force alone. Our intelligence will be better than ever, and we need to use it to our advantage."

"I know, but brute force is more satisfying."

Raúl disconnected from Plan Colombia thirty-five minutes outside of Bogotá and turned his thoughts to GEM. They were still on his mind well into his second whiskey at the hotel bar. GEM provided cover and had a violent wing Raúl liked to use. Establishing reliable contacts with the Latin American terrorist groups was tricky, and GEM was an excellent liaison with Sendero, FARC, MST, and others like them. GEM was even making inroads with the Central American drug gangs. Still, Raúl did not trust GEM. Goodnature and his kind were unprofessional, soft, and cowardly. They were too far out on the fringe. A perverse primitive ecological ideology permeated everything about them. They wanted a plague to sweep "the evil that is man" off the face of the earth. Raúl thought they were unstable and dysfunctional. They talked the talk, but they let others do the walking. Ecological revolution was great as long as the right people survived.

Raúl reluctantly brought Goodnature on board, but only because he could be a convenient tool. He dealt exclusively with Dávila, however, as Raúl did not want his role exposed. Goodnature thought Dávila was no more than a petty drug runner, and openly disrespected him during their first meeting by questioning his judgment. Dávila soon thereafter kidnapped Goodnature's girlfriend and traveling companion. His men gang raped her, bludgeoned her to death, drew and quartered her, and fed her to Dávila's farm animals. They video taped everything and showed it to Goodnature. He begged for his life and never again questioned Dávila's instructions. It appeared, however, that Goodnature had gone back to his old ways. Even before meeting with Pérez, Raúl had indications that Goodnature was working with U.S. soldiers and the paramilitaries on side deals. American servicemen were the ultimate professional soldiers, but they were amateur drug dealers and gun runners. Dealing with amateurs was dangerous. He did not mind if Goodnature occasionally free-lanced, but would have to replace him if he continued to stray off the reservation.

Goodnature was from another planet, but Raúl and Steven Price were cut from similar cloth. They had the same business vision and goals. Price was exceptionally bright, but was a political animal who loved schmoozing diplomats and politicians at U.S. embassies around the world. He had strong political connections and patrons who looked out for him—and for Phoenix. Many observers believed that he harbored political ambitions. He topped the U.S. diplomatic circuit's invitation list for important functions, as bureaucrats catered to a possible future boss or committee chair. Raúl did not understand Price's need to be in the constant company of powerful politicians.

While Raúl made sure his operations ran smoothly, Price dined with the ambassador at the U.S. Embassy in Bogotá. Raúl looked at his watch and wondered if he was still there. Raúl smiled. Pulling Price away from a diplomatic function was like pulling teeth. Each in his own way, they liked the good life. Raúl finished his whiskey, and finally felt relaxed and tranquil after a long day. It was late and he decided to call it a night.

31

A slow mist fell gently in the San Borja neighborhood of Lima as Aníbal Carrasco stood at the back door of the Sendero safe house. The damp, luminescent dial on his watch showed 2:07 A.M. It was time to move. Carrasco and his team reviewed their checklists and loaded two blue Volvo sedans with weapons and explosives.

This operation would take pressure off Sendero's drug trade and Carrasco was upbeat. Sendero had been dormant for some time, and he loved blowing things up. A few old-style leftists still wanted to "liberate" Peru, but the Sendero leadership was more pragmatic and understood that terrorism was about money. They also understood that killing Peruvians turned people against them. Property was a much more attractive target. If they had to kill, it was better kill police, military, or foreign businessmen.

Tonight's target was the elegant Excelsior Palace Hotel in San Isidro. Police patrols were light near the hotel, and they only occasionally stopped drivers to ask for ID papers. Sendero knew the police never stopped the hotel's blue Volvo sedans, and that the underground parking garage gave discrete and unobstructed access to the entire complex. The also knew that the garage was the entrance of choice for businessmen bringing prostitutes into the hotel.

The Sendero men dressed like respectable businessmen, the women like not entirely respectable ladies. Carrasco led in the first car, and his long-time companion Mónica Artigas followed in the second. They all reviewed each person's responsibilities one last time a mile from the hotel. Three blocks from the Excelsior Palace, they came to a dead stop.

"Shit!" Carrasco's driver muttered.

"What's wrong, Javier?" Carrasco leaned forward from the back seat.

"The MP at the intersection has his hands up. He's telling me to stop!"

"Take it easy," Carrasco said calmly, "and show him your documents. You're okay."

"Is there a problem, sir?" the driver asked, handing his papers to the policeman.

"None." The MP focused on the driver's license and registration while his companion raised a flashlight to the car, then lowered and turned it off when he saw the vehicle was a blue Volvo. "There is a French Embassy party at the hotel. Only hotel cars get through. You're in order. Is this other car with you?"

"Yes. They're registered guests from England with friends from Play Women Lima."

"I see," the MP grinned. "You may go."

"Damn the French," Carrasco growled. "That party wasn't on the schedule."

"Thank the Vírgen María for our documents," said the driver.

"Aníbal, is everything okay?" Artigas radioed from the second car.

"We're fine. They're waving us on. Follow us into the garage."

Sendero's documents were on Government of Peru paper and were identical to officially-issued ones. With a visit to the Ministry of Interior facilitators who sold government documents for cash,

Sendero had national identification cards, driver's licenses, and auto registration papers under false names. It was one-stop shopping.

"Okay, Javier, slow down when you get to the ramp," Carrasco told the driver when they reached the Excelsior Palace's side entrance.

The driver eyed the security guard twenty feet ahead. "What if he stops us or asks for room numbers?"

"He won't. He'll see two hotel sedans with guests bringing in lady friends. You won't even have to roll down your window."

"Son of a bitch!" Javier exclaimed under his breath as the guard waved them on. "That was easy!"

"I told you," Carrasco said. "Okay, go ahead slowly to the right and down one level. Park in front of the elevators, and make sure the car is even with the concrete columns so the security cameras don't see us when we get out."

The men had 9mm semi-auto pistols in shoulder rigs, and their companions carried the same model in purses. Each driver had a concealed pistol plus a short-barreled FAL carbine in the back seat. The couples carried overnight bags full of explosives.

Carrasco originally thought to attack with an ammonium nitrate and fuel oil (ANFO) air blast device hidden in a delivery truck, but he abandoned the idea since it would not cause enough damage. The bomb would kill people outside the hotel, but the blast wave would dissipate too rapidly to cause structural damage. Sendero engineers knew that even a huge ANFO device would not do the job. That meant they would have to attack from inside the building. The Excelsior Palace had three rows of steel-reinforced structural columns along its long axis and the floor panels were only lightly reinforced. The columns and beams had reinforced steel fill, but nothing like a U.S. project.

They left the cars in couples, flirting and carrying on like people getting ready for a night of amorous engagement. The drivers stayed with the cars.

"Good. Still no security cameras in the elevators," Artigas observed as all four took the same elevator and punched the buttons for the fourth and tenth floors.

"Remember," Carrasco said before he got off on four, "do this quickly and get out. If you see somebody, embrace until they go away. Radio me if you have trouble."

"Good luck," Artigas said as the door closed.

Carrasco and his partner turned left, hurried down the hall, and picked the lock to the service area that led to the hotel's structural support members. They would work unobserved.

"Ana, bar the door," Carrasco said as he unpacked explosives, primers, blasting caps, and fuses from the overnight bag.

"Done." She knelt by Carrasco and helped take inventory of their gear.

"We've got everything," Carrasco said.

"Is this all of the C-4?" Ana asked, unwrapping a block.

"Unfortunately." Carrasco picked up another block. "This is the last of it. We've got enough for today, but we need to get more from Mansour soon."

Holding the C-4 three feet off the ground, Carrasco asked, "Ready?"

"Ready." Ana placed her block on the other side of the column, directly opposite Carrasco's.

"Okay, I'll set the primary trigger first." The delay device would detonate the explosives at 5:05 A.M.

"Don't set the secondary until we're packed up and ready to move," Ana said. The backup mechanism would detonate the explosives if it detected a heat signature or movement within ten feet.

"It's late, but I'm not asleep. Let's finish the other columns."

Carrasco loved C-4 and trusted "Made in U.S.A." to explode as advertised. The Russian stuff was garbage, and he eagerly accepted

Mansour's offer to be Sendero's sole supplier. Carrasco expected trouble when he switched providers, but relaxed when the Lima police found four Russians in the Pacific surf with multiple bullet wounds. Mansour meant business.

"Have we got everything?" Carrasco asked. Ana nodded yes. "Now!" he said as he activated all the devices and locked the door behind them.

The tenth floor team finished at the same time as Carrasco. The blast would not bring the hotel down, but would cause substantial damage, maybe enough to have it demolished. The attack would not, however, kill many people. To kill people, Sendero had another plan.

"I've got the rooms on the left and you've got the right," Ana said. She took a fragmentation grenade from her pouch and taped it behind the canvas bag holding the morning paper. Elegant Latin American hotels hung papers from the doorknob, believing that leaving them on the floor was bad form.

"Remember," Carrasco said firmly, pulling a grenade from his overnight bag, "only doors with newspapers. That means a guest is in the room."

After duct taping each grenade behind the bag, they partially removed the pin and attached it to a short wire taped to the door frame. Carrasco knew hotel guests would open their door when the C-4 detonated and the hotel evacuation alarm sounded. The grenade would detonate at waist level. Easy kills.

The teams rendezvoused on the mezzanine to place additional explosives in the travel offices and the communications center. It took less than ten minutes to rig the floor to detonate simultaneously with the structural columns. It was 4:26 A.M. Time for Sendero to go home.

"Easy does it, Javier. Pull out slowly, the same as when we came in," Carrasco told the driver.

"We're right behind you," Artigas radioed.

"Same guy, same stupid smile," Javier said as the guard waved Carrasco's car through.

"Time to go home and watch the news. Well done, everybody." Carrasco relaxed against the headrest and closed his eyes.

The cars eased out to the street, turned left, and disappeared into the mist. Lima would soon awaken with a bang.

32

Steven Price closed his eyes as he and Raúl rode to the Bogotá airport. It had been a long night. Instead of returning to the hotel from the U.S. Embassy party in his own car, Price accepted a ride from the Colombian general who sat next to him at dinner. Price's car followed ten minutes later and was rendered a mass of twisted metal and flames several miles from the hotel. Two RPGs tore through the left front side of Price's sedan and killed the driver and bodyguard in front. Hand grenades and hundreds of small arms rounds obliterated the bodyguard in back. The lightweight armor and ballistic glass of Price's car was no match for the level of the attack. The embassy RSO got Price out of bed and told him that he narrowly escaped being killed. It appeared the attack was directed at the general, since the two sedans were virtually identical and followed the same route.

"It looks like they were after the general, but they nearly got you," Raúl said. "I'll have my people talk to the army and the CNP."

"Thanks. The embassy will jump on it too."

"I know, but I'll check anyway. We can't take any chances."

Raúl thought Price's primary concern would be his narrow escape the night before. It was not. Price was angry with Phoenix CEO Geoff Whitworth for ordering the company plane back to

Chicago so he could fly to Seattle, leaving Price and Raúl to fly commercial. That meant meeting someone else's schedule, and Price was furious.

After forty-five minutes in traffic, narrowly avoiding two wrecks and a dead motorcyclist, they finally reached the airport. Security was always tight in Bogotá, and police dogs gave them a quick sniff as they got out of their car. After checking in, they were patted down twice and asked for their passports several times before reaching the gate. They finally boarded after walking through a metal detector at the door of the plane.

Raúl sipped champagne two rows ahead of Price, pleased that the trip went well. He was still growing coca under everybody's nose, refining and exporting more cocaine than ever. The chemicals business let him move precursors at will, and his legitimate partners gave him cover and up-to-date information. All was well.

He wanted more, but had no illusion about dominating the drug trade on his own. It was better to manage his current position and expand slowly rather than "going for it." Pablo Escobar "went for it" and paid with his life.

U.S. Customs dogs checked everyone at the American Airlines baggage carousel in Miami. Anyone coming from Bogotá was a target. Price loved Latin America, but he was glad to be home.

"Playing golf this afternoon, Raúl?" Price asked.

"If it doesn't rain. I should get in a round and make tonight's flight to La Paz easily."

"Stay focused when you get back. Don't fight Blackstone over petty shit."

"That's easy for you to say. You should see the way he acts sometimes. The guy is a pain in the ass."

"I'm sure you've said the same about me. Just keep your eye on the ball."

Traveling was exhausting and telling Raúl to ignore the small personal stuff was even more so. Price failed to understand why little things upset Raúl. Worse, they affected his judgment. With time to spare before boarding for Chicago, he eased himself into a chair in the American airlines lounge. The words *Shining Path Terror Attack* drew his eyes to the television screen. A young reporter stood in front of a building smothered in smoke as she described how a Sendero bomb rocked a Lima hotel at dawn. The police had a preliminary casualty toll of fifty-two dead and thirty-nine wounded. Most of the dead were guests killed by grenades. The Lima fire chief evacuated the hotel and said the damage might be severe enough to require demolishing the building. Price felt lucky. He cheated death in Bogotá, and could have easily stayed in the Excelsior Palace and been a victim of the Sendero attack.

Aníbal Carrasco liked what he saw on CNN. His effort achieved its objective, no Sendero were hurt, and the police were baffled. Carrasco was especially glad they got a good kill rate, but left the building standing. The furor would die down soon. The operation was perfect. It was right on the edge.

In his Chicago office, Price checked his computer for news on the Lima attack. None of the major services had anything substantial. His phone rang as he logged off the Internet.

"Mr. Price," his secretary said, "it's Senator Carlson. I thought you might want to take the call before you go home."

"Thanks, Tracey." Price picked up the handset. "Yes, senator."

"Steven, I got a call from State this morning about the attack on your car last night. Are you okay?"

"I'm fine, and am just glad I rode with the general. Otherwise, I wouldn't be talking to you right now."

"Does the embassy have any idea who it was?"

"None. They figure the general was the target, not me, and the attackers made a mistake."

"Lucky mistake for you."

"No kidding. I know it's dangerous there, but I never expected it to happen to me."

"Are we still on for dinner next week?"

"We are."

"See you then."

Price scanned his e-mail to see if there was anything pressing. Only two messages were tagged High Priority. The first was from Barry Leiffer, the senior partner at Phoenix's accounting firm. He wanted to review a recent takeover proposal. Price replied that it would have to wait a couple of weeks. The second was from Blackstone titled "Raúl Issues—Your Eyes Only." Price shook his head. "Not this crap again," he said out loud. He deleted the note. The last thing he wanted to fool with was the latest spitting match between Blackstone and Raúl. They would have to sort it out on their own.

33

Over lunch in the living room, Chris brought me up to speed on Hugh Gacki, the systems whiz, who seemed perfect for the task. He was a University of Pennsylvania English and math major who worked for several years as a Peace Corps volunteer in Latin America, then as a consultant with the U.S. Agency for International Development. He was not out to save the world, but believed that hard work could make people's lives better. After five years, he returned to the U.S. disgusted with the way graft and corruption kept millions of people in poverty. He earned a Ph.D. in artificial intelligence from Carnegie Mellon and headed up a cutting-edge marketing research firm in Miami where he made sure his clients knew their customers' preferences before the customers themselves did.

Chris met him when the U.S. government retained Gacki's firm to model, forecast, and influence the political decision-making process in several Latin American countries. Chris in turn hired Gacki for his own research projects, and what started as a professional relationship became a friendship. Gacki's frustration with the impunity of Latin American elites had grown over the years into full-blown rage as he watched Latin American countries flounder. Chris said that while Gacki researched the untouchables, he champed at the bit to hack some computer systems and nail a few high-level people. Without source data, though, he was hamstrung. He was so good he did not worry about getting caught, and would work on this project for free because he wanted to expose prominent tin soldiers. Chris knew Gacki would jump at the chance, especially when he learned I had source data and that Raúl Orellana was the fish on the hook.

Gacki arrived at Chris's house shortly after lunch and absorbed more about the idiosyncrasies of Phoenix's operations in half an hour than most people would in a day. According to him, hacking the chemical companies' databases was the easy part. To find something on Raúl, however, he had to match the exact production cycle to the invoices we had. That was the only way to follow it through the chain. As to hacking the banking systems, that was a piece of cake. I handed over the invoices from Gustavo's package and we left him alone so he could get to work.

We heard pages flipping and then a loud whistle. "Hey, Richard," he called, "I'm not sure, but you may have a lot more on your hands than someone skimming profits."

"Why do you say that?" I went back to the study, with Chris right behind me.

"You might want to look at the products he's moving," Gacki said handing the invoices to Chris.

"Well, well," Chris said. "This is interesting."

"Do you two mind cluing me in?" I asked. "This feels like a party I wasn't invited to."

"Raúl's moving a bunch of chemicals on this invoice," Chris said, "but three in particular stand out. Acetone, ethyl ether, and potassium permanganate."

"So?"

"They all have a variety of industrial applications," Gacki said. "Acetone is a common solvent used in nail polish remover and cleaning fluid. Ethyl ether is a pharmaceutical solvent used to extract fats and oils. Potassium permanganate is a water purifier, disinfectant, and bleaching agent. Each has a legitimate use—but they're also precursor chemicals for making cocaine."

"No way." I grabbed a chair.

"Yes way," Gacki said. "Unless he's engaged in a business that uses those chemicals, he's got no reason to be working with them."

"Plus," Gacki added, "even if he had a legitimate use for one, it's unlikely he'd need all three."

"Exactly," Chris shot back.

"Guys," I said, "it looks like this changes the dynamic of what we're dealing with."

"I'll say," Gacki said. "Time for me to get to work."

Chris and I went to the back porch to unwind with a few beers before I had to catch the flight to La Paz. After several hours of probing, Gacki hit on an identifier that made his eyes light up and his fingers type faster. He found unique alphanumeric tags on the invoices that pinpointed chemicals, process batch numbers, production and shipment dates, and final destinations. That was the key he needed to pull the pieces together. He shouted for sustenance, and Chris took him a second six-pack of Dr. Pepper while I gathered my gear to head out. Gacki did not even look up from the keyboard when I said goodbye. He said it would take time, but those tags gave him a pipeline into the heart of the system. It proved nothing, but it was a start.

I checked in for my flight, and bought Q-tips. I hated late night deep ear itches. A seatmate once told me I should never put foreign objects in my ear. I asked her about domestic objects. She said nothing to me for the rest of the flight. No sense of humor. I asked for a beer at the Admiral's Club, and saw a sound bite about a Sendero bomb. The experts speculated about the true intent of the attack. This was not plasma physics. Terrorists liked notoriety, fame, and influence. Many liked money and comfort. They liked to blow things up. It was a mistake to consider them in a normal context. They were seriously screwed up people and they needed to be shot. Simple.

Only two paragraphs into my book, I heard a familiar voice from the front of the plane. My stomach turned when I looked up and saw Raúl. He threw me a consummately disdainful look, then recovered and said he was pleased to see me. About as pleased as I was to see him, I didn't doubt. As luck would have it, he sat across the aisle from me.

I slept surprisingly well, woke up refreshed, and had some orange juice before we started our descent. Raúl looked dragged out. His seatmate got sick half an hour into the flight, and threw up all night long. That would teach Raúl to get on a plane with me. I got off quickly when we landed in La Paz, and my Bolivian ID papers had me through immigration and in the car with Lucho in under fifteen minutes. With some luck I would be home soon.

34

The traffic from the airport was light, and the children were thrilled I arrived in time to take them to school. Julie had breakfast ready when I got back from dropping them off and said I needed a nutritious meal. She knew I never ate on the plane. We sat on the living room sofa, and she gave me my protein shake along with a plate of scrambled eggs and sausage. Julie could see that I was worried. She asked what was going on.

"Something's seriously wrong at Phoenix, and I think it's going to get worse before it's over."

"Talk to me." She rubbed my arm.

"Do you remember the conversation I had with Gustavo before I left for Lima?"

"I sure do if it's the one where it looked like Raúl was getting kickbacks from BLI."

"The same. I asked Gustavo to keep digging, and I talked to Chris about Raúl,"

"Does he know him?"

"Yep. Said he was a mean and nasty guy. No news there. Here's some news though: Raúl was the Bolivian head of Operation Condor."

"Wonderful," she said, raising her eyebrows. "I would never

have expected that."

"Neither would I, but that's not the biggest surprise."

"How so?"

"Well, there's a story here, so bear with me. Chris wrote a white paper on Latin American corruption, and Raúl was one of the people the State Department wouldn't let him mention. He's dying to catch Raúl with his hand in the cookie jar, so I gave him the information Gustavo found. Chris brought over a systems guy to look at the data, and we found out Raúl's importing cocaine precursors."

"What do you think he's up to?"

"There might be nothing to it, but I have to believe something is going on when it's tied to a guy who's getting a million dollars a year in kickbacks."

"Have you told anyone at Phoenix yet?"

"I sent Price an e-mail that I was concerned about some conflict of interest issues with Raúl, but didn't give him any details. Embezzlement is bad enough, but I'm not sure I'm ready to talk about drugs. I'll wait for him to call me back on this one."

"How about talking to someone at the embassy?"

"Even worse. What would I say? That I suspect Mr. Squeaky Clean Eradication Man of running coke? I don't think so."

"I know. I just want you to get some help. What are our options?"

"Well, I could drop it and ride off into the sunset with a promotion in a couple of years."

"My love, ninety-nine point nine percent of the people in this world do that every day without blinking an eye. You can't."

"You sound like you've been talking to Chris. He said exactly the same thing."

"That's because I know you better than you know yourself, and so does he. You two are alike. That's why you get along so well. Anything else?"

"What I do depends on what Chris's guy finds out. At the very least I know Raúl is embezzling, so I'll take that to headquarters when I have better information. If there's drug activity, that's an embassy matter and it goes straight to John Denning."

"Señor Richard," our housekeeper Lucy interrupted, "es el señor Chris en el teléfono."

"Hey Chris," I said, taking the handset from Lucy. "Anything new?"

"Listen, Hugh was up for hours last night. That alphanumeric code on the backup data is exactly what he was looking for, and it let him drill into the system. Our problem is that it's only one data set. He needs more info. Can you help us out?"

"I'm not sure. I gave you everything we had. Anything else will have to come out of their office. It would look funny if I went over there and asked for the last two years of that stuff."

"Yeah, I agree—but we really need it."

"I've got a thought, but I need to cook it a bit. I'll call you later."

"Sounds good. Bye."

"More problems?" Julie asked.

"Maybe yes, maybe no. Did you ever schedule a meeting with BLI to apply for your import-export permits?"

"I meet with Solís next Friday. We were going to meet tomorrow, but he's at El Alto all week."

"My love, I sure could use your help." I explained my idea to Julie.

35

The Cessna Citation carrying the four FARC crossed unnoticed from Brazil into Argentina a hundred miles north of Monte Caseros and flew inland west of Buenos Aires. One phone call and $200,000 to air force general Ricardo Silva ensured that no radar monitored the plane in Argentine air space. That same payment bought landing rights and lodging at Silva's four thousand acre ranch in western Buenos Aires province.

Argentina was the last leg of a three-country trip. On the first, the FARC established a permanent training facility in northern Bolivia after three years of training the locals at makeshift sites. They next spent twelve days training the Brazilian MST in basic guerrilla tactics. Both groups would soon conduct small operations against their governments. Among the FARC on the Citation was Alberto Maure, the number two man in the FARC. He did not come to train Bolivians or Brazilians. Maure instead traveled to visit important partners in Argentina.

"Look at this place," he said, admiring the countryside as they drove the ranch SUV to Buenos Aires. "These people had everything, and they pissed it all away."

"Like the rest of the continent, hermano," his top lieutenant observed.

"No, not like the rest. The country is so rich. They waste everything and still manage to keep from drowning. It should be a world power today, but never will be."

The FARC Ford Expedition negotiated the spaghetti bowls on the approach to Buenos Aires and pulled off into the residential neighborhood of Belgrano. They turned onto 3 de Febrero and pulled in through the electric wrought iron gate at a house in the middle of the block. The car rolled forty-five yards down the driveway and parked in the garage at the back. The FARC piled out and greeted friends they had not seen for some time.

"Alberto, salaam aleikum," Rafik Hamza said as he embraced his old friend Maure.

"It's been too long," Maure said. "You know everyone with us."

Within minutes, they were drinking coffee in the seclusion of the Libyan embassy. It was a low-key two story house built in the 1930s, with a plain brick exterior that did not draw attention to itself. Belgrano was an upper middle-class neighborhood, a preferred area for foreign diplomatic missions. Like many Argentine houses, it was built so prying eyes could not tell if there was activity inside. With its windows always closed, one would think the diplomats wanted to keep out the searing Libyan desert heat.

Maure first met Hamza when the Libyans trained with the FARC in Colombia for three months in late 2002. Before that, they trained with the IRA for a month. Hamza believed there was no such thing as too much training. Infidels relied on technology and weapons while he and his brothers relied on skills. This meeting, however, had nothing to do with training.

Maure explained to Hamza that the FARC directorate had authorized an increase in operational funding, not revealing that GEM was the source of the money. The purpose was to increase terrorist activity in Colombia so the security forces would concentrate more on terrorism and less on drugs. The FARC wanted to stop a run of drug losses to Colombian authorities, having lost two planes in the last four months. Though there was no love lost between them, the seizure of $300 million of paramilitary cocaine was worrisome. The Colombian police, with American money and equipment, were kicking in more doors than ever. Maure said more guerrilla attacks inside Colombia would not be enough, and they needed the Libyan's assistance for something more significant. He proposed that the FARC fund a Libyan operation against the United States. Hamza loved the idea of hitting the U.S. hard, but he asked the obvious question. "Why don't you do it yourself?"

"We can't carry out the level of attack we need," Maure said. "You have greater access to weapons and better cross-border movement than we do. Plus, we don't want to get credit for it."

"And it's okay for us?" the Libyan wondered. "Why?"

"You have no real exposure, but we do. The pressure on us increases every day, and the government has publicly invited foreign bounty hunters into the country. When the U.S. president visited Cartagena last year, the Colombian president and defense minister publicly stated that we plotted to assassinate the American leader. We're not that stupid. It was a lie to get more Plan Colombia aid money. The announcement came a few days before the Colombian congress voted on a constitutional amendment to allow the president to run for re-election. The lies and scare tactics worked. The Americans sent more money and advisors, and the congress amended the constitution. A major hit on the U.S. would shift the attention away from us, but we would sign our own death warrant if we did it."

"And we wouldn't?"

"Rafik, you don't get it! The U.S. would take over the country. As they say, 'we know who you are, and we know where you live.' They have no idea who you are or where you live. On top of that, your leader has renounced everything he ever stood for. You're under less scrutiny than ever. Now is your moment."

"What do you propose?"

"We'll fund an attack on major U.S. interests. Unless something has changed, you could use the money, right?"

"We need it more than ever. Our situation is worse since Qadafi let international weapons inspectors into Tripoli. They found the plans for our ten kiloton nuclear device, and Qadafi is afraid cash for weapons purchases will be traced to him."

"If you take this on, you can hit the U.S. and take responsibility yourselves or blame anyone you want. It's a win-win situation for all of us."

"How much are you talking about?"

"Twenty-three million dollars."

"That's a lot of money," Hamza observed. "Are you serious?"

"I wouldn't joke about it. I need to know if you're up to it, Rafik. Are you?"

"We are. We already have several plans drawn up. This comes at a very good time, and we have a lot of help in this part of the world."

"I don't mind if you get help, but it can't be another Israeli Embassy or AMIA attack. I don't want you working with Hezbollah. I want an attack on an important American target, one actually in the U.S., on their soil. *Sí o sí.* Do we have an agreement?"

The March 1992 bombing of the Israeli Embassy in Buenos Aires killed twenty-eight people and injured more than two hundred. A July 1994 bomb destroyed the seven story Argentine Jewish Mutual Association center in Buenos Aires, killing eighty-six people and wounding dozens more. Argentine authorities never charged anyone, but most intelligence services attributed the attacks to Hezbollah or other Islamic extremists.

"We do," Hamza said. "We will have no further contact once we receive the money. You'll know when we have struck."

"Done," Maure said.

"Do you want access to some of our arms deals in return?"

"No. We want you to do something we can't do ourselves. We

need you for this, just as you needed our help in Madrid, Berlin, and London. We want a good hit."

Hamza was ecstatic. For the first time in years, he could finally carry out a major operation. He and his colleagues joined Qadafi, trained under his aegis, swore allegiance, and risked their lives for him. Qadafi abandoned them without a second thought. Hamza and his colleagues wanted to break with their leader, but continued in his service because of threats against their families in Tripoli. He hated Qadafi because he disbanded the Islamic Call Society in 1992 and then eviscerated the Islamic Martyrs and the Fighting Islamic Group. Qadafi broke trust again when he fingered Meghari and Fhima as the perpetrators of the Pan Am flight 103 attack. The final blow came when Qadafi let infidels into the country to look for weapons of mass destruction. He was a traitor. Finally, they could operate without him.

As much as he hated Qadafi, Hamza hated the Americans even more. His rage was now more fervent and personal than ever. Pakistan's security forces, with help from U.S. intelligence, had captured Abu Faraj al-Libbi. He was Libyan, a regional al Qaeda planner in Pakistan, and got caught because he was careless. The Americans trumpeted him as the al Qaeda number three operational planner, when in reality he was a small fish who was more of a threat to Pakistan's President Musharraf than anyone else. Al-Libbi was not nearly as important as the Americans thought. He was, however, extremely important to Rafik Hamza; he was Hamza's cousin. America would pay for this atrocity.

36

The Café de la Ciudad, an old-style La Paz coffee shop dating from 1900, was convenient for discrete conversation. The tables were set comfortably apart, the wood paneled walls and tall ceilings muted sound, and the service was attentive and efficient. I stepped through the tall doors and was temporarily blinded by the contrast of the bright sunlight outside and the restaurant's dark interior. My eyes adjusted, and I took a table at the rear against the wall. The place was perfect for the occasion. I was downtown and close to everything, could work the phone, and would eat lunch with Julie. The restaurant was one of Klaus Barbie's favorites, and it seemed ironic that I would work to bury Raúl where he and Barbie shared their favorite meals.

Klaus Barbie was a Nazi SS officer who fled Germany after the war. He was a Café de la Ciudad regular. Known as the Butcher of Lyon, he was responsible for the torture and murder of 26,000 French civilians, as well as the deportation of thousands of French Jews to concentration camps. The American Counter Intelligence Corps protected and employed Barbie because of the unique "police skills" he put to use in postwar West Germany. Barbie had to run when the French sentenced him to death in absentia for war crimes. The CIC helped him and his family escape to Latin

America. He finally settled in Bolivia in the mid 1950s and worked as an interrogator and torturer for several Bolivian and Peruvian dictatorships. His last significant job was the 1980 Luís García-Meza narco-coup in Bolivia. Authorities deported him to France in 1983, and he died in prison. Even Raúl could not save Barbie.

I put my reader file on the table, but chose instead to read the latest *Road and Track*. My cell rang at 1:15 P.M., right on schedule.

"Honey, are you there?" Julie asked.

"I'm here, darling, and I can hear you loud and clear. Are you in Solís's office?"

"I am," she said, her voice slightly hushed. "It worked like a charm."

"How did it go?"

"Great. I got here as they were shutting down for lunch. I told Solís's secretary I came to talk about my import-export permits. When she said that Solís wasn't here, I apologized and told her that I had made a mistake and had come on the wrong day. I said you were on your way in, and I would wait for you to pick me up."

"And?"

"She made me a cup of coffee, put me in Solís's office, and told the security guard I would wait for you. She apologized again and left for lunch. I'm ready. Tell me where to look."

"When I met with Solís, he pulled Phoenix documents from the file cabinet near the door and the credenza beneath the window. Try the file cabinets first. Look for a Phoenix label, and then we'll try Raúl's company."

"I've got it," she said quickly, "but the cabinet's locked."

"Do you have the letter opener?"

"Of course."

"Okay. I'll walk you through it. Whether or not this works depends on the kind of locks they have. Ready?"

"As ready as I'll ever be."

We had rehearsed the procedure at home, and I reminded Julie to push the letter opener hard between the drawer catch and the bolt mechanism on the side of the drawer. With luck, she could pull on the drawer and the catch would ride on the letter opener right past the bolt. Julie said she knew what to do. I heard nothing, then a faint sound of metal on metal.

"It keeps slipping, and then I can't find the catch," Julie said.

"Take your time."

"Okay. Got it, yes! It's open."

"Great. Now look for Phoenix imports from either Guangou Chemicals Ltd. or Phuket Global Chemicals. Take your time."

Several minutes passed. I saw no reason to miss the opportunity to drink a beer, so I ordered a Paceña and a plate of fries. More than half the beer was gone when Julie came back on.

"Found a bunch here. Looks like they go back three years."

"Great! Now do the same thing for Raúl. Look for the BolChem S.A. file cabinet."

"I already did that. The lock was the same as the other one. There are dozens of invoices from Guangou and Phuket to Raúl."

"You're incredible. Copy everything, and leave the office the way you found it."

"See you soon," she said hurriedly. "Order some wine for me."

"Done."

Julie walked in half an hour later with an armful of documents. We could have gone home for lunch, but we enjoyed the irony of eating there. I had in front of me a detailed three year history of chemicals shipments, volumes, the originating party and country, and the destination party and country. Some showed the transshipment location and method of payment. The last four shipments went from China to Houston to Iquique, Chile and then overland to La Paz. All shipments originated with a Phoenix subsidiary in the U.S. or Asia, and the final destination was a Raúl-controlled subsidiary in Latin America. There was not one single reference to precursors on anything. That made the initial data seem even more like a mistake, but I knew that was impossible.

There were strings of alphanumeric codes attached to every chemical listed, but I had no clue if they meant the same thing as the codes Gacki found on the invoices I gave him. As we ate, Julie and I realized we had only one option.

"Have we unpacked the scanner?" I asked.

"I set it up last week."

"We need to get this information to Chris, and I don't want to FedEx it. The authorities open packages before they leave, and this might not get out. Can you scan this so we can e-mail it?'

"I think I can manage that," she said, sipping red wine. "Let's finish lunch and head home."

Julie scanned the BLI and BolChem invoices while I called Donovan & Mason for an update of Phoenix's and Raúl's company structures. As we spoke, they faxed me the names of Phoenix's subsidiaries and joint ventures around the world, as well as a list of Raúl's companies. There were more than two hundred entities. He had companies all over Latin America, but the Brazilian operation stood out. He owned one hundred percent of Brasil Chemical Products S.A. in São Paulo, and it made all three precursors. Since the company was privately held, Donovan & Mason could not get any production or sales data. They would keep digging and update me when they had something. Grant & Company found little on Raúl, but determined that some of his companies disappeared in the chain after several transactions. They would get back to me in a few days. I was frustrated but realized that both companies had been working the problem for less than forty-eight hours.

A half dozen phone calls later, it was 7:30 P.M. and was time for a drink. The scent of sliced limes filled the kitchen, and I was reaching for the Bombay Sapphire when the phone rang. Any other day, I would let it go to voice mail so I could attend to the more important task of drink making. Today was different.

Gustavo was on the line. "How was your trip, Richard?"

"Good, thanks. I got in this morning, but had some catching up to do so I didn't go to the office."

"Did you receive the e-mail I sent you?"

"I did, but haven't had a chance to open it. What's up?"

"It has wire transfer information from headquarters and our banks. Can you look at it soon and call me at home?"

"You bet. Give me a few minutes."

Julie was in the study and had almost finished scanning the documents. I asked if she would like a gin and tonic when I was done talking to Gustavo. She said I could not make it fast enough. Gustavo's file was huge and took several minutes to download.

"Gustavo, I've got your e-mail in front of me. There's a bunch here."

"No kidding. You've got over two years of wire transfer information that picks up all the Phoenix corporate entities, joint ventures, and holding companies as well as most of Raúl's business accounts."

I scrolled through several screens. Some of Raúl's transactions were huge. Millions of dollars flowed to businesses in Bolivia, Brazil, Colombia, Ecuador, and Peru, companies Grant said likely did not exist.

"Gustavo, how did you get the banks to turn this over?"

"They're paranoid. Citibank got so burned on the Salinas money laundering deal in Mexico that all you have to say is 'potential impropriety,' and they'll hand over anything. They don't want to get caught with their shorts down again, and they actually expect us to help them stay clean. They gave me everything."

"Man, he moves a lot of money," I said as I clicked through more screens. "I can't believe this is for just the operations we know about. He must be moving it other places we don't see."

"I'm sure of it, but I don't know where. I still can't find the payments for those chemicals we discussed, but I'm certain they're buried some place. That bothers me."

"Bothers me too. I'll look at this and let you know where we need to go from here."

"Thanks. Call if you need anything else."

Life was not generally full of infinite choices; it was either one way or the other. I had the luxury of three options. I could ignore what I saw, I could be a good corporate employee and take it to Phoenix, or I could try to put the pieces together and get it to law enforcement.

I would not ignore what I saw. I had already fulfilled my obligation to Phoenix by sending Steven Price an e-mail about Raúl. I was glad he had not responded since I was not prepared to come clean with what I had seen. Left alone, Phoenix would bury the problem, obfuscate it, or blame me. Corporations and managers survived and progressed by the absence of waves. This was a big one.

That left my third option, which was to pull the data together and get it to law enforcement. My gut told me there was much more to this than embezzling and it would all end up on someone's desk at the U.S. Embassy.

37

The reception at the U.S. Ambassador's La Paz residence in honor of Rep. Mike Blaine and a small U.S. Congressional delegation had the usual complement of foreign diplomats, Bolivian government officials, foreign and local businessmen, and a couple of journalists. I tried to avoid most of them as I looked for something cold to drink. Jennifer DiAngelo, the U.S. Embassy Commercial Officer, had the same idea and was already at the bar. She had just heard that her next assignment was Madrid, and was thrilled. I suspected she would have infinitely better prospects in Madrid than in La Paz.

"Hi, Richard. I haven't seen you for a while. Been out of town?"

"I was in Lima last week and got in from Santa Cruz an hour ago."

"Raúl is here," she said apologetically, "and he's pissed at me."

"Maybe he's constipated or hasn't gotten any lately."

"No, really," she laughed, "it's about the invitations. My secretary didn't see your note that we weren't supposed to invite him. She sent the invitation, and it was too late to call it back."

"Don't worry. It's fine if he comes to these on his own account, but I don't want him invited as the Phoenix representative next time."

Raúl reveled in being the Phoenix representative and attending U.S. Embassy functions. It demonstrated his special status in the business and diplomatic communities, and he played on it to secure personal, business, and political favors. Image was everything. He had tried to cut me off at the knees, so it was time I returned the favor. The game was more fun when two played, and I was more than ready to jump in.

I spoke briefly with the U.S. Ambassador and the Deputy Chief of Mission, both good men with a wealth of Latin American experience. Everyone wanted their time or a favor, and no one was ever completely satisfied. The topic of the evening was how to get more visitors to Bolivia. Selling the country to American tourists was a chore, since most people had no idea where it was or what it offered.

"Hell," said the DCM, "we just need to show people that they can have a great time in a country that doesn't have a fast-food restaurant on every block!"

As usual, the conversation turned to the drug trade and the dire Bolivian economy—insufficient tax revenue to pay debts, underachieving development, and continuing social unrest. On top of that, Bolivian troops killed several cocaleros recently when they broke up a demonstration in Cochabamba.

Though civil unrest forced two presidents to resign in the last two years, Bolivia had seen no serious terror attacks yet. Several car bombs at oil and gas company offices in Santa Cruz resulted in only minor destruction of property, but the frequency of the attacks was of increasing concern. In addition to the attack on the Excelsior Palace, Sendero killed over thirty people in two disco attacks and almost twenty at a bus station. During the previous week, the FARC bombed a supermarket in Medellín, killing a dozen, and kidnapped the head of the Cali power company. A grenade attack on an expatriate bar in Bogotá killed seven and injured twenty the night before. The Colombian National Liberation Army (ELN), Colombia's second largest guerrilla group with 4,000 combatants, had blown up three oil pipelines in two weeks. After months of quiet, terrorism had suddenly spiked.

"It almost makes you wonder if they're coordinating their activity," the DCM observed.

"Let's hope not," the defense attaché said. "They're tough enough to handle as it is. If they're working together, they might run cross-border attacks. That would be a nightmare."

"Who is Sendero again?" asked Representative Blaine's chief of staff. The attaché rescued us as he took the staffer by the arm and invited him for a drink.

"The Bolivians don't have a terror problem like the rest of the region," I said, "but the coca issue won't go away."

"You know what they should do?" the DCM asked rhetorically. "They should legalize drugs and tax the exports." The DCM had a drink in him and was telling it as he saw it. Despite his qualifications, candor would never get him the top job.

"That might be the only solution," I responded, "and it would provide a steady cash flow."

It was no joking matter. Bolivia had huge gas reserves which generated no income. The billion dollar Bolivia-to-Brazil gas pipeline was below capacity because the lagging Brazilian economy could not bring gas-fired power projects on line. Bolivia was years from realizing its gas potential, and it appeared that coca was the current solution to its economic challenges.

38

Back from the party, I stretched on the sofa and held Julie's hand. I knew Raúl was into illegal drug operations, but could prove nothing. Law enforcement, Denning in particular, would say I was crazy. The corporation would eat me alive. Even in the face of obvious evidence, corporate America expertly ignored such things. Corporations talked sanctimoniously about conflict of interest and ethics, conducted employee training, and made employees sign letters that they understood and would abide by strict policies. CEOs issued serious letters describing their personal commitment to a code of ethics, but it fell apart when one of their own senior executives actually faced a problem.

The process was meaningless because corporations thought ethics was about business school courses, buzzwords, policies, and procedures. They missed the point. It was about people. All the guidelines in the world were useless if people did not know right from wrong, and were unwilling to do right when confronted with a problem. If CEOs run and hide from the tough ethical work, their employees will likely do the same. Leadership comes from the top.

Not only was Raúl engaged in crime, he was doing it right under Phoenix's nose. Corporations frequently ignored what their representatives did because it was convenient to do so. Companies hired them precisely because they had close ties to government. They got things done. If a corruption scandal erupted, corporations could cut and run claiming no knowledge of what happened locally. What did the average American CEO think representatives did or how they did it? Could all American corporations really think they had one of the few honest reps in the country?

Julie and I were in bed and drifting off to sleep when I was jolted awake by what sounded like someone yelling after he stubbed his toe. I reached underneath the bed for my pistol and flashlight, and made sure my shotgun was there too. I looked to my left through our open second floor balcony door and saw someone climbing the telephone pole behind the house two hundred feet away.

The climber shouted as the sliver dug deep into his finger, and then bit his lip, wishing he could reel in the sound of his own voice. He knew Blackstone could see the pole from the house, but hoped the gringo was sound asleep. The job should have been finished earlier in the day, and having to work after dark made him angrier than the splinter. A man climbing a telephone pole at noon did not arouse much suspicion, but one at 2:00 A.M. did. He was exposed, but had no choice. The kit should have arrived by mid-afternoon, but an equipment mix-up resulted in a midnight delivery. He promised the phone tap would be ready the next morning, and not delivering on time might shorten his life expectancy.

In a whisper, Julie asked me what was going on. I told her to turn slowly and look out the window at the guy on the pole. I dropped out of bed and got the binoculars from the bookcase.

The night crawler slithered down the pole after twenty-five minutes, and I knew this was not good. Someone wanted to watch or listen to us, and the visitor had doubtless installed something to do just that.

I slept little and pulled myself into the Mitsubishi at seven, well before Lucho came to take the children to school. I needed to find a phone to call Denning, and turned left out of the gate and drove down Avenida Strongest while I analyzed my options for protecting Julie and the children. One was extra security, but that didn't stop phone taps. Plus, I was stuck with Raúl's security company. Another was to get my family out of the country. Molotov cocktails were bad enough, but a phone tap was an intimate intrusion. Someone was targeting my family and our private lives. Running away was not the answer. We had to confront it head on.

"Good morning, John," I said from the pay phone at a supermarket. "Did you leave the party last night walking or crawling?"

"Walking," Denning answered slowly. "Well, mostly walking. As usual, I ate too much, drank too much, and got to bed too late. These postings are bad for your health. What's up?"

"I need to talk to you about something. It's pretty urgent."

"I'm really tied up today. The DEA Chief of Operations will be here in a few weeks," he said. The DEA chief was responsible for the agency's worldwide drug enforcement operations. "I've got planning meetings and all sorts of crap to work up before he gets here. Can it wait a couple of days?"

"It can't. Listen, I need five minutes. I can swing by your house when the children go to school."

"You got it."

"Thanks, John."

39

"Yeah, Richard, I'd be concerned too," Denning said after I told him about the nocturnal telephone repairman.

"Can you tell me if my phone is tapped?"

"Yes and no. I have the technical capability to see if it's tapped, but I'm not supposed to do that. Since you're not attached to the embassy, all I can do is point you to the local authorities."

"Great. They won't figure this one out. Plus, they wouldn't act against someone so powerful."

"You know who did it?"

"Raúl," I said matter-of-factly. "I think he's dirty, and he may suspect I'm on to him. I wouldn't put it past him to tap my phone."

"Neither would I. What have you come up with?"

"You know the drill, the local rep who takes better care of himself than his U.S. partners and does other things on the side, some of them illegal."

"He wouldn't be the first. He's one among dozens."

"I know, but the others aren't my problem. He is."

"You could have a local security company look at your line."

"John, the only competent security group is Raúl's. You know that."

"Sorry. Kind of ironic, isn't it?"

"Ironic perhaps, but not funny. I'm in a real bind. Can't you do something?"

"This stays between us." Denning looked straight at me. "I don't like how deep Raúl is into the embassy's affairs. Sometimes the ambassador listens more to him than he does me or the DCM. It pisses me off, and I'd love to help you nail him. I'll send one of our guys over this afternoon. His name is David Fountain, and he's on loan from the FBI. Technically he works for me, so I can cover."

"Thanks a million, John. I won't forget this."

"No need to thank me. Just some advice. Be very careful," Denning said seriously. "Raúl has a lot of friends and tremendous influence."

"Tell me about it."

After a morning of meetings, I went home to make phone calls I did not want to make from the office. I had a satellite phone for emergency use, and it sure felt like an emergency. I convinced myself the tap would not pick up my sat calls and dialed the first number. I had known Tom Barrett, an independent chemicals consultant in his mid seventies, for over twenty-five years. He knew the chemicals business better than anyone.

"Richard," Barrett started, "your wholly-owned subs or joint ventures have no reason to work with those three chemicals. Pure and simple."

"Then why did one of our joint ventures buy them?"

"Are we discounting the possibility that someone is running drugs?"

"For purposes of this discussion, yes. That's the obvious explanation. I'm trying to find others."

"Fair enough," Barrett said. "Could be they were sold by mistake."

"That doesn't look like the case. The chemicals were labeled correctly. My finance manager said that part of the shipment went to a local company, and the rest was re-exported to Colombia. Our rep paid for the shipment and the end user paid him."

"Okay. The other possibility is that he's selling the chemicals legitimately to make some money on the side."

"That could be," I said. "His contract doesn't restrict him, and he can engage in any sort of business he likes."

"Beyond that, there's not much I can think of."

"I know governments monitor those chemicals. How closely?"

"It depends. They watch them if they suspect the manufacturer or end user of something or if they don't know the purchaser. They don't think twice if someone like Phoenix is involved."

"So this stuff walks right through if it's tagged to a well-known company?"

"Basically, that's right," Barrett replied. "Phoenix's reputation protects them from scrutiny."

"What if it's not well-known?"

"A registered inspector would look at it. Foreign governments hire private companies to be sure that goods exported to the final destination country are what they say they are. They control the paperwork and can walk it through the system or freeze it in its tracks.

"Thanks Tom. I owe you a bottle of wine."

Next, Donovan & Mason told me that the principal Phoenix chemicals groups were in Kuala Lumpur, Singapore, Santiago, São Paulo, and Rosario, Argentina. They had a chemical trading company in Houston, but no manufacturing in the United States. Donovan & Mason believed Phoenix located the companies overseas to put them beyond the scope of U.S. legal and regulatory authorities. It also let Phoenix keep certain acquisition debt off its consolidated balance sheet, hidden from banker's prying eyes. A Donovan source said the Phoenix audit partner, a fellow named Barry Leiffer, overruled his audit firm's oversight committee several times to approve Phoenix's accounting methods. They also reported that Raúl owned two chemical companies in the region, one in Brazil and another in Uruguay. I called Chris, hoping he had come up with something solid.

"Chris, has Gacki found anything?"

"Not yet. He's been in their systems for two weeks. All he's been able to work with so far is the first data set you gave him. It wasn't enough to see a pattern."

"How about the data Julie pulled from BLI and what Gustavo got from Citibank?"

"The identifiers look the same, but he hasn't had enough unrestricted time on the system to test it. He has a window opening after 11:00 P.M. tonight, and he'll be deep in their data files most of the weekend. That should be enough time to get some answers."

"Great. Hey, forgot to tell you, I had a pole climber outside the house about two this morning."

"Phone tap?"

"You're as paranoid as I am. An embassy tech is coming over this afternoon to check it out."

"Which phone are you using?"

"Sat phone. That's all I've got."

"Good idea. If we're lucky, Hugh might crack this tomorrow or Sunday night. I'll call you as soon as we're done."

"Thanks."

The telecommunications security panel on the 44th floor of the Phoenix Tower flashed Richard Blackstone's name for the fifth time in less than two hours. The security group monitored and logged all satellite phone use. Calls from remote locations, like Bolivia, might mean an emergency. More than five calls in three hours generated an exception report requiring a supervisor's review. The supervisor determined that Blackstone's office, home, and cell phones were operational. The sat phone user keyed the correct identification code each time, and the signal originated in La Paz. The headquarters log showed that the phone had never been used. The supervisor concluded that Blackstone was testing his phone to make sure it worked. He took it off the watch list and told the analyst there was nothing further to pursue.

The FBI technician arrived at precisely 4:00 P.M., young and eager to fight bad guys. I showed him the pole our late night visitor climbed. He left to check it out, and I went up to the bedroom to watch through binoculars. The sun was setting, but there was still plenty of light to see what he was doing. Someone else could watch him as well.

Fountain was back after an hour with good news and bad news. The good news was that I was right: my phone was tapped. The bad news was that it was a state-of-the-art device, expertly installed. He traced the tap and found it ran into a line used by Raúl's air transport company.

"It's sophisticated, but low maintenance. That means they're not likely to come back."

"Where does that leave me?"

"I've made some adjustments so you can bypass the tap. They'll never know unless they disassemble the unit. That's pretty unlikely."

"Are you sure they wouldn't know?"

"Completely. Here, I'll show you."

After my crash course in telecoms, I let Fountain out and called Denning on my sat phone since I was still hesitant to use the land line. He was on an emergency trip to the Chapare until Monday, so I left a message thanking him for his help. Steven

Price's secretary said he was playing golf, and I left a voice mail asking him to call me. We were beyond personal dislikes, and Price needed to know about it.

Julie poured two glasses of champagne, I put together a snack tray, and we went out back to enjoy the sunset. By the third sip, we still had not said a word to each other. I had to unload.

"What on earth did I get us into, Julie? This seems like a nightmare."

"Not you, we. We took this job together. We came here as partners, and we'll work through this as partners."

"I know, but this is beyond anything I expected. Stealing from the company is bad enough, but Raúl tapped our phone and might be running drugs. I didn't say so before, but I don't think the stolen tires, the Molotov cocktails, or the gunshots were coincidence."

"I wondered too."

"Don't worry. I promise that I won't let anyone hurt you or the children. Is that clear?"

"Crystal."

"Do you know what bothers me the most? It's not that some jerk takes a company for a ride or that he's doing something illegal. It's not even that he tapped our phone. What disturbs me is the black hole we would be in without Denning. Embassies don't normally help people the way he's helped me."

"Not everyone is the president of a large U.S. corporation tied to the eradication program. That's incentive enough for them to keep you safe. Plus, we're already in a black hole. We'd just be deeper without them. The company wouldn't lift a finger to help you."

Each individual had to assume responsibility for morals and ethics and not charge or trust some bureaucrat with the task. Taking a serious problem like this to the company was out of the question. Corporations never resolved them. They covered them up or just let them fade away. People had to either solve serious problems on their own or get them to law enforcement.

Latin American justice systems were often corrupt, and some were black holes no one should fall into. There was no consistent rule of law, transparent process, or baseline of ethical behavior. Judges and their political cronies often used the systems for political advantage, persecution, and personal gain. People without millions got stuck in a legal swamp I would not wish on anyone. Then again, I would wish it on Raúl. The problem was Raúl would never fall into the system. He owned it.

Perhaps there was no need for a system in my case. Maybe I could bring some justice to him on my own.

40

Several weeks after learning of the FARC funding, Hamza and three colleagues met in a two story house in the Palermo Viejo section of Buenos Aires. At forty three, Hamza was the senior man in Latin America. He had waited years for this opportunity. Libyan intelligence recruited him as a University of Michigan civil engineering undergraduate and trained him in Libyan and Syrian camps during his junior year summer vacation. The school's multicultural atmosphere and large size made subversive activity easy and let foreign agents act with unusual freedom. Hamza operated around the world for seven years, then returned for graduate studies at Michigan and to recruit his own agents for Libya.

At thirty-five, Mohammed, the communications and explosives expert, was the sharpest intellect of the group. Hamza's first recruit at Michigan, he earned an MS in computer science from Berkeley. Hamza recruited the other two, Ahmad and Faysal, at NYU while he attended a U.N.-sponsored NGO non-proliferation conference in New York. They had less experience in direct action operations, but both were excellent planners and intelligence gatherers.

Tripoli had always decided the target, the timing, and how to execute an operation. Qadafi, however, was no longer giving the orders. Those decisions were now up to the team. Hamza knew a nuclear strike against the U.S. was a high risk. The unique challenge of nuclear weapons was to select the right target, coordinate the delivery and detonation, and spread the blame. If not, it could be a retaliation nightmare. Though the team had lost respect for Qadafi, they hesitated to tie him to the attack. They had family in Tripoli, so they decided to attribute the blame to a new radical Islamic group. Hamza was confident the U.S. would not launch an indiscriminate conventional or nuclear retaliatory strike if they had no idea who had attacked them.

After the meeting, Hamza cell phoned his banks to see if the FARC money was deposited. He normally avoided land lines as it was not unusual for the Argentine state security agency (SIDE) to indiscriminately tap hundreds of lines at a time to see who or what they might pick up. The SIDE routinely listened to the phones of senators, representatives, federal judges, and prominent private citizens on behalf of the dominant political party. They rarely monitored cell phones, so there was little risk on the airwaves. Hamza had to be careful, but Libyans were not considered an internal security threat. A former president was of Arab extraction, and Arabs moved freely in Argentina. Despite having the proof, the country had made no arrests for the Israeli embassy or AMIA Center attacks. Hamza confirmed twenty-three million dollars of deposits through an automated system and rang off.

Money complicated things when it came to nuclear weapons. Black market nukes were expensive, and large amounts of money were traceable. Middle East heads of state with money were afraid it would be traced to them. Small Islamic terror groups could hide easily, but had no money. Thanks to the fortuitous FARC funding, Hamza's disaffected state-trained group could afford nuclear weapons.

Hamza made another call. "I can pay for the packages."

"Excellent," Hassan Ali replied from Ciudad del Este. "You will inspect the merchandise before proceeding?"

"Of course. I want to make sure it meets our specifications and that we understand the technical requirements before we take delivery."

"I'll meet you at the warehouse with one of our technicians. What time can you be there?"

"Five this afternoon."

"See you then."

The team took two separate flights from Buenos Aires to Ciudad del Este. Hamza and Mohammed went to meet Hassan Ali while Ahmad and Faysal attended to logistical issues. Ali was a well-respected Ciudad del Este merchant, a family man devoted to his children. He cherished his adopted country and was exceptionally committed to his Arab brothers. Publicly he was the epitome of the low-profile businessman, but privately he was a serious player in the international terror and arms trade.

In 2003, Ali bought two transportable North Korean nuclear devices for $3.7 million. With Chinese and Pakistani assistance, the North Koreans developed several low yield 10-kiloton Medium Atomic Demolition Munitions (MADM) weapons during the 1990s. The Chinese acquired the plans from an unidentified source in the mid 1980s and produced almost sixty bombs. Once their production cycle was complete, the Chinese quietly offered the technical specifications on the open market for the right price. The North Koreans bought the plans, acquired the matériel, and built five bombs.

In late 2002, the general responsible for the North Korean MADM program discovered his retirement pension would be modest. Over the years, the government bought his loyalty with cash, vacations, cars, and houses. With only two years of active duty left, he would soon have no power to yield and no loyalty to sell. As a precaution, the North Koreans revoked their generals' nuclear weapons control a year from retirement. The general knew his window of opportunity was closing.

Various Middle East and Far East countries had approached him to buy weapons, but he always declined for fear of jeopardizing his career. With little service time left, however, he saw that selling bombs was the only way to a secure financial future. He discretely contacted potential clients, but there were no takers. The Americans watched them too closely.

The general learned from a Venezuelan government intermediary that Ali was looking for nukes at a discount—for cash. The general did not drive a hard bargain. He was running out of time, and the money was on the table. Ali made immediate offshore deposits, and arranged safe passage to Argentina for the general and his family where the Buenos Aires Korean community could assimilate them.

Hamza and Mohammed deplaned in Ciudad del Este and took a circuitous one-hour route to the least known of Ali's storage locations. They were taking no chances. Ali and his son Rahim greeted the Libyans at the warehouse door and went straight to the financial terms.

"We agree on the price then?" Ali asked once the door was closed.

"Seventeen and a half million. We'll wire the full amount after we inspect the units and you train us. I want delivery as soon as you confirm the transfer."

"I could sell them for much more, but I believe in you," Ali said solemnly.

"I know that, and we are very grateful." Hamza knew Ali wanted to move the weapons fast because he was afraid the Americans were closing in on him. It was just a matter of time, and it was a buyer's market.

Hamza and Ali shook hands sealing the purchase as Rahim

pulled the tarps off two large footlockers bearing the stickers and markings of the original North Korean metallurgical and fish shipments that camouflaged their ocean transit to Paraguay via South Africa.

"I can train your people in a couple of days," Rahim said, handing Hamza and Mohammed a set of operating and maintenance manuals.

"You trained almost four weeks with the North Koreans," Mohammed said. "We get a couple of days?"

"Most of that was maintenance training. You only need to deploy the bombs."

"I want basic maintenance as well," Hamza insisted. "The footlocker is fully transportable?"

"It is," Rahim replied, "but it's heavy. The entire package weighs over 350 pounds. It includes the warhead, the packing container, the code-decoder unit, and the firing unit. The warhead itself is not large, and as you can see from these diagrams"—he pointed to an exploded diagram from the North Korean manual—"it's twelve inches high, eight inches in diameter, and comes inside a thirty-inch high container."

Hamza and Mohammed thumbed through the manuals, gave the weapons a cursory examination, and said they were satisfied.

"We start tomorrow at 8:00 A.M.," Hamza said.

"See you then."

41

For a break, we decided to take a weekend trip out of La Paz with our Australian friends. I packed and tried not to think of Raúl lurking around every corner. By the time we got to the airport, I had forgotten about him and cocaine.

Our destination was Trinidad, a jungle town in north-central Bolivia, where we would spend two days on a restored cattle barge on the Mamoré river. The sediment-laden brown water was full of pink dolphin, cayman, and piraña. The accommodations were primitive. There were four beds to a room, one bathroom to share with neighbors, mosquito nets, and no air conditioning. Forget cell phones and faxes. We were so remote that only satellite phones worked, and I brought mine for emergencies. We at least had Bombay Sapphire gin to ease the stifling heat and humidity.

Two days of fishing and swimming flew by, and we were soon back at the Trinidad airport for the Sunday evening return flight to La Paz. After checking in, I went outside with Kathy to buy water from a sidewalk vendor. She spotted a twin-engine prop plane approaching and asked if we could watch. Kathy loved to watch planes as much as Sean did. She found Julie's digital camera in my backpack, and I pulled out the binoculars.

We leaned on the chain link fence as the pilot dropped his

wheels and lined up to land. The plane touched down smoothly, tires screeching. The pilot made a right turn off the runway, taxied to the terminal, and came to a stop 150 feet directly in front of us. Three Toyota Land Cruisers pulled alongside the plane as the propellers stopped, and a couple of men piled out of each car. The binoculars gave me a close-up of everyone, and the steady breeze revealed pistols underneath baggy cotton shirts. Oscar Dávila, the drug lord I saw at Las Palmas in Santa Cruz, stepped out of the middle car.

The aircraft door opened, and Raúl appeared. He walked quickly down the stairway and embraced Dávila. Next off the plane was a slightly overweight man with light brown hair. The third person was a distinguished older gentleman who looked more suited to a polo match than a hot and dusty Bolivian runway. Despite the heat, his clothes were impeccable and his demeanor regal. Last off the plane was a thin fellow with dark skin and a goatee. He sported a shoulder rig and a stainless steel semi-auto with an extended magazine.

Raúl, Dávila, and the other two stood in a semi-circle facing me, chatting while a young fellow loaded luggage into the vehicles. I took Julie's camera from Kathy and gave her the binoculars. I zoomed in on everyone around the plane, and shot as many pictures as I could. No one ever looked away from their immediate surroundings. I snapped the plane's tail number as they broke off and got into their cars. They cranked the Land Cruiser engines, and I realized that Kathy and I were next to the gate they would soon drive through.

"Daddy, isn't that Raúl? Should we say hello?"

"Not now, Kathy. We need to get back to the terminal fast."

I pulled her with me as we turned away and were through the terminal door before they started to roll.

42

The Land Cruisers arrived at Dávila's nine thousand acre ranch less than an hour after leaving the airport. Dávila hated the drive, but it was necessary. His father died seven years earlier when a business associate sabotaged his helicopter. Dávila never flew in them again. He almost put a landing strip on the ranch to avoid the drive, but was paranoid about giving his enemies easy access. He owned the roads, so he felt safe on the ground. He could not, however, control the airspace.

Dávila headed Raúl's drug operations and a few of his legitimate investments. Unlike Raúl, he could not move easily in polite society, and he would never have Raúl's political influence. Raúl was one of the old guard with a status few enjoyed. Though once mayor of Santa Cruz, Dávila would never be entirely legitimate. Ultimately, none of that mattered when it came to business.

Raúl and Dávila talked on the phone throughout the week, but they discussed troublesome issues in person. Today they had a thorny one, the Brazilians. Dávila struck a deal three years earlier with Guilherme Fonseca, the biggest and most powerful drug dealer in the Rio favelas. Fonseca owned most of the Rio police and ran little risk of arrest. Dávila was Fonseca's sole cocaine supplier, and all was well. Until now. Dávila had hot information that Fonseca intended to bypass him and cut a deal with the Colombians.

"Is the information reliable?" Raúl asked.

"Very reliable, Don Raúl. Rogério Neves called me from São Paulo after he met with Fonseca to confirm a purchase. Fonseca has no idea Neves is one of ours and he told Neves he would lower the price on their next deal because he has a new Colombian supplier. He flies to Colombia in two days to close the deal with Vargas."

"What else do we know?"

"He'll take a Hawker Horizon jet from Rio to Medellín and arrives at 8:10 P.M. We know the car service that will pick him up."

"Good. Tell Captain Ramírez to use high caliber long guns on Fonseca. I don't care if his entire family is with him. I want them to look like hamburger meat. Okay, what's next?"

"We're getting pressure in the Yacuiba and San José de Pocitos to Salvador Mazza and Tartagal corridor. We need to reroute or back off. The volumes aren't huge, but getting them through is becoming a headache."

Yacuiba and San José de Pocitos were small southern Bolivia towns, and Salvador Mazza and Tartagal were right across the border in Argentina. Raúl moved a hundred pounds or so per month by truck through the area. Eduardo Molina, the Yacuiba Municipal Council leader, and most of the local police were on Dávila's payroll. Authorities knew of Molina's drug activity, but had not been able to bring him to trial. A prosecutor once formalized charges against him, but several 9mm bullets to the side of the young attorney's head while he sat in confessional cut his career short. Oscar Dávila had created a job opening in the local prosecutor's office, but no one applied. Molina bought a seat on the city council and a year later landed the job of mayor of Yacuiba and the District of San José de Pocitos. He ran unopposed in both races.

Despite an iron fist, Molina could not control all the dynamics of the drug trade. One was the method of payment. After the

Argentine peso devalued, dealers along the border insisted on U.S. dollars or hard assets—imported sedans, SUVs, and motorcycles. A new moto-cross bike bought two pounds of cocaine and an SUV got between nine and ten. The devaluation of the peso brought barter back to life along the Bolivia-Argentina border.

The drug trade was invisible when cash changed hands, but was painfully apparent when imported high-end assets were the currency. Pressure from the federal law enforcement authorities increased in the corridor. Molina controlled the local cops, but not the federal police. To keep them away, Molina needed to slow the flow of cars, move vehicles at night, or find other routes.

"Oscar," Raúl said as he got up from the table to stretch, "I'm not going to reroute just because some assholes are flaunting SUVs."

"Do you want Molina to take care of this?"

"Tell him to kill a couple of local dealers. Let everyone know what's coming if they don't listen. They're testing him. He can solve the problem quickly."

Raúl punched the intercom on the table and told Dávila's secretary they were ready. Three men came into the conference room. Two sat down, and the third stood next to Raúl.

"Gentlemen, this is Donald Kinkaid," Raúl said, nodding to the man in his early thirties beside him. "Dr. Kinkaid teaches economics at MIT and consults for the U.S. government. He joined us two years ago when our offer seemed better than tenure or a government pension. His relationship with the government is invaluable. On the flight we discussed some planning tools that give us a competitive edge. Now you'll now see why. Donald."

"*Señores*," Kinkaid started, picking up the remote control, dimming the lights, and bringing a laptop computer to life, "please turn your attention to the flat-panel display on the wall to your left. The GALAXY computer model is our primary planning tool. It's based on a similar model I built for the U.S. drug enforcement and counter-narcotics agencies a few years ago. A number of refinements, however, make it more powerful than the original. GALAXY is an integrated model that lets us market cocaine based on a number of interlinked supply factors. Although the model is integral, it's not linear. That means that we don't have to run it from start to finish to generate a result we trust. We can start in the middle, run it backwards, back in to results, or ask intermediate questions. The model recommends actions to take based on what law enforcement, the military, or other players, including our competitors, may do. Since my company provides the base data to the U.S. government, we know precisely what actions their model will suggest. We'll always be one step ahead of them.

"There are two parts to the model," Kinkaid continued, clicking to the next screen. "Phases 1 through 4 include the production and processing of coca leaf into cocaine, and Phases 5 to 8 cover the delivery and availability of final product to the market. Each phase is connected by transition points that strengthen or disrupt subsequent phases. Coca leaf is grown in Bolivia, Brazil, Colombia, Ecuador, and Peru. Our emphasis has been and will continue to be on the most valuable source leaf. Since the alkaloid content of coca leaf determines the yield, we focus on plants with the highest alkaloid content. That means we will concentrate on coca leaf grown in Bolivia, Peru, and Colombia—the BPC Corridor.

"The base data for the first two phases, coca cultivation and production, come from our own cultivation, from U.S. government ground and satellite intelligence, and from Sendero and the FARC. We have additional sources in Andean military and intelligence services. The data for Phases 3 and 4 come from our own intelligence instead of from the U.S. government. It's hard information for us, but the U.S. only guesses at it. Since the U.S. government is aware of every loss, and we only know about our own, we include their data for the rest of the model.

"Phase 1 starts with net coca cultivation for the current year.

Net production is simply gross production plus new growth less eradication and field abandonment.

"Phase 2 derives a net leaf amount, the forecast yield from Phase 1. We estimate by each growing region. The model applies leaf yield factors to reduce the net coca forecasts to determine the net leaf amounts.

"Phase 3 generates coca base available for processing, calculated directly from the net leaf amount.

"Phase 4 calculates the coca base processed at labs. We focus on all four geographical exit corridors. The U.S. government model doesn't incorporate the eastern exit corridor, but ours does. The government model has focused on lab production in Colombia the last several years, but our main processing labs are in Bolivia and Brazil, along with some in Peru, Colombia, and Argentina.

"Phase 5 is cocaine flow from South America. This first node connects cocaine production to distribution. We assume losses from spoilage, source country seizures we don't anticipate, source country seizures we generate, and interruption in the supply chain due to labs moving or accidents. The source country seizures we generate are the labs and processed cocaine we tip off to the local authorities. It's just a cost of doing business.

"Phase 6 incorporates transshipment points for delivery to U.S. and non-U.S. end markets. Europe is the major non-U.S. market with others in Argentina and Brazil growing quickly. We move fifty-two percent more cocaine to Argentina and Brazil than the government estimates. Our preferred methods are commercial and noncommercial air and maritime. The government model leads the authorities to do two things. First, air interdiction efforts have been so successful that most shipments are primarily and increasingly moved via water. As a consequence, the U.S. concentrates on interdicting maritime shipments. Second, cocaine leaving Bolivia, Ecuador, and Peru goes through Mexico and into the U.S. overland. That means the government watches the overland route like a hawk. As a last observation, we had nothing to do with the Southern Winds airlines fiasco. Some small Argentine players thought they could hide cocaine shipments on commercial flights to Madrid. We knew better.

"Our model results and our subsequent actions differ in two important respects from the U.S. government's. First, since we control the radar infrastructure, we send the majority of shipments via non-commercial aircraft instead of by normal water routes. The last piece of this was put in place last year when we upgraded the radar systems in Lima and Guayaquil through our German subsidiary. Our ability to turn planes on and off to various radar systems means we can move unimpeded through multiple Andean air corridors. We will soon have the same unrestricted access to several U.S. air corridors. Second, we move considerable volumes from our processing facilities to Argentina, Brazil, Europe, and the U.S. via two new methods instead of overland through Mexico. We have a perfect record shipping cocaine in construction equipment, and we have moved two shipments on liquefied petroleum gas tankers.

"Phase 7 is the availability of cocaine at the U.S. border, and Phase 8 is availability at retail locations. Smugglers prefer to use commercial maritime vessels, but we don't transport that way. We operate where the authorities aren't looking. Also, non-commercial air is almost statistically insignificant for the authorities at four percent of seizures. They no longer include this method in their model since most non-commercial flights stop short of the U.S. border. So, that's where we focus. We'll soon start using Raúl's international air fleet to transport cocaine when we rotate DEA agents back to the U.S. We have total control of those flights from departure points to final destinations. No one checks them when they leave or when they arrive."

"So," Raúl said as Kinkaid sat down, "there are several things to note. First, yield is increasing considerably. Second, my legitimate businesses give us cover. Third, we can go after the Bolivian, Peruvian, Argentine and Brazilian markets because the authorities are watching Colombia. Fourth, they watch sea routes, so we move a lot more via air than they imagine. Fifth, we've got new ways to ship—international moving containers, construction equipment and heavy machinery, DEA flights—that are very effective. We execute better than anyone else. You'll be glad you joined us."

"Raúl, your reputation precedes you and this presentation confirms it. I am impressed," said the elegant man sitting to Dávila's left. "Your access to our operations in the Far East and the Southern Cone is assured."

"Molto bene," said the other guest, "and you have a guaranteed pipeline to our businesses in Europe."

"Thank you," Raúl replied graciously. "Would you like to join Dr. Kinkaid for a drink? Oscar and I will be with you shortly."

"This way, gentlemen." Kinkaid led the pair out of the conference room.

"What do our next deliveries look like, Oscar?" Raúl asked after the door closed.

"Aside from the Van der Bors shipment to Chicago, we have five hundred thirty pounds arriving in Miami in ten days, two hundred seventy pounds two weeks later in Houston, and four hundred pounds three weeks after that in Hamburg. The Miami shipment is stored in the back panels of kitchen appliances exported from Brazil, and Houston's is in SUVs assembled in Mexico. The Hamburg delivery will leave Argentina in a cargo of LPG containers originating at the Bahía Blanca plant. Unless there's something I don't see," Dávila said, scrolling through several spreadsheets, "that's it."

"Time to call it a day, Oscar."

They put their notes away, turned off the lights, and headed for a dinner of Argentine beef and red wine with their new partners.

43

Hamza and his team reviewed their mission notes in a Ciudad del Este apartment as Ahmad prepared to give a final review of the attack on the United States. Success depended on exhaustive intelligence, precise planning, tight coordination, attention to detail, seriousness of purpose, and flawless execution. Toward that end, Ahmad prepared with the professionalism of a first-rate military planner.

"The nuclear devices give us unique targeting and destructive possibilities. Much as we might want to strike places like Boston, New York, or Washington, such attacks would likely not succeed for two reasons. First, the U.S. authorities expect attacks on national landmarks and monuments and they have already hardened them. Second, though the emotional and visual impact would be great, the economic consequence would not. They can replace monuments, train stations, and financial centers, and can certainly elect more politicians to replace dead ones. So, we have chosen two relatively soft targets with disastrous economic consequences.

"The TransAmerica Oil and Gas Company refinery processes 515,000 barrels of crude oil per day," Ahmad said as he pointed to the first PowerPoint slide, *Houston Target Overview*, "and it's in the

Houston Ship Channel foreign trade zone. U.S. Customs inspects no cargo when it enters the zone, only when it leaves. The *Evening Star* cargo ship will sail from Guayaquil, Ecuador, and dock and unload at the zone cargo storage area adjacent to the refinery. Our team will disembark with the weapon and arm it in a van on the eighth floor of the zone parking garage. The garage overlooks the refinery, less than a hundred yards from the catalytic cracking unit and major liquids storage facilities. The team will leave the facility in a car parked on the floor below the van, and will be on a flight out of the country before the device detonates. We took these photos last month from the garage, and you'll see that there is line of sight to the refinery."

Ahmad clicked through several ground-level pictures of the Port of Houston, the ship channel, the foreign trade zone, and finally the TransAmerica refinery itself. He then brought up several satellite photos of the port plus detailed overheads of the refinery and the surrounding area. The first photos were at sixteen meters resolution. Ahmad clicked through the same photograph at eight, four, two, and finally at one meter. He had drawn several concentric circles on each photograph.

The photos revealed a massively dense matrix of almost 300 plants and installations that included refineries, petrochemical and other industrial facilities, silos, wharves, warehouses, storage units, containment vessels, and dozens of docked ships—many of them huge LPG carriers. The entire complex produced almost half of the nation's supply of gasoline and petrochemicals.

"Placing the device on the eighth floor produces a modified low altitude burst and is more effective than a pure surface blast. The next photos and the superimposed lines show you the effects of the explosion. The air blast overpressure destroys the refinery and causes fifty percent mortality out to 650 yards. That's the innermost solid black circle on the photo. The heat wave fireball ignites everything in its path and causes fifty percent mortality for anyone unsheltered within a mile. That's the dotted black circle farthest out. Initial radiation generates fifty percent mortality out to twelve hundred yards and secondary radiation out to six miles. The first is the solid red line, the second is the dashed red line.

"The explosion creates a domino effect because of the high industrial density. Remember, this is not a population dense area—it's packed with industrial operations and we destroy and shut down far more than we kill. The cascade of explosions will not only cripple facilities but will also release massive amounts of hydrogen fluoride, chlorine, ammonia, and methyl isocyanate that will affect between half a million and a million people. Since we have no idea what the wind speed and direction will be on the day of the attack, we can't forecast the deaths resulting from these toxic clouds. It could, however, be significant. Finally, detonation near the channel vaporizes large amounts of water and carries it up in the radioactive cloud. That's a longer term effect, and we have no idea how many deaths might result.

"We estimate the attack will kill 19,500 people, destroy a two billion dollar refinery, and incinerate between eight to fifteen billion dollars of nearby installations. The authorities will close the Port of Houston and the ship channel to all commercial traffic. The next chart shows you the impact."

Ahmad clicked on a chart titled *Houston Target Economic Statistics and Impact* that summarized the target's economic importance. The Port of Houston is a twenty-five-mile long complex of public and private facilities near the Gulf of Mexico. It ranks first in the United States in foreign waterborne commerce and sixth in the world in total tonnage. Almost 200 million tons of cargo move through the port yearly, and over 6,600 vessels call each year. The port provides 75,000 direct and 135,000 indirect jobs, and the Houston area economic impact is almost eight billion dollars. Petroleum products, chemicals, iron, steel, cereals, and fertilizers all move through the port. The annual value of foreign goods transiting the port exceeds forty-five billion dollars.

"The losses in the greater Houston area will be enormous. All commercial traffic will stop, but even more important is the shutdown of all area refineries. Since refineries are 'just in time' production processes that rely on continuous tanker calls, refining operations will stop until tanker runs resume. That removes an additional 2.4 million barrels of refining capacity a day for at least several months. The permanent TransAmerica loss plus the short-term losses due to port shutdown comes to almost three million barrels per day. That's seventeen percent of total U.S. refining capacity."

Ahmad brought up more photographs showing the New Orleans and Baton Rouge port facilities and refineries. He had drawn circles on the pictures of Baton Rouge. The photos revealed an area densely populated by refineries, petrochemical plants, industrial facilities, storage units, and ships—similar to Houston.

"Our Louisiana target is the International Petroleum Corporation's (IPC) 497,000 barrel per day Baton Rouge refinery. The *Flying Eagle* oil tanker will deliver the weapon on a scheduled run to the IPC refinery. The team will board the tanker at the Colombian Caribbean port of Coveñas and sail to Baton Rouge with the weapon in their passenger compartment. They will arm the device in their quarters and it will detonate on board several hours later. A workboat will take the team from the refinery dock directly to a waterway public access. They won't enter the refinery complex itself or pass through any security checks. Their boat driver goes off his shift six hours later, so he will die in the blast. As you can see from this photo taken from the docking facility, their compartment will face the refinery only eighty-five yards away. We will wipe it out."

Human damage would resemble the Houston disaster, with an estimated 14,500 people dead. Physical damage would include the destruction of a two billion dollar refinery, ancillary damage of seven billion dollars, and a permanent cut in U.S. refining capacity of half a million barrels per day. As with Houston, authorities would close the New Orleans and Baton Rouge ports. The next slide showed the attack's economic impact. New Orleans controlled cargo access to the 14,500-mile Midwestern inland water system for steel, grain, containers, and manufactured goods. More than 2,400 vessels called at the port each year, and more than 6,000 reached the Mississippi River through New Orleans. The port hubbed rail service, fifty ocean carriers, sixteen barge lines, and seventy-five truck carriers which handled 11.5 million tons of cargo and sustained 110,000 jobs, two billion dollars in earnings, and thirteen billion in spending per year. Along with coffee, rubber, and half a million tourists a year, a great deal of oil moved through the Port of New Orleans. Shutting down water-borne traffic would stop the flow of oil and indefinitely remove an additional 1.5 million barrels of refining capacity per day. The permanent IPC losses plus the temporary losses reached two million barrels, twelve percent of total U.S. refining capacity.

"Any questions so far?" Ahmad asked as he turned off the laser pointer.

"Are we sure we can get the bombs to the targets?" Hamza asked.

"We can never be completely sure, but it's unlikely the Coast Guard or counter-terror measures will affect us."

"Convince me again."

"The Container Security Initiative focuses on just that, containers. Other governments let the U.S. inspect high risk containers at foreign ports before they're loaded onto ships headed for America. That doesn't bother me for two reasons. First, nobody can really define a high risk container, so they have no idea what they're looking for. Second, their container inspectors are in the twenty or so biggest and busiest international ports they think are the likeliest to handle high risk cargo. We'd never be that stupid.

Ports like Guayaquil and Coveñas are not on their radar screen.

"They also have something called The 24 Hour Rule. Complete manifest data for sea cargo has to be turned over to the U.S. twenty-four hours before loading. Again, that's just containerized cargo vessels.

"Finally, the National Targeting Center identifies high risk containers. What's high risk? Besides, we don't use containers."

"How about radiological detection?"

"They've deployed something like eight or ten thousand personal radiation detectors plus a few hundred isotope identifiers and portal monitors. The radiation detectors and monitors are activated by everything from cat litter to bananas so they ignore almost all the alarms. Also, the portal monitors check vehicles leaving ports—we'll detonate inside the facilities. Finally, they're going after containers. They're consistent, and nothing they do concerns us. Plus, there is another reason we're invisible."

"And that is?"

"They've actually created an exception for us. The Americans want to protect lives, but they're afraid tough security measures will hurt the economy. To keep traffic moving, they exempted two categories. Bulk cargo is product loaded loose or packed in bags, boxes, or barrels, like fuel, grain, crude oil, or coal. The tanker from Coveñas is a crude carrier and is not subject to any control measures. The second category is break-bulk, non-containerized cargo, packed or crated items, or loose cargo. The Coast Guard exempts it on a case by case basis. The vessel from Guayaquil has been exempt for a year because it always carries bulk and break-bulk cargo. We are covered."

"Excellent," Hamza said.

"If there are no other questions, I'll summarize and move on to the logistics," Ahmad said as he brought up the last slide, *U.S. Attack Summary Effects.* "The attacks will obliterate two refineries, permanently remove six percent of U.S. refining capacity, temporarily remove twenty nine percent, and shut down all traffic in two of the busiest ports in the world. Direct property losses will be at least nineteen billion dollars and maybe as high as twenty-six billion. We kill thirty-four thousand people. On top of that, we create two separate economic impacts.

"First, shutting down the ports and refineries will cost from three hundred to six hundred billion dollars in commercial losses. Maybe more. Gasoline prices will double, maybe even triple. People will panic. The stock market value of the major oil and chemical companies will fall, and the rest of the market will drop due to the ripple effects in the real economy. It's safe to say the market will lose from half a trillion to a trillion and a half.

"The U.S. economy might not survive the attack. We're using their wealth against them, and we'll bleed our enemy to death. Plus, an attack with nuclear weapons will terrify them. The American psyche is already defeated by fear and will never recover from this attack. They are already weak. Their citizens blindly trust their government to protect them, are unwilling to defend themselves, don't trust pilots with guns, and shut down airports when an old lady forgets scissors in a bathroom. Look at the way they panicked and fled in Washington when a student pilot strayed off course. We are striking a soft underbelly. Quite simply, my brothers, we own the country."

"That's great Ahmad, but it only works if the delivery teams put the devices on target."

"Correct, but they know what they're doing."

Two Libyans living and working in Buenos Aires for the last six years would take one bomb with them on the *Evening Star* from Guayaquil to Houston. Their Argentine textile company had a joint venture with an Ecuadorian manufacturer that exported to the U.S. They would accompany a shipment as dead-head passengers without raising any eyebrows. The bomb would look like personal effects. Both men had impeccable identification papers, and no one would inspect what they brought aboard.

The team taking the bomb to Baton Rouge lived in Rosario, Argentina, and worked as contract engineers for the largest integrated oil companies in the world. They had extensive experience with U.S. refining operations, and had blanket security clearances under false IDs from IPC.

"This could be our weakest link," Hamza said. "APIS and U.S.-VISIT might shut us down from the start."

The Automated Passenger Information System (APIS) and U.S.-VISIT were Department of Homeland Security measures designed to capture and review data on foreigners at U.S. ports of entry. APIS required sea carriers on voyages longer than ninety-six hours to provide most passenger and crew data to law enforcement agencies. U.S.-VISIT mandated that immigration authorities digitally photograph and fingerprint scan every foreign visitor.

"We're not worried," Ahmad said. "Neither measure affects the crew and passengers on either ship. The Ecuadorian textile venture is fifty percent owned by a prominent North Carolina family whose son is a U.S. Senator. He pressured U.S. Customs to exempt ships carrying their products from all federal security controls. The Baton Rouge tanker is also exempt because the authorities already reviewed and approved IPC's security measures. Even if they checked on our teams, it wouldn't make any difference."

"Why is that?"

"The Americans compare APIS data to federal databases, like the Interagency Border Inspection System or the FBI National Crime Information Center. Our people aren't in those systems. We've been sleeping with the Americans for so long they have no idea who or where we are."

Everybody on the hit teams had citizenship under three false names and carried authentic Argentine papers. Their U.S. visas were legitimate documents obtained through a collaborator at the U.S. Embassy who later paid cash for two ocean resort houses in

Punta del Este, Uruguay.

"Remember, both attacks must take place as simultaneously as possible, no more than an hour apart. We don't want the first to jeopardize the second. Our teams have to make their flights to Guatemala City and Rio because the FAA will shut the entire aviation system down after the attacks. We have only one chance to do this and we better get it right. The teams will be on the high seas with no secondary targets if we have to abort the attack or if we are discovered. Once the *Eternal Star* passes through the Panama Canal and the *Flying Eagle* leaves Coveñas, there will be nothing to hit until they reach their targets.

"My brothers, if there are no questions, Hassan Ali is waiting for us."

44

"Why on earth is the alarm going off?" I asked Julie as I pried my eyes open. It was 3:28 A.M.

"That's not the alarm, sweetie," she said as she kissed me and went back to sleep.

"Damn, it's my sat phone." I jumped out of bed and grabbed it from the study desk. "Hello?"

"Richard? Chris. We've got news for you."

"Man, you guys are burning some serious midnight oil. What's up?"

"A bunch. Hang on, I'm putting Hugh on the speaker phone."

"Hey, Richard," Gacki said. "Looks like your boy Raúl is running precursors big-time. And that's not all."

"I'm all ears." I sat down and turned on the desk lamp. "Careful guys. You know the computers will red flag this call."

"Probably," Chris said, "but it's not like you're involved or are going to hide it. You'll turn all this over long before an analyst gets to the tape."

"Okay guys, shoot."

"I got into the chemical companies' manufacturing systems and the customs clearance database in Houston," Gacki said. "After a couple of passes, the only place I saw precursors was on the first invoices you brought up."

"How about the data Julie copied?"

"That saved us, because it confirmed that the six digit codes were the key to tracking all of this."

"What does that mean?"

"The code tied to specific production runs," Gacki said excitedly, "and identified every chemical. That's how they could label them as something other than precursors and still keep track of them. The people on the receiving end just had to look for the alphanumeric code stamped on the container and they knew what it was. The name on the invoice was irrelevant."

"Hugh, slow down, because I'm confused. If they could call them by another name to mask their identity, then why did the invoice use the correct names in this case?"

"They made a mistake. Raúl's company requested those chemicals and the manufacturer sent them to him. They just forgot to change the names on the invoices."

"A simple clerical error?"

"Sure looks like it," Gacki said, slurping a soft drink. "I dug into six years of their production and shipping records. Until two years ago, the Far East companies manufactured and shipped precursors to Raúl's company on a regular schedule. All of the shipments were tagged with similar six digit tracking codes."

"What happened two years ago?"

"They stopped shipping precursors to him. I figured something had to be going on, so I hacked into all of Phoenix's and Raúl's chemical subsidiaries and joint ventures around the world. Guess what I found?"

"Another provider?"

"Bingo. It was a good thing you told us to look at the Brazilian company in the Donovan & Mason package. Brazil started to ship to him the same month the Far East companies stopped, and that's where it's coming from now."

"But I didn't see that in any financial records," I said, "and no shipments from Brazil show up in the files."

"I know," Gacki said, "and none ever will. The Far East shipments showed up in the BLI files because they went to the U.S. before they arrived in Bolivia. Raúl had to pay for that shipment through a company he didn't control. Not so with Brazil. Since Raúl controls the Brazilian company, he clears all the payments through inter-company accounts. He pays himself, and no one sees any money moving. They still tag the chemicals with the six digit codes. It looks like he moves the chemicals into Bolivia by truck, but it's not clear how he gets them across the border. I suspect he bribes the border guards. That's why there's no customs record."

"That all begs the question," I said slowly. "Why did he drop the Far East supplier?"

"Good question," Chris said, "and we're only guessing, but I think the change makes sense. With the Far East supplier, he shared a joint venture with Phoenix. That meant he had to run funds through several companies he didn't control and had to bring the chemicals through the U.S. to be certified. That was too much to explain. Right now he just deals with himself, and he sneaks the chemicals across the Bolivia-Brazil border unseen."

"I get it, but that doesn't explain why he would go back to the Far East when he has such a cozy deal in Brazil," I said.

"That's an even better question," Gacki said, "but we think we figured that one out too. About six months ago, Raúl needed more precursors than the Brazilians could supply."

"So he had to go back to the Far East for a while to make up the difference."

"Exactly," Chris said. "Five months to be precise. It looks like they screwed up on the first invoice, but they got with the program because the next four relabeled the chemicals to hide what they were."

"How did they make it through the chain from the Far East?"

"The manufacturer told U.S. Customs they were something else, and they automatically certified them as whatever the manufacturer said. The agent entered the name in the system, and that's what appeared on the manifest, just like any legitimate product. The manufacturer separately transmitted the six digit tag to the end user so they knew exactly when and where shipments would arrive. It flew through the system."

"Do you think the customs people and BLI were in on the deal?"

"Maybe. They certified chemicals as something other than what they were, but that doesn't mean they were in on the scheme. They're probably only guilty of trusting one of the best known corporations in the world."

"I think we've got him," I said.

"Put it this way," Chris said, "you don't have him running drugs yet, but he's going to have to explain what he's doing with all these precursors."

"Man, it can't get any better than this."

"Oh, yes it can!" Hugh shouted. "I also got into the Citibank, HSBC, and Merrill Lynch systems. Raúl wasn't just dealing this stuff to himself, he was selling it to Colombian and Peruvian companies."

"Can you tell who they are?"

"The payments to Colombia and Peru are accounts the DEA has long suspected are FARC and Sendero fronts," Chris said. "They've been chasing this since I was at State, but could never close the gap. Plus, it looks like Raúl is funding some of Dávila's companies."

"Why would Raúl funnel money to FARC and Sendero fronts? Protection?"

"That's our guess. Oh, and he has bits and pieces of money flowing to an organization called GEM. Green Earth Movement. Seems like they're out to save the earth by blowing people up."

"Can you guys get this to me securely and fast?" I asked.

"You bet," Gacki said. "Give me an hour and it's on the way."

"Thanks, guys, I really appreciate it."

"Where are you going with this?" Chris asked.

"I'll get it to the RSO. Hey, I almost forgot. We were at the Trinidad airport coming back from the Beni today and saw Dávila and his goons meeting Raúl when he got off a private plane. Raúl brought some other people with him, and they all hugged like long-lost relatives. I got it on Julie's digital camera."

"Excellent. Be careful until you turn this over."

"I'm going to scan and e-mail the pictures to you by morning. I want you to have them in case something happens to me."

"Good move," Chris said. "Call me as soon as you talk to the RSO. If I don't hear from you after forty-eight hours, I'll take everything to the FBI and DEA."

"Thanks, Chris. I hope you don't have to do that."

"Me too."

Julie was awake and sitting up when I got back to bed. She heard the entire conversation.

"Sounds like you've finally done it, darling."

"I hope so. I think I can turn this over and let it go, but I have to be more careful than ever."

"My love, that bastard will have to go through me to get to you. Got that?"

"My guardian angel. Raúl wouldn't know what hit him."

"John, good morning," I said into the sat phone in as even a tone as I could manage.

"Richard. How was your trip?"

"Great except for the heat, the humidity, and the mosquitoes. I can't believe I actually paid to sweat for two days in the jungle."

"Oh, come on. We've done that trip, and you know it was fun."

"Well, if you say so. John, I need to see you."

"Okay. Anything we can talk about over the phone?"

"I'd rather not. Can we meet in your office around ten?"

"You bet."

I closed Denning's office door and laid out everything. I showed him the data on Raúl, how he brought in precursors, and the money flows to the FARC, Sendero, and GEM. I also brought the digital photos of Raúl and Dávila at the Trinidad airport.

"How did you get all this?" Denning asked as he thumbed through everything.

"I had some help."

"Yeah, I'll bet you did. This is pretty incredible. Can you tell me who?"

"No, especially since they got into some proprietary systems to do it."

"I can imagine. Quite frankly, I really don't want to know. Richard, the DEA needs to see this. Do you want me to take over from here?"

"Part of me wants to dump this on you and move on," I said, contemplating what I was about to commit myself to, "but all of this is tied to Phoenix and our business in Bolivia and Latin America. As the top person here, I need to see it through."

"Fair enough. I want you to know that even with what you have, it won't be easy to find a receptive ear. Everyone around here thinks Raúl walks on water, and the ambassador thinks he's got a halo."

"Yeah, I hope he chokes on it. John, what are you saying?"

"I'm just warning you that it's going to be a tough sell, and don't be surprised if you get some hostility. Understand?"

"Got it. Can you set me up with the DEA?"

"You bet. You'll need to talk to Torres, but he's in the field. He'll be back in a couple of days to get ready for a visit from the DEA Chief of Operations."

"Is this something Torres can handle on his own?"

"Under normal circumstances yes, but Raúl isn't ordinary. This is above Felipe's pay grade. You need to talk to the chief of operations during his visit. I'm out that week at a meeting in Miami, but I'll get you on his agenda."

"Thanks, John. Do me a favor?"

"What's that?"

"I don't trust anyone except you and maybe a couple of others. Tell Torres I have something for DEA eyes only. If there's a spider's web, that may keep you from getting tangled up in it."

"No problem, amigo. I leave Sunday, and get back the following Saturday morning."

"A full week of meetings?"

"Three days of tough sessions poolside in Miami, then two hard days on the golf course. It's a dirty job, but someone has to do it. Hey, be happy! It's your tax dollars at work."

"Why does that fail to inspire my confidence?"

45

Steven Price settled into the Falcon for the trip to D.C., still pissed that Whitworth called the plane back to the U.S. in the middle of his Latin America trip. He would remember that power play. His new plane would arrive soon and Whitworth could have the Falcon to himself. The Falcon was an excellent aircraft, but the Gulfstream 550 was the best in the world. Price wanted one desperately, but until recently Phoenix was near the bottom of the delivery list.

Phoenix held the counterparty positions on energy trades with a gas pipeline company that was first in line for a G550. Price knew that if the company suffered a cash crunch, they would have to cancel their forty-five million dollar extravagance. Phoenix called in the trades unexpectedly and the pipeline CEO was a desperate man when Price offered to take the plane off his hands. The CEO thanked Price profusely for allowing him to escape a five million dollar order cancellation penalty. Steven Price was brilliant.

Price reclined the leather seat and put his feet up as the cabin attendant told him the galley was stocked as he expected with pink salmon, Argentine red wine, Tanqueray, and Cohiba cigars. She turned her attention to Whitworth when he boarded the plane, and brought him an assortment of Belgian chocolates once he settled in. Watching him ponder which to pick, Price was reminded yet again that Whitworth was a wimp. The Phoenix staff sweated bullets when Price flew on the corporate plane. Their careers depended on his having a smooth flight with all the creature comforts he expected. Phoenix had a corporate VP of Business Development whose sole responsibility was to ensure Price was happy when he traveled.

Price and Whitworth registered at the D.C. Four Seasons and went straight to dinner. Their car stopped a half block from Senator Carlson's house, security verified their names against the invitation list, and each guest produced a picture ID. The agent asking for ID was backed up by a partner ten feet behind him. Both had M-4 carbines slung across their chests and .40 caliber SIG 226 pistols in thigh rigs. Things had changed in Washington.

The agents escorted the car to the residence and stood guard as the driver opened the rear door. The Phoenix executives stepped out onto the curb with the measured nonchalance and indifference that each of them had perfected to an art form. Such was the confidence of corporate chieftains who answered to no one. That was, unless they looked to the beneficence of a politician to cut deals. That willingness was just another cost of doing business. Steven Price knew that demeaning yourself was transitory and appearing to sell your soul was illusory.

The guest list was limited to the senior Phoenix executives, two senators, one representative, two political powerbrokers, and a couple of two-stars. They all shared the same goals and ambitions—money, power, influence, and control. Price enjoyed the power and influence during his short stint in Congress, but he hated catering to constituents. There were more satisfying ways to power. For now, he had to deal with politicians, and that meant sharing a dinner table with them.

"I need some issues gentlemen," the senator said, already exasperated. "Things are not good for us, and we need some good press."

The senator had fallen into the trap of trying to change the battlefield rather than accepting it. Trying to make things happen led to political discomfort at best or political suicide at worst. There were many ways to ruin a career, and pushing too hard and too soon was one of them. Phoenix had cultivated Carlson for years, and would not see their investment fail because of impatience.

"This is a temporary setback," Whitworth said. "You have plenty of time."

"Terrorism and the war on drugs," Price interjected.

"Excuse me, Steven?"

"Your issues, senator. You said you needed some issues."

"Okay, I'm listening."

"Terrorism and the war on drugs are your domestic and international issues."

"Terrorism I can understand and accept, but the war on drugs is old."

"Senator, it's a real-live issue, and they're connected."

"Keep going."

"RAND has come out with another study, just as damaging to us as the 1994 study. You'll remember that the administration initially rejected the 1994 findings but then adopted a few of them quietly."

"Of course I remember. It came with a bang and died with a whimper."

The 1994 study determined that treatment of hard-core users was the most effective and efficient method of reducing cocaine consumption, seven times more cost effective than law enforcement. The killer conclusion was that the treatment option was even more attractive when compared to interdiction programs.

"This latest study," Price continued, "determines that we have failed to reduce the availability of drugs and have jailed low-level dealers, not kingpins. It notes that a gram that retails for twenty-five dollars today would sell for a couple of dollars if it were legal. Some analysts have called the war on drugs a taxpayer funded government subsidy to foreign cartels and domestic dealers."

"I wouldn't worry too much about that report," Carlson said offhandedly. "It'll go away on its own."

"I'm not so sure, senator," Price said, as skeptical as Carlson was dismissive. "Many Americans believe the war on drugs is no war at all. A crisis like terror attacks focuses attention on the real issues and away from the bogus ones. The terror threat is real, so we have to keep up the pressure on drugs. We need to link the two, and we are exposed in two critical areas if we don't."

"And those are?"

"First, we lose considerable profit. As long as there are drugs, we make a lot of money eradicating them. The more pressure we put on drugs, the more money we make. The second is that federal, state, and local agencies employ thousands of people whose livelihood depends on the war on drugs. If they don't have a war to fight, they don't get budget money. If they don't get budget money, they're out of jobs. That means thousands of angry voters. Many in your own state of New York."

"Good points," the senator said. "I would hate to disappoint a lot of loyal government employees."

"There is one other matter, if we may, senator," Price said as he nodded to Whitworth. "We will soon be the largest supplier to Pakistan's nuclear energy and weapons program. It means significant revenue, and we have a chance to expand our business with them. We've picked up a few hints of resistance on Capitol Hill and would greatly appreciate your staff helping us pave the way so our near term deals go through."

"Ever since Khan came clean, it's been a bitch when it comes to Pakistan and nuclear weapons," Carlson said. In 2004, Abdul Qaddeer Khan, the father of Pakistan's nuclear weapons program, admitted passing nuclear technology to Iran, North Korea, and Libya.

"I wish the bastard had kept his mouth shut," Price said.

"Can he be tied to you?" Carlson asked.

"No, he can't," Whitworth responded. "We paid him through intermediaries and he never knew anything. No one else does either. He thought he was dealing with the Chinese."

"Didn't you pay him enough to stay quiet?" asked one of the two-stars.

"We paid him over a million a year," Price answered. "The problem is that he developed a conscience. Beats me why that happened."

"The U.S. government," Carlson said, "will stand by Pakistan because it's in our interest to do so. Notice that even after Khan's admission we agreed to sell them F-16s. The inescapable reality is that President Musharraff has factions inside his government that are sympathetic to al Qaeda. If he were assassinated, it's highly likely that radical Islamists would get their hands on Pakistan's nuclear weapons. *That's* our real problem. Hell, why do you think we helped them nail al-Libbi? The guy was no direct danger to us, but was a huge threat to Musharraff. The Pakies can't afford the political backlash of going after bin Laden, but they'll take our help to eliminate significant internal threats. The bottom line is that I can take care of your problem. Don't worry."

Phoenix established joint ventures in the early 1990s with mainland Chinese and Hong Kong companies to develop new business and markets in the Far East. The mainland companies concentrated on manufacturing and high-technology enterprises dedicated to military arms and telecommunications programs. The Hong Kong companies concentrated on software and services. One mainland project resulted in the production of ring-shaped magnetic bearings made of samarium-cobalt alloy. The rings underwent a precision manufacturing process to endure the ultra high speeds of gas centrifuges making fuel for nuclear explosive devices. Clients paid dearly for the rings since they were a key component in making nuclear weapons fuel.

Phoenix's financial and technical contributions made the Chinese world leaders in the manufacturing technology. The U.S. government knew the joint venture sold several thousand rings to Pakistan in 1994 and 1995, and ignored it so business could proceed as usual. The joint venture sold several thousand rings to Iraq and Iran from 1995 to 1997, but they hid the sales better than previously. Phoenix wanted to push the rings to a wider market, like India. It was always more profitable to sell to both sides.

"Let's try one more on for size," the senator continued. "Is there any way you can be tied to the SCOPE fiasco?"

He meant Malaysia's Scomi Precision Engineering (SCOPE), implicated in black market trafficking of nuclear technology. CIA had established that SCOPE was not merely a manufacturer of innocuous oil and gas industry parts. They had employed their precision milling and cutting expertise to manufacture and export to Libya special parts for centrifuges, the machines used to enrich uranium for nuclear weapons production.

"There's no way we can be tied to SCOPE," Whitworth said. "We invested in one of their early joint ventures, but those products aren't part of this latest investigation. They couldn't cover their tracks as well as we could, so we opted out."

"Good. That's one less headache. How's your telecom venture with the Chinese coming along?"

"Great," Whitworth said. "We've extracted more concessions than we thought possible."

"How so?"

"We put $620 million in equity with their telecom and satellite company, and we're fully funding their research and development operations in California, Texas, and India," Price answered. "In addition to the equity participation, we have exclusive rights to build two manufacturing plants on the mainland, we operate tax-free for twenty-five years, and the Chinese government guarantees to take our entire output for the first fifteen. It's a huge deal for us."

"Where are they concentrating most of their activity?" the representative wondered.

"They'll put a quarter of the telecom infrastructure into Beijing, and the rest will go to operations in Central and South America, West Africa, and Europe. The Chinese want to be big players in foreign markets over the next decade, and we intend to get them there."

"How about their satellite systems?" asked one of the power brokers.

"They want to upgrade their littoral environment resolution and scanning capability," Whitworth continued. "They're looking primarily to monitor weather patterns in humid and tropical environments. It sounds as though they may have finally gotten serious about protecting their people from floods."

"How about your oil and gas ventures with them?" Senator Foster asked.

"Even better than telecoms," Price said with a smile. "The oil and gas business is hard to break into, but our close relationship with the Chinese let us short circuit the barriers without having to set up our own operations. As you recall, the Chinese National Petroleum Corporation was short of cash in 2002. We helped them out with a $585 million bridge loan to buy the Indonesian producing assets of a European oil and gas company. That made us equity owners in the biggest offshore oil producer in Indonesia. Ever since then, they have welcomed our participation in other deals. We financed the CNPC's $225 million acquisition of some Peruvian blocks in January this year, and that makes them the second largest oil producer in Peru. We close our third Chinese deal the week after next with a global investment and participation agreement. For an investment of $970 million, we'll be a fifty percent joint owner in new exploration and production ventures world-wide. Our first priority is Africa, and Geoff and I travel next month to Chad, Nigeria, Angola, and Sudan. This will be extremely profitable for us."

"You didn't have any involvement with the Unocal deal did you?" Carlson asked, referring to the China National Offshore Oil Corporation's (CNOOC) bid to take over the ninth largest U.S. oil and gas producer.

"No way. We knew they were listening to their investment bankers more than they were to their political advisors. They had a hard-on for that deal and were going to make a bid no matter how much it blew up on them. They wanted to make a point, and that's the last thing we needed. Trust us, we're smarter than that. Our deals will be low profile."

"I'm glad to hear it," Carlson said as he sipped his coffee. "Let's hope those profits keep flowing so you can afford to keep up your political contributions."

"I wouldn't worry about that, senator," Price said.

46

There was quiet talk in Ciudad del Este that something *pesado*, heavy, was going to happen. That normally meant a sizeable arms deal, drug deal, or both. Even those not directly involved suspected that something was going on. Jamil Mansour sensed there was a hot deal, but it was unusually quiet. Things would turn up if he kept working it. He wanted to be in on every big sale, and hated being left out. Mansour had completed a transaction in Ecuador and was negotiating his first sale of small arms to the MST in Brazil. His preliminary agreement for RPGs and explosives with the FARC was almost done when they suddenly went quiet. The silence disturbed him. If competitors were stealing his customers, he would deal with them appropriately.

Even though business had backed off a bit, there was never a shortage of action in Ciudad del Este. Somebody always wanted to buy, sell, trade, or steal something. Mansour had a pending order to supply mortars to Hassan Ali, and it was time to follow up with him. Perhaps he could pick up some information while he closed the sale. He pulled up to Ali's house and two bodyguards stopped his car short of the entrance. They checked the vehicle for explosives, patted him down, and asked for his pistol.

Hassan's son Rahim greeted him in the courtyard and apologized that his father was out and would not return for several hours. Rahim invited Mansour to dinner and said they could discuss business as they ate. During dinner, Rahim confirmed the current order and asked for another forty RPGs. Rahim never drank alcohol in public, but drank like a fiend in private. Mansour liked a drink as much as anyone, but paced himself to keep his senses keen. Rahim was soon on his third whiskey, and Mansour needed to keep up with him. He would have a killer headache in the morning, but throwing a few back was part of the business and one of the best ways to get information and deals.

"Praise Allah. The Americans will get what they deserve," Rahim said defiantly.

"Praise Allah. May they burn in hell forever," Mansour rejoined vehemently.

"Jamil, my friend, they will. Very soon. Shortly they will feel the wrath of Allah as a firestorm burns them from the face of the earth."

Rahim continued to drink, regaling Mansour with stories of his father and how they grew up poor. His father educated two sons, cared for a family, and accumulated wealth and influence. He could strike a blow at America that no one else could. Mansour knew there was a huge deal out there, and he was missing out on it. Despite his best efforts, Mansour got nothing meaningful from Rahim.

"Damn," Mansour muttered as he slapped the Land Rover steering wheel and pulled onto the main road. "I know that bastard is working something without me." He took a deep breath and reminded himself that the business worked that way. Patience and hard work would eventually pay off.

Once he arrived home, Mansour went to the refrigerator for a Brahma beer, watched late-night ESPN sports, caught the news on Al-Jazeera, and decided to call it a night. He brushed his teeth, washed his face, and leaned against the wall to relieve himself. Each final drop fell in slow motion, and he was transfixed by the concentric circles in the toilet bowl. They expanded symmetrically to the edge, just like an explosive blast wave. Then it hit him, and all sense of time and urgency froze.

"I know what he's done! That prick has sold nukes!" He slammed his fist against the wall hard enough to break the tile. He shook himself off as his mind raced back to a late night card game with Hassan and several other arms dealers five months earlier. By three in the morning, Hassan had downed almost half of a bottle of scotch and was certifiably drunk.

Before he passed out, he said that a nuclear firestorm would strike the United States and burn the Americans off the face of the earth. Mansour knew Hassan was a possible player in black market nukes, but never thought he was well enough connected to get access to the devices. People talked about black market nuclear weapons long before the Russian army officer Ledbed testified to the U.S. Congress. Some believed his testimony about a hundred missing suitcase bombs was fantasy. Others believed it was true. There were also rumors about North Korea or China selling nukes on the black market. How on earth could Hassan Ali do such a transaction without help? The sale would be enormously profitable, and Mansour wanted part of it.

47

"Good morning, Mr. Ling's office. May I help you?" asked the secretary of the Chinese National Petroleum Corporation (CNPC) president in Beijing.

"Yes, this is General Manager Yi calling from Lima. I would like to speak to Mr. Ling."

"Does this concern Peruvian operations, Mr. Yi, or is it in regard to corporate business?"

"Corporate business."

"Wait one minute please, and I will connect you."

Chinese intelligence, the Ministry of State Security (MSS) and the Military Intelligence Department (MID), operated freely in the world and unusually so in Latin America. Their Latin American intelligence unit headquartered in Lima worked through a wholly-owned local energy subsidiary whose managers, engineers, and analysts traveled unrestricted throughout the region. The CNPC started with small coastal oil blocks in northwest Peru that produced enough oil to justify a full-time presence in the country, but industry watchers never understood why the Chinese paid several times market value for properties with no exploration upside. What observers did not know was that the fair market value was a non-issue for Beijing. The CNPC had recently increased its

Peruvian profile by acquiring interests in several large production blocks and a gas-fired power plant. A silent partner financed both deals. China's interest in Latin America was stronger than ever, and the CNPC would be in Peru for a while.

Beijing was more than willing to fund loss leaders to gain strategic military, intelligence, economic, technological, geographical, and political footholds around the world. While Lima was its beachhead, China had long-term designs on Brazil and Argentina. The Chinese president visited both countries and signed letters of intent to invest $30 billion there over the next decade. Brazil sat on the world's sixth largest uranium reserves and agreed to sell unprocessed uranium to supply eleven nuclear reactors in China. The proceeds would let Brazil finish the $2 billion Angra 3 nuclear reactor outside Rio.

The Brazilians claimed the reactor was for peaceful purposes but refused International Atomic Energy Agency inspections. While the world wrung its hands, the Chinese saw an opportunity. They set up the uranium sale agreement under a nuclear development joint venture in Brazil administered by Chinese managers. The first contingent of managers had arrived a year earlier to monitor, control, and oversee Brazil's nuclear development and report every detail to Lima and Beijing.

In Argentina, the Chinese negotiated a telecommunications agreement, but the real goal was an outlet for their exploding population. In exchange for the investment, the Argentine president gave privileged immigration status to Chinese citizens. The MID calculated that within three generations, a third of Argentina's population would be Chinese. Argentina would not be a client state, but would be an extension of the mainland. While the U.S. was preoccupied with the Middle East, China was building a long-term base in America's backyard.

Saying he wanted to discuss corporate business, Yi signaled to Ling's secretary the topic was intelligence, not Peruvian oil and gas operations. While Yi waited, she connected him to a secure encrypted line.

"Yi, I understand you had a productive trip to the zone this week," Ling said. He meant Panama.

"I did, but it was disturbing," Yi said, clearly worried. "I met with our managers at Balboa and Colón, and there is more activity than I am comfortable with."

"So I gathered from your e-mail last night. Do you think it's a ruse or is it real?"

"We know that at least five two-man Arab teams passed through both ports and the locks in the last three weeks. We have photo surveillance of them taking pictures, shooting video, asking about docking and clearance procedures, storage facilities, and vessel schedules."

China monitored Central America through a port management and logistics company that operated the ports of Balboa and Colón, as well as others in the region. The company controlled all traffic and storage facilities. Two other Chinese subsidiaries managed most of the zone's telecommunications and infrastructure, including several local regional airports. The Chinese were exploiting a gaping hole. American intelligence capabilities in the zone dropped off after the December 1999 turnover of the Panama Canal. U.S. surveillance activity in the area suffered a death blow when the 2001 terrorist attacks redirected virtually all American on-the-ground intelligence assets to the Middle East and other regions with a heavy Muslim presence. After that, the Chinese operated at will and unchecked.

"Did you make contact with them?" Ling asked.

"The audacious dogs actually came to us! They requested a meeting with our Colón general manager and said they represented wealthy Arabs looking at manufacturing investments in Central America and the zone."

"What do you think?"

"They're interested in our port and storage operations, not manufacturing. The pieces don't fit. They said they were from Egypt, but we can't confirm that. I think they're advance teams scouting an attack on the ports, the locks, or the storage facilities."

"To what end?" Ling asked.

"Maybe nothing more than to choke off northbound traffic. They kept asking how many ships go through the locks to the U.S."

"I was afraid they might do something stupid like this," Ling said. "You have good reason for concern Yi. This is worrisome."

The possibility of an attack on the canal made Ling take a long, deep breath as he contemplated his options. While most of the world's nations were satisfied with five-year economic plans, the Chinese were methodically laying the groundwork for the next two to three centuries. The political leadership knew their population of 1.4 billion and market size virtually guaranteed they would become the world's dominant economic power. That is, if they could contain incipient social unrest that threatened to explode the country apart.

They also realized they would not achieve their goals as long as the structural remnants of failed socialist and communist economic experiments hampered them. The law of large numbers guaranteed success, but only under the right conditions. Political philosophy was holding them back, and they knew it. China could not replicate the ingenuity, creativity, and entrepreneurship that made America the most powerful economic engine in history all at once. They needed time. While the Chinese caught up, war and future social costs were draining the U.S. economically, immigration was creating severe political strain, and the children of foreigners were going home with degrees in hard sciences while Americans were becoming lawyers and accountants.

China put out cautious feelers to the international community, and foreign investment started to trickle in during the 1980s and 1990s. The Chinese gradually implemented structural and legal changes they knew would entice foreign businesses. Billion dollar proposals and deals started to come in. The National People's Congress revealed they were serious when they approved landmark changes to the constitution protecting private property. Deals and money rolled in faster than ever.

Western manufacturing, computing, energy, telecommunications, and service companies were willing to cut virtually any deal with the Chinese to get at a market too big to ignore. Their needs for corporate growth played into Chinese hands perfectly. Western corporations and governments justified giving away proprietary technology and know-how, lending money at below market rates, and accepting lower than normal returns for the privilege of gaining access to China. Some deals granted exceptionally favorable business terms, though China limited those to companies that provided strategic technology or privileged U.S. political access. China's plan was simple: use the West to gain technological and economic prominence, then gradually turn and crush their opponents. The West thought only *they* had long-term vision. China had already surpassed the U.S. as the largest recipient of foreign direct investment in the world and it would only get better.

China needed time and luck to achieve its goals but was not so naïve to think their quest for hegemony would go unchallenged. They were engaged in full fledged economic war, a fact the West did not yet entirely understand or appreciate. Yet the West, the United States in particular, would eventually take measures to protect itself. While U.S. corporations were among the first to invest, Washington would be the first to complain, and then act, if they thought China was getting too big a slice of the global economic pie. Beijing knew the U.S. would first complain publicly, then take feeble economic counter-measures, multi-lateral sanctions, and finally unilateral action. When those failed, America would resort to military force to protect its way of life and standard of living. It always had, and always would. China would not back down from anyone, and would be prepared.

The Chinese had long understood that high technology, as much as men on the ground and ships on the seas, would decide future wars. They gradually developed two complementary capabilities to help them face down America. The first was a stronger and more technologically advanced military with enhanced telecommunications. Through numerous acquisitions and joint ventures, they developed the technology to monitor world-wide message traffic and hack any computer system in the world. A loss or serious degradation of telecommunications and computing capability would cripple the U.S. Another series of acquisitions gave the Chinese world-class laptop technology that they were rapidly integrating into all military units. The second capability was their array of port management and logistics companies that controlled key ports and geographic choke points. China could move weapons and technology unchecked by the United States, and deny key water routes to its enemies during the inevitable future war.

Beijing had little interest in stopping potential attacks for America's sake, but a strike now might cost them years of groundwork. China was still ramping up its economy and was years from having the commercial, technological, military, and operational capability to wage a war against the U.S. An attack by anyone on the canal would be catastrophic, since it risked exposing Chinese military capability in the zone. In early 2002, China started moving nuclear tipped ballistic missiles to the area in container vessels. They were specially modified Dong-Feng 31s, designed with technology obtained by espionage and illegal technology transfers from the U.S. Each road-mobile ICBM carried a 1.0-2.5 megaton thermonuclear warhead and had a launch preparation time of fifteen minutes. There were seven nuclear missiles in the zone, each with a five thousand mile range. They were hidden in storage yards along with several thousand similar containers from around the world.

A recent port acquisition package secured facilities and operations in Mexico, Costa Rica, Buenos Aires, Lima, Recife, and São Paulo. The Mexican operations put them 700 miles from the U.S. border and 1,000 miles from Houston. After closing the transaction, the Chinese placed two nuclear missiles in Mexico and aimed them at the U.S. That made a total of nine nuclear missiles targeted at the United States that could be deployed, armed, and launched on short notice. If the U.S. played too fast or too hard, China had nine aces up its sleeve right on America's doorstep.

"What would you like us to do?" Yi asked.

"Do you have them under round-the-clock surveillance?"

"We assigned two of our teams to each Arab team. We monitor all their movements and communications."

"Yi, we can't take any chances with this. Be very careful, and don't let them out of your sight. Kill and dispose of them as soon as possible. It's good that they're giving the Americans hell around the word, but we can't let the Arabs interfere with our long-term plans. Is that clear?"

"Very clear, sir. Thank you."

"Good day, Yi."

48

DEA Chief of Operations Brett Simpson shook my hand and thanked me for coming to see him. With my heart pounding and sweat trickling down my back, I wondered if he would thank me once I was done. I asked myself what I was doing here, but it was too late for that. Simpson sat at the end of the table to my left and Felipe Torres was directly across from me. Simpson said he understood from Denning that I wanted to talk directly to the DEA.

I laid it all out. Phoenix subsidiaries manufactured the precursors, exported them to the U.S., then shipped them to Bolivia and several other countries around the world. I showed them the wire transfers from Raúl's companies to suspected FARC and Sendero fronts, that Raúl was skimming close to a million a year from the BLI contract, and that he tapped my phones.

"That's it guys," I said. "I'm here to turn it over to you."

Simpson was impassive, but tapped his pencil rapidly while Torres made notes. "This is quite a story, Mr. Blackstone," he said. "Have you passed this on to Phoenix yet?"

"No," I answered. "I sent an e-mail to Steven Price, my boss in Chicago, when I first suspected Raúl was getting kickbacks from BLI. That was the extent of it. I haven't spoken to anyone at the corporation about what we've discussed, but I will after this meeting."

"Why now and not earlier?" Simpson wondered.

"When I sent the e-mail, I had only a corporate conflict of interest and business ethics violation. It soon became a problem with potentially serious legal consequences. Quite frankly, I didn't tell Phoenix about the precursors because I didn't trust them to pursue it. I thought U.S. law enforcement should see this first."

"Fair enough," Simpson said uneasily.

"I can't believe Raúl is involved in anything like this," Torres said, shaking his head. "We've checked him a dozen times and never found anything."

"These are very serious allegations," Simpson observed. "There will be criminal charges involved if this plays out, but it appears you have some problems as well."

"I do. I'll present my board with allegations about someone they believe beyond reproach. That's not going to be easy, but I suspect that my political problems pale in comparison to yours."

"Mr. Blackstone," Simpson started slowly, "Raúl is a successful businessman, has tremendous influence in the Bolivian government, and has the U.S. government's full trust and confidence. He receives strong support from federal agencies, senior military officers, and congressmen. You've really stirred the pot, sir."

"Look, it's not as though I made this happen," I said, looking at my folder and realizing I had forgotten something. "Sorry, guys, I've got one more thing to show you. I took these pictures two weeks ago when I was with my family in the Beni. Dávila came by car, and Raúl and the others got off the plane that's behind them."

"Oh, shit," Simpson said softly as he looked through the pictures with Torres. "This has just gone from bad to worse. When did you say you took these?"

"Two weeks ago. Anyone you recognize?"

"I should say so," Simpson said slowly. "Raúl and Dávila are obvious. The short guy on the left is Ricardo Agostini from Milan, one of the three most wanted drug bosses in Europe. He hasn't been seen for two years, and there's an international arrest warrant out on him. The older man to his right is Javier Burgos. He's the most powerful drug and arms dealer in Argentina. Do you have an extra set of these?"

"Those are yours."

"Brett, we need to close on Raúl fast," Torres said.

"Not yet, Felipe," Simpson said, handing my documents to an embassy secretary who left to make photocopies. "This is damned sensitive, and we'll have to do it quietly. I can't do a thing about Raúl until I talk to Washington."

"As you say, boss."

"Does this mean you won't take any action until you've seen more data?" I asked.

"Not at all," Simpson said, pulling a business card from his wallet. "I'll take this up with my boss tomorrow afternoon in D.C. If you don't hear from me by Monday, call the cell phone on my card. Mr. Blackstone, I wish this had never happened, but I'm glad you brought it to us. Thank you for your time, sir."

Simpson used an embassy computer to send an e-mail to the DEA Administrator requesting a Saturday afternoon meeting. He gave no specifics. Knowing how difficult it would be to get a weekend meeting on such short notice, he later sent a message from the hotel with details of the discussion with Blackstone. He did not mention Raúl's name, but would do so in person. To add emphasis, he called the administrator from his sat phone and left a voice message telling him to check his e-mail.

49

Raúl's cell phone rang shortly before 10:00 P.M. as he ate dinner with friends at the Círculo Militar, a century-old social club in downtown La Paz. Membership was restricted to an elite group of Bolivian military, political, and business leaders. He excused himself from the table.

"Don Raúl, we have to meet tonight." The caller was quiet but insistent.

"I won't be home for a while. Can it wait until tomorrow?"

"No. Tonight."

"Come by the house at midnight. Call my security when you're a minute away and they'll let you in."

"Thank you."

Raúl's men looked under the car and checked the back seat and trunk before they let the vehicle through the gate. They disarmed the garden perimeter intrusion sensors, a guard accompanied the visitor to the west entrance and into the living room, closed the door, and returned to his post. Raúl looked relaxed as he sipped a cognac on the sofa. His eyes were intense and he said nothing. The guest poured a glass of white wine and slid into the Swedish leather chair opposite the sofa.

"We've got trouble, Raúl. Blackstone went to the embassy today and talked to the DEA Chief of Operations. He had copies of your precursor import documents and wire transfers to what he says are FARC and Sendero fronts. Blackstone was in Trinidad two weeks ago and has pictures of you with Dávila, Agostini, and Burgos at the airport."

"What did the chief say?"

"Not much, but he's worried. The embassy secure communications log shows he sent an e-mail to the DEA Administrator asking for a meeting at five tomorrow afternoon. The good news is that he mentioned no details and no names."

"Do you think anybody other than Blackstone knows about this?"

"I doubt it. There were initials on the documents, but they were photocopies of originals so it doesn't mean much. DEA was the only agency at the meeting, and it was closed doors. John Denning is still in the U.S. on business and has no idea what's going on."

Raúl got up from the sofa and walked to the bar. He said nothing as he poured another drink and went into the study adjacent to the living room. The door closed behind him, he sat down at his desk, and put the drink on a coaster. He turned on his desk lamp and sat back to consider his alternatives. An encrypted e-mail would be safest, but any delay could be fatal. Raúl hated to expose himself over the airwaves, but time was short and he was running for his life. He unlocked the desk drawer and pulled out the satellite phone. After swinging the antenna into position, he pressed the icon to make a call, waited for the beep confirming he was linked to the system, and then dialed the number.

Raúl relayed the information as he understood it, and they agreed on a course of action. He disconnected the call and locked the phone in the desk. Before returning to the living room, he speed dialed the third number on his cell phone directory and conveyed succinct instructions. *Was there any misunderstanding?* There was none. He turned out the light, got up, went back to the living room, topped off his drink, and told his guest that all was well.

Julie and I had dinner alone after we put the children to bed, and spent two hours talking about my afternoon at the embassy. It was time to call Price and let him know what was happening. I reached him at home and gave him the details of the meeting with the DEA. He said nothing for several seconds.

"Richard, you did the right thing. We've worked too hard for something like this to bring us down. Damn."

"I had no choice, Steven."

"No, not you Richard. Raúl. Did the DEA give you any idea that they might view us positively for being so forthcoming?"

"We didn't even touch on that, but I don't see why not. They were thankful that I brought it to them."

"Good, maybe candor will help. This isn't going to be easy, but maybe we'll get lucky. Have you told anyone else?"

"No one." I did not want to implicate Denning. I knew Price might try political pressure to keep the affair low-profile, and I wanted to keep John out of that crossfire.

"Good. Keep it that way for now. We don't want this getting out. Let me know as soon as Simpson gets back to you. I'll call Geoff and our legal department right now to schedule an emergency board meeting. We've got to plot a course so we know how we're going to respond as a corporation. Be careful. These are dangerous people."

"Thanks. I appreciate the support."

Julie listened to my conversation and gave me a big smile and a kiss when I cut the phone connection. It was exactly what I needed. I was nervous and my stomach churned, but her touch soothed me.

50

The cold La Paz morning air filled his lungs as John Denning stepped off the American Airlines flight Saturday morning. The altiplano chill bit and he stuffed his hands in his pockets as he walked down the steps to the tarmac. Seventy yards to his left several people prepared a private plane for departure. Denning looked closer and recognized the white U.S. government Gulfstream that would take DEA Chief of Operations Simpson back to Washington.

Rather than go through immigration, Denning walked over to the aircraft as Simpson arrived in a convoy of three embassy SUVs. Denning approached quickly, and the DEA protection specialists picked him up as they piled out of the vehicles. Since Denning was in the U.S. during Simpson's visit, the protection team did not know him by sight. One moved forward to cut him off, and another swept his coat to acquire a firing grip on his pistol. Simpson knew Denning and called the team off, shouting that it was the U.S. Embassy RSO.

"Morning, Brett!" Denning called from twenty feet away. "Sorry I missed your visit."

"Hey, no problem, John," Simpson said to his friend. "It's not like I won't be back."

"How was the trip?"

"Well," said Simpson, shivering in the wind, "it started out great, but took a twist I never expected."

"What happened?"

"Torres and I met with Richard Blackstone yesterday, and he told us a pretty incredible story. It looks like our number one local man in the war on drugs has bamboozled us. Blackstone didn't mention you, but I know you scheduled the meeting. I'm not going to ask you to betray a confidence, but this is serious stuff. We've got some work to do."

"Yeah, I know what's going on, and it's pretty much a disaster from what Blackstone showed me. What's your plan?"

"I've got a meeting with the administrator this afternoon as soon as I get to D.C. Don't do anything until you hear from me, but get ready to bring the ambassador and the DCM as well as the FBI Legal Attaché in Santiago up to speed fast," Simpson said. "For now, watch your back, and make sure Blackstone's safe."

"Will do."

"I'll call you at home after the meeting. Gotta go, John."

"Take care Brett. Good luck."

Simpson had been a private pilot for many years and knew to expect a long takeoff because of the thin La Paz air. He clocked what seemed to be an eternity before he felt even the faintest sign of differential pressure building enough to lift the wings. He closed his eyes as the nose rose and the aircraft pitched up to pull the wheels off the highest runway in the world. He came to Bolivia for a routine field operations review. Never in his wildest dreams did he anticipate an outcome so bizarre.

Denning's diplomatic passport got him around the immigration line quickly, and he sipped mate de coca in his embassy car as

Simpson's plane roared overhead. The Gulfstream's noise was so fierce that Denning knew he had a call only because he felt his phone vibrate on his hip.

"Sandy, what's up?" he asked Sandy Lombard, the assistant RSO.

"Urgent stuff, John. NSA picked up a satellite phone call last night originating in La Paz that mentioned Simpson's name. They're cleaning up the tape now, but we wanted to make sure he's okay."

"He is. I just talked to him, and you can probably hear his plane right now. If those guys don't know it, tell them that he carries a sat phone with him all the time. It was probably his own call."

"Okay, John. Thanks. Sorry to bother. See you Monday."

"Call me if you need me."

"Will do."

The aircraft climbed out of La Paz, and Simpson asked the pilot to fly close enough to Mt. Illimani so he could take pictures. He leaned over to pull the camera from his briefcase, and an explosion from the right side of the plane threw him out of his seat onto the floor. The plane lurched violently, and he cursed for not keeping his seatbelt fastened. Simpson pulled himself into the seat as the plane shook hard. His first instinct was to scream on the phone to the pilots to ask what happened. No need. It was obvious. His mind rushed as he tightened the seatbelt and clutched the arm rest. He knew the pilots would adjust the thrust on the remaining engine and extinguish the fire so they could return to El Alto.

There was an explosion from the left side of the aircraft before he finished the thought. People scrambled and shouted as the plane lost altitude. The pilots fought hard against impossible odds.

With neither engine working and nothing but dead weight, the plane crashed into the side of Illimani in a bright fireball.

Denning was in the shower when his phone rang, and was told that the DEA plane had crashed. The crisis was in full swing when he arrived at the embassy. Maps of the presumed crash area covered the conference room walls, and everyone held a phone or a radio. He would normally have handled the briefing, but told the DCM to start without him so they would not lose time.

"Eyes and ears front and center, everyone," shouted the Air Force Defense Attaché. "Simpson's plane took off from El Alto this morning at 06:01 hours. The pilot reported starboard engine trouble at 06:05, that he had control of the plane, and was returning to La Paz. He reported port trouble almost immediately. That was the last communication. They went off radar, and a Beechcraft pilot carrying tourists around the cordillera said he saw a plane flame out and crash into Illimani. We'll have the FBI, FAA, NTSB, Gulfstream, and others all here within twenty-four hours, so get ready for visitors. John, you've got a message on your desk. Washington is sending a Mobile Tactical Support Team to beef up security just in case this was not a one-time event. That's all we know."

Denning packed his briefcase and gathered his gear before heading to El Alto to meet with airport authorities. Once in the car and on his way, he dialed Blackstone.

"Richard, got some news," Denning said as he turned onto the Prado.

"What's going on?"

"Simpson's plane blew up this morning just after takeoff and crashed into Illimani."

"What the hell happened?"

"We don't have a clue. All we have is the tower report of engine trouble and a Beech pilot who saw the crash."

"John, I'm not the guy you would normally call in a crisis like this."

"I know, but it's not every day the DEA Chief of Operations hears what you told him yesterday and dies in a plane crash eighteen hours later. I saw him at the airport this morning and he was disturbed."

"I smell Raúl big time. What do you think?"

"I don't know what to believe. What I do know is that I have to get up to El Alto to help coordinate the search and rescue, not that we're going to find any survivors. I've really gotta go. I'll call you later."

"Thanks, John. Bye."

I told Julie about Simpson and we agreed it was no accident. My gut told me it was Raúl, but I could not believe he would be so brazen. Killing his own people was one thing, but attacking a U.S. law enforcement official was something else. Instinct told me it was only a matter of time before he came after me and my family. I was in no mood to wait around, so I got seats for everyone on the Sunday morning flight to Miami. We could at least eat dinner tonight knowing we had done something to protect ourselves.

My phone rang as we started appetizers, and I swore under my breath. I thought I turned it off before we sat down. By the third ring, my family was ready to climb down my throat unless I answered it.

"Richard," Denning said, sounding very tired, "it has been a killer day. Sorry, no pun intended. It looks like the initial information we got on Simpson's plane was spot on. The aircraft flamed out and flew right into Illimani. We've got a planeload of stateside experts on the way right now. Tomorrow is going to be even busier than today. Where are you?"

"La Venenciana. Eating dinner."

"Is Lucho with you?"

"Nope, told him to go home. The guy needed a break. I'm my own driver tonight. Why?"

"I'm sending someone over to drive you back. I'm worried."

"Are you sure it's necessary?"

"Sure? No, I'm not sure. Will it make me feel better? Yeah, it will."

"Okay, John, I understand. Who is it?"

"Adam Jefferson. He's with the MILGROUP and has some force protection experience. You met him a few weeks ago at the embassy. I know you can take care of yourself, but another set of eyes and ears never hurts. He'll be there in twenty minutes. Oh, I got your voice mail. It's a good move to fly out of here as soon as possible."

"Thanks, John. Tell Adam to come on in when he gets here."

51

He arrived twenty minutes early at the well-appointed 29th floor suite in New York City, despite a late connecting flight and the time it took to shower and change clothes. He eased into the blue cloth chair next to the coffee table, and his eyes darted to the double doors to his left. In a matter of minutes, he would be behind those doors telling the story of a lifetime. It was no time for nerves, but they rolled over him like mini-tsunamis. His boss's administrative assistant brought him a cup of freshly-brewed coffee. He sipped it and gathered his thoughts. The coffee was comforting, but he was still anxious.

Everyone in the world thought the organization was a bunch of idiots running around the world screwing up everything they touched. Nothing was farther from the truth. They were hamstrung by bureaucrats who did not understand the business and by politicians whose only idea of the world outside of the U.S. was a ten-day junket with first class plane tickets, five-star hotels, chauffeured limousines, and airtight security. Despite their ignorance and inexperience, those same politicians tried to make international policy and told him how to do his job.

It was a tough business, and it was the real world, not a beltway fantasy land. Keeping your successes quiet in a real-life but secret business was frustrating. The public heard only about the failures—like missing one person in a million. The problem was, one asshole could cause a lot of damage. His life had never flashed before him, but it did with a vengeance as he waited. He always scoffed when people said certain events made you wonder how you got to a particular place and time. No more.

He interviewed the standard corporate possibilities in the fall of his University of Kentucky senior year, but with little satisfaction. He gravitated towards the banks and the major corporations because of his economics major, but they were worried about his political science and history course work. They could not understand how it was relevant to anything they did.

The only interesting recruiter was a fellow who had worked all over the world for a large oil and gas company. He said that corporate life provided a good dental program, but was not the place for those who wanted to be valued. The recruiter suggested the young man make a list of what he liked to do, and then figure out how to do it. The oil and gas man's advice sounded great, and he drew up the list as soon as the interview ended. He liked traveling, the outdoors, shooting and hunting, speaking foreign languages, and meeting new people. Above all, he wanted to be challenged. The corporate world did not come close. The U.S. Army wanted him, and he wanted them.

Only a few months into his first overseas deployment as an intelligence officer, it became apparent he was on the wrong career path. The Big Army bureaucracy drove him crazy, and he knew there had to be a better fit somewhere. A sympathetic commanding officer suggested that he might find a home in Special Forces. After a bit of homework, he realized his CO was right. The first challenge toward a new career was to negotiate the six phase selection, qualification, and training program.

The Phase I Special Forces Assessment and Selection Course

was a grueling twenty-four day program that evaluated a soldier's fitness, motivation, and ability to cope with stress. His performance put him in the six week Phase II Special Forces Qualification Course concentrating on land navigation and small unit tactics, and then the twenty-six week Phase III Officer Qualification Course where he excelled at reconnaissance, direct action, and counterinsurgency operations.

During the Phase IV unconventional warfare training he demonstrated an uncanny ability to assess and negotiate complex operational and interpersonal challenges. His natural language ability allowed him to blow through the Phase V Serbo Croation course. He completed the Phase VI Survival Evasion Resistance and Escape course by making it a mental instead of a physical challenge. Then came forty weeks of specialty training in military free-fall, advanced free-fall, combat diver, waterborne infiltration, advanced reconnaissance, target analysis and exploitation, and special operations target interdiction. After almost two years of training he went back overseas, but this time as a force multiplier.

After ten years in Special Forces, he was a highly experienced Tier One asset. He identified, formed, trained, and led foreign armies in unconventional warfare. Because of his unique abilities, he moved from the 7th Special Forces Group to another SF unit for a six-month training cycle and then joined an assault group that focused on direct action operations. When terrorism moved to the front burner, he became a member of a reconnaissance and surveillance squad to find High Value Targets (HVT) in the Middle East. He and his *recce* buddies could move undetected through enemy lines or urban environments better than any soldiers in the world. Twelve years into his career, he was gearing up for the reason he joined SF—to hunt, find, and kill bad guys. His enthusiasm and faith then took a couple of hits.

Frustration at not being in the fight turned to rage when the head of the Joint Special Operations Command (JSOC) ordered his squad withdrawn from the HVT rotation, and instead deployed another service's unit perceived by those on the ground to be less capable of completing the mission. As if that were not enough, JSOC then placed in command of his overall task force an Air Force general who had no direct action experience. Although the general had a solid aviation background, it seemed that a politically correct promotion trumped giving the door-kickers the best leadership available. Even the hunter-killers were victims of bureaucratic wrangling and ass-kissing.

On the verge of renewing his commitment to the U.S. Army, a senior CIA officer asked him to consider another branch of government. The approach was timely. For the first time in his career, he was ambivalent about the Army. He liked the idea of expanding his tool kit. He had deployed several times with CIA field officers, worked well with them, and respected them. The agency's history and mission appealed to him. Even though it was the focus of attention, CIA was not to blame for the September 11 attacks. There were much better places to point accusing fingers. The agency did a superb job—the public just did not know it.

His unit finally deployed to hunt HVTs, but his decision was made. He accepted CIA's offer and resigned his U.S. Army commission several months later. Despite looking forward to his new career, it was the hardest decision he ever made. He planned to take three months off to relax, but changed his mind when a Southern senator he had worked for as a summer intern called him with a temporary job offer. The senator wanted a "no holds barred" white paper on U.S. intelligence and military efforts to fight terrorists. An ex-intern with SF experience headed to CIA was perfect.

A month after finishing his white paper he started the Basic Operations Training Course in Virginia where he was taught weapons handling, explosives, infiltration, and exfiltration. His next courses were in North Carolina where he learned covert entry, intelligence gathering, applied explosives techniques, "snatch and grab operations", electronic eavesdropping, surveillance and counter-surveillance, and evasive driving. He polished his firearms skills through courses at private facilities in Arkansas, Arizona, Georgia, and North Carolina. After a year of training he was ready to roll.

Born and raised in the U.S., his Syrian immigrant father ensured that he spoke fluent Arabic. It was a slam dunk CIA would send him back to some of his old Middle East haunts. He was surprised when they sent him to learn Spanish, then Portuguese, and stunned when his assignment was Latin America. CIA said they wanted to monitor and infiltrate the terrorist groups operating in Latin America and posted him with "non-official cover" (NOC) to Ciudad del Este, Paraguay, as an import-export agent dealing in manufactured goods. His real business was terrorists and the arms, drugs, and counterfeit money associated with them.

After two years, he was connected to a continuous flow of illicit arms, drugs, cash, and stolen property. He moved eleven million dollars in arms in the last year, and had a number of deals working. Most of the arms went initially to CIA front organizations in the U.S. and the Far East, but over the last year he dealt directly with Latin America's most notorious terrorist groups. The small players who bought arms and carried out attacks were the stepping stones to the big fish.

He finished reviewing his notes a third time, and his watch told him he was less than sixty seconds away from the most important meeting in his life. He knew his material backwards and forwards, but still he was nervous. His hands were damp, his heart raced, and measured breathing did only so much to slow his heart. The door to his left opened, and the secretary stood. The familiar face of Roger Harrington, his boss and CIA's Latin American Division head, appeared in the open doorway. The man who brought him into CIA gave him a smile and a thumbs up. Waiting for him standing around the conference table were the Deputy

Director of Central Intelligence (DDCI), the Deputy Director of Operations (DDO), and the head of the Counterterrorist Center (CTC).

"We don't normally conduct meetings like this because of the extreme risk to our NOC assets," Harrington said as they sat. "The circumstances, however, require that we do this face to face. Gentlemen, meet Jay Mansour."

52

Adam Jefferson approached Blackstone's red Mitsubishi Montero outside La Venenciana carefully. He lit up the exterior with a flashlight to see if he noticed anything unusual. He used white light to look for improvised explosive devices since it would pick up colored wires. Jefferson looked for explosives even though he thought a small arms attack was most likely.

He avoided an initial touch on the car to keep from setting off a vibration or motion sensor. He looked underneath the vehicle, in through the windows, along the door edges, the hood, trunk, exhaust, wheel wells, spare tire, and around and behind the license plates. He saw no wires, filaments, or anything reflective. As he looked, he reminded himself that bomb planters were ingenious. His favorite was the Range Rover in Bogotá that had explosives connected to a wire in the wheel well. The terrorists drank coffee as they watched their victim drive away and detonate himself after the eighty-five yard filament ran out.

Jefferson ran the edge of a business card along the gaps in the hood, doors, trunk, gasoline cap, and the sunroof. A business card was soft and pliable, a credit card was hard and more easily tripped devices. There were no wires or obstructions. He carefully opened the driver side door a half inch, and then fully. He did the same with all the doors, the trunk, gasoline cap, sunroof, and the hood. He stuck his hand into the hood welded panel open areas. Hot engine air would detonate hidden Semtex. Simple and effective. He continued to look for filament wires, something ajar, shiny surfaces, powder residue, light switches, and pressure pads. He sniffed the car, looked under the seats, in the glove compartment, under the dash, in the CD player, ran a card in the overhead visors and opened them, and checked the center console storage bin. As a last check, he pushed his palm against the floor, door panels, seats, seat backs, headrests, interior roof, and the headliner. The car was clean. He would wait to crank the engine until Blackstone and his family were ready to leave.

We paid the bill and said goodbye to the owner and the waiters. One waiter stood outside and held the door open. I waved to Jefferson that we were ready to go and turned to tell the children to hurry up. The Mitsubishi engine came to life, and I saw a brilliant flash as a deafening roar and intense heat obliterated my sense of space and time. The shock wave blew me off my feet and through the door against the wall several feet behind me. I was on my hands and knees, my ears ringing fiercely. I could not see through the dust and dirt, but knew I was not badly injured. I called to Julie and the children, and got hands on them to make sure they were not hurt. I told them to go back to the kitchen, the safest place in case there was another blast.

I crawled back to the door, and saw that the front of the restaurant was blown out. Wood and glass was everywhere. The waiter who held the door was decapitated, his body blocked the doorway. I poked my head slowly around the corner and saw the car in flames. I backed up, sat against the wall, and called Denning to tell him I needed another car and driver.

"Hey, John, I've got some deep shit over here at La Venenciana. My car just blew up."

"What?"

"We were headed out the door, Jefferson started the engine, and it flew all over the block."

"Are you guys okay?"

"Yeah," I said, wiping blood from my face. "Julie and the kids are shaken, but they're not hurt. Jefferson's dead, there's a headless waiter, and I think the owner's in bad shape. Can you get a doctor over here and get us some transport?"

"Hang tight. I'm on my way."

"Thanks. We're not going anywhere."

I wanted to pull out my pistol and shoot whoever did this. Looking around was pointless and dangerous, since there might be another device somewhere. Plus, whoever planted the bomb was long gone. Since there was no back door into the kitchen where my family was, I stayed out front to make sure no one came in until Denning arrived. As for who did it, landing on the prime candidate did not take long.

"He tried to kill all of us, John!" I shouted as Denning walked toward the restaurant.

"It's hard to believe, but I've got to agree with you. Plus, there's more."

"What's that?"

"NSA intercepted a satellite call from La Paz last night that they took for a threat on Simpson's life. We called stateside a couple of hours ago, and voice analysis says the person was Andean, a long-time English speaker, educated in the U.S., and between fifty and seventy years old. They sent the tape over to Intelligence and Threat Analysis at State to see if they agree."

"We both know it's Raúl, John. Can you get a copy of the tape?"

"I asked for it, but don't know when they'll get it to me."

Ilidio Quevedo adjusted the volume on the police scanner in his office at the El Alto hangar. Three police units and a fire truck had been called to investigate a car explosion in downtown La Paz. Quevedo chuckled. Maybe they should use the fire extinguishers. Not even a trained professional would suspect that the Mitsubishi's fire extinguishers were packed with Semtex. For good measure, he took the car tools out of the rear storage area and packed it with explosives as well. Even though the Czech government owned Explosia, the company that produced Semtex, it was ridiculously easy to buy. Ironically, it was harder to purchase from private companies than it was from a government. The wireless relay connected to the transmission detonated the explosives exactly as planned. A good night indeed, and Quevedo opened a Paceña to toast himself. *Adios,* Sr. Blackstone.

"Richard, give me all your documents," Denning said as we huddled in his living room. "I need passports, driver's licenses, ID cards, all of it. I'll roust a Consular Affairs friend out of bed and should be back in a few hours."

"Here you go." I gave him all our papers.

Latin American police routinely ask their own citizens and foreigners to produce an ID, so part of daily living includes having all identity documents within easy reach. With Denning off and running, I focused on what Julie and the children needed to travel. We could not go back to the house, so Lucho and Lucy would have to pack for us. I caught Lucho at his house in the middle of a card game and told him we had an emergency. He was out the door as we spoke, and I warned him to watch his rearview mirror. With luck, Julie and the children would soon be safely ensconced in our northern Michigan cottage.

Next came the hardest part. I hate waiting. John's wife helped Julie get the children to bed while I made checklists. Everyone was agitated, but the adrenaline rush was gone and they were asleep instantly. I took a shower and was resting on the sofa when Lucho and Lucy arrived with several suitcases and duffle bags of clothes and books. Lucho saw the concern on my face and told me not to worry, since he left his two brothers to watch our house. He also brought my other 1911 and my shotgun.

A sense of desperation, an overwhelming helplessness, replaced rage. I pulled a cold beer from the fridge, and went to John's study to listen to music and relax. I put my head back, closed my eyes, and floated through space and time. More than ever, I knew I was in a third world country and targeted to die. What was worse, they had tried to kill my family as well. I felt paralyzed.

By the end of the third beer and the CD, I threw off the frustration and locked it in a box. I went back to the living room, sat on the sofa next to Julie, and put my head back to rest my eyes.

"Whoa, guys! What time is it?" I asked the two fuzzy figures standing over me.

"5:00 A.M. on the nose amigo," Denning said with a huge smile. "Time to get up and moving. We've got some goodies for you."

Bill Wilson of the Consular Affairs Section handed me a packet of documents and identification cards. I was astonished. In only hours, they had generated U.S. passports, Bolivian ID and residency cards, and U.S. driver's licenses, all under new names. Wilson had also paid for American Airlines tickets from a Department of State account. Business Class no less.

"Guys, this is huge," I said. "I don't know what to say."

"My pleasure," Wilson beamed, so excited he could hardly contain himself. "Too bad I can't say anything about it. Maybe you can tell the story some day. Put me in your book."

"Thanks a million. How long will you burn in bureaucratic hell for this?"

"Forever if they find out," Wilson said, "but they won't. We altered the records the same way we do for our guys who don't exist. The Bolivian documents are better than the originals."

I turned to Julie, kissed her cheek to wake her, stroked her hair, and whispered that I would not travel with them to Michigan.

"What?" Her eyes flared, wide awake.

"I'm not going with you. I need to take care of things here first."

"You need to take care of your family first. You told me we would get out of here if something serious happened. Well, it happened, and we're getting out of here."

"Yes, you and the children are, but I can't just yet."

"Don't split any damned semantic hairs with me Richard Blackstone! You know exactly what I'm talking about."

"Listen love…"

"Don't 'listen love' me right now, because I'm not in the mood for it. Damn it Richard, Raúl tried to kill all of us. Sean and Kathy are terrified, and so am I."

"I know you are, but I have to stay," I said, wiping the tears from her face. "You'll be safe in Michigan, and I have to make sure Raúl doesn't come after us again. It'll be only a few days."

"I swear you can be difficult sometimes. When will we see you?"

"Don't know sweetheart. I'll get out as soon as I can."

"There will be hell to pay if you don't." She jabbed my chest.

"I love you, Julie. I'll be there soon, and I promise you'll be safe."

53

"Boy, that didn't go very well yesterday, did it?" Jay Mansour asked as he drank a large mocha and looked dejectedly at his boss across the kitchen table in suburban Maryland.

"Quite frankly, Jay," Roger Harrington answered, "it went about as well as we could have expected. With our history, it's a minor miracle we even got in the door to explain what you've come up with on the nukes."

"Does that mean I should be thankful I got my audience in a five-star hotel suite?" Mansour asked sarcastically. As a NOC he could not be seen near a CIA installation, but he expected nothing more than a basic safe house.

"I'm not sure thankful is the right word, but I'll take what I can get. The suite was to make us think they were serious. The only reason they showed up was to cover their asses. They're not going to take any action based on what we told them. They consider this case closed."

"This shit all goes back to your time in Saudi and my paper for Rutledge, doesn't it?"

"I'm afraid so," Harrington said with disgust.

Roger Harrington and Jay Mansour had run headlong into CIA's risk-averse, politically correct bureaucracy. Harrington in particular, had waged a pitched battle inside CIA over the last decade. He was paying for it. As he saw organizational constipation set in, he fought to change attitudes, perceptions, and decisions. The perils facing America had been around for years, but no one paid much attention. CIA headquarters and their intelligence counterparts at the Department of State ignored the Islamic threat when field officers identified it in the 1980s. The danger went back to the Muslim Brotherhood founded in the 1920s to fight British colonial rule. Harrington marveled that no one saw the warning signs decades before. He considered both CIA and State professionally negligent.

As station chief in Islamabad, he openly criticized State Department officials who believed they could pressure the Taliban to hand over Osama bin Laden in exchange for diplomatic recognition. He was furious no one saw or admitted that Pakistan's Inter-Services Intelligence (ISI) covertly supported the Taliban. It was obvious what they were doing. Harrington's written communications to headquarters named and derided senior State Department officials who thought they could fight terrorists with diplomacy. They were dangerously out of touch. Harrington knew the only way to deal with the Taliban and bin Laden was to hunt them down and kill them. He told his superiors as much repeatedly. Headquarters saw Harrington as a fanatic who endangered U.S. diplomacy and operations overseas.

After three years in Islamabad, Harrington was recalled to CIA headquarters for an attitude adjustment desk assignment. Judged to be back in line after one year of being kept away from anything controversial, he was named Chief of Station in Riyadh. He spent more time in the streets than he did behind a desk. The high level of underground Islamic militant activity alarmed him. The royal family and Saudi intelligence discounted his concerns, but Harrington knew what he saw and heard. The radical clerics who in 1991 sent a "Letter of Demands" to King Fahd grew stronger and more active by the day. They wanted to topple what they perceived as anti-religious and corrupt governments around the world. Harrington believed the Saudis facilitated radical Islamists to preserve power.

He urged CIA to take the Saudis to task for their support of Islamists, to pressure them by denying them critical Middle East intelligence, and to have the Department of State quietly register displeasure. He received a phone call from Virginia that he was to "cease and desist" his behavior as it was "not conducive to productive international relations." After Pakistan, he was not seen as a "team player" and his e-mails from Saudi were hurting his career. Harrington put his boss on hold, and got up to pour a glass of scotch. He took his first sip, put his boss back on the line, and told him that they could screw themselves if being a "team player" meant selling out America's security. Harrington's response was too much for headquarters. He was a star, but they could not reign him in. They had only one choice. They promoted and isolated him. In late 2002, CIA named Harrington head of the Latin American Division and effectively exiled him from the Near East and Middle East locus of the war on terror. CIA headquarters believed they had closed the file on Roger Harrington.

Whereas Harrington hit a wall mid-career, Jay Mansour's problems started before he was even on CIA's payroll. His position paper for Senator Rutledge took on, among others, the White House, Congress, Pentagon, Department of State, Justice, and CIA. As a former SF operator he had intimate knowledge of military matters, and with Rutledge's connections he had unrestricted access to everyone in the government. Congressional oversight or special investigative committees touched on institutional problems but never blamed anyone. Formal hearings and commissions were nothing but ass-covering exercises. Journalists never asked public officials the tough questions because they feared being denied access to privileged information sources and leaks that fueled their columns. They were both caught up in incestuous relationships to keep their jobs. Jay Mansour identified problems, called for action, and named names.

The White House failed from the beginning by designating the FBI as the lead agency to pursue a legalistic approach that treated terrorists like common criminals. They promoted putting terrorists in jail as a victory even when Osama bin Laden said he feared no jail—only God. The Pentagon put together untenable covert action plans because they did not want the "dirty business" of hunting terrorists that were not worthy of facing a professional army. The State Department continued to coddle "friendly" nations that harbored terrorists. If anyone was to blame for September 11, it was Congress. They were publicity hounds who leaked confidential information to aggrandize themselves, had no concept of the threat, and no idea how to deal with it. While terrorists plotted, politicians posed for photo opportunities and pontificated at public hearings. Congress was responsible for CIA's becoming a risk-averse community. CIA itself did not escape criticism. The Counterterrorist Center never infiltrated an Islamist group and did not recognize the shift from state sponsors of terrorism to insurgent groups. It all came back to bite the U.S.

Everyone failed when it came to Osama bin Laden. OBL financed training camps in the Sudan and in 1995 put together a plot to kill the CIA Chief of Station in Kharthoum. CIA complained to the Sudanese government, and bin Laden backed off. The White House and Justice washed their hands saying there was not enough evidence to indict him. OBL left the Sudan unmolested. In 1995 he offered a million dollars for the assassination of Senator Hank Brown, scheduled to visit Afghanistan. The White House, State, Justice, and CIA sat on their hands and told Brown not to travel. The Director of Central Intelligence undercut paramilitary and covert programs to chase OBL asserting they were too risky. The U.S. had reason and opportunity to kill bin Laden many years ago, but did nothing.

Senator Rutledge ran with Mansour's report and confronted organizations and people. The assessments, the conclusions, and the names of the individuals responsible were on the mark. The people he named, especially those in Congress and at CIA, resented being exposed as incompetent. Rutledge was so senior that he suffered no repercussions. Mansour, however, was an easy target. Rutledge had enough political muscle for Mansour to keep his CIA job offer, but not the stroke to keep him from being in deep organizational trouble before he walked through the front door.

The Deputy Director of Operations personally kept Mansour away from the Middle East Division, the Osama Bin Laden Task Force, the Counterterrorist Center, and all terror-related issues. He isolated him within the organization with a non-official cover assignment in a remote location. Despite the disappointment, Mansour looked at the assignment as an opportunity. Harrington and Mansour were professional soul mates, and Harrington protected and nurtured his charge. Through a fortuitous twist of fate, CIA sentenced two of its most capable men to the same organizational perdition.

"Okay chief, what do we do now?" Mansour asked.

"Good question. Of the three people who heard us, two were against us and one was with us. The deputy directors hate our guts and won't lift a finger to help. The CTC head is our ally, but his vote doesn't count for much."

"Yeah, but we've got a serious problem."

"What we have is a serious but unsubstantiated allegation about transportable nuclear devices coming from a NOC at the top of the official exiles list. To top it off, your boss is not far behind you on that list."

"What have we got to do for them to act?"

"We need some no shit eyes-on actionable intelligence that forces their hand. Under any other circumstances, they would run full bore with what you have. We'll need to meet a far higher standard. We may never get there."

"Is there any way you can get SAS to help me out?" Mansour referred to the agency's Special Activities Staff, the covert paramilitary arm that put together specially designed Military Special Projects teams skilled in counter-terrorist hostage rescue operations, raids, and personnel and matériel snatches.

"They'd never approve it. Plus, they've cut our paramilitary capability so deep that there's not much we could do even if we wanted to. Everyone available is deployed to the Middle East."

"Can you pull any strings from your buddy at DIA to run some guys from the SSTs my way?" Mansour asked. The Defense Intelligence Agency had recently christened an operational wing to increase the Pentagon's intelligence capability. Top-level analysts formed Strategic Support Teams and worked closely with high-speed military units around the world.

"He'd love to help because he knows exactly what we're going through over here, but he's so overloaded with requests that he has no one to spare. Plus, they're analysts and you need boots on the ground."

"What if I have my own plan to get eyes-on? Can you get me the money?"

"Tell me what you're thinking."

"I've got a bunch of SF and SEAL buddies I deployed with who are doing private contract high risk security work. They've all been out less than a year, so they're up to speed on anything we can think of. I'd put a team together to visit Hassan Ali and follow the trail of those nukes. You get whatever eyes-on we come up with and run with it from there."

"How much do you think you'll need?" Harrington asked as he pulled out a notepad.

"Well, we need to pay them at least what they're getting now. I'd figure a team of ten operators at six hundred a day for thirty days. That puts personnel costs at $180,000. On top of that we'll need weapons, tactical gear, communications equipment, transport, living costs, and bribe money. Half a million, give or take, and we should be good to go."

"Tell you what I can do. I've got $740,000 left over in my budget for 'miscellaneous consulting and advisory projects.' It's yours. I'll get it down to some of your front companies."

"The sooner the better."

"Go get your laptop. Write up an Op Order and lay it all out. I'll let you handle the contract details. Make sure you have an ironclad confidentiality agreement. I want these guys to keep quiet for fifty years. If they don't, we hose them for eternity in court. I'll ruin their grandchildren if they even think of coming clean with a 'tell all' book about how they did contract paramilitary work for us. Got it?"

"Got it, boss."

"How soon can you put it together?"

"I'll have them on the ground in a week. How fast can you get the money to me?"

"Faster than that. You need to get cracking, Jay. If you can get something solid, I'll make so many waves they won't have any choice but to move."

"I'm out of here," Mansour said as he got up from the table and shook Harrington's hand. "Talk to you soon."

"Good luck. Do whatever it takes to get this done."

54

Because of Raúl's influence in La Paz, Denning told no one I survived the Saturday night attack. The first few days were probably the most dangerous, and Lucho offered to put me up at his house so I could keep a low profile. Denning offered as well, but Lucho's house, buried in a maze of El Alto structures, was the better choice. Denning lived across the street from the American School, and it would be too easy to spot me there. As soon as I settled my things in Lucho's workroom, I called Chris and told him about the attack on us the night before. "Chris, it had to be Raúl. Someone told him that I met with Simpson."

"Okay, who are the possible candidates?"

"You, Julie, Lucho, Gacki, Denning, the DEA, the FBI, and probably everyone at the embassy. The whole damned world knows!"

"Not exactly a secret, is it?"

"No it's not. But I have a plan."

"And that is?"

"Raúl thinks I'm dead, so he's not looking over his shoulder any more. I'm not going to let him walk away from this. I think I can find out who he's working with if I can get to his laptop."

"Why do you say that?"

"Raúl's technologically literate, but he's used to having people wait on him. His secretary does everything for him except his e-mail. That tells me there's more on that laptop than routine Phoenix business."

"You're probably right. Can you get to it, or do you need Hugh to help?"

"I think I can do it from here. I'll call you as soon as I'm done."

"Good luck, and let me know if you need anything."

I made a few notes while my laptop booted up, and then dialed Gustavo's cell phone. I needed his help, and it was time to trust my instinct.

"Gustavo, do not, I repeat, do not say my name," I said slowly. "Do you understand?"

"Yes. You're not dead?"

"Not yet. Are you where you can talk?"

"I'm on the Prado reading the paper. I talked to Raúl this morning and he said a car bomb killed you last night."

"Yeah, he wishes."

"What's going on?"

"I've got proof that Raúl is deep into some illegal crap, and it's much worse than the kickbacks we talked about. I think that's why he blew up my truck. I need your help."

"Raúl blew it up? Tell me what you need."

"This isn't a game. Raúl's nasty, and it could get ugly."

"I know, but I don't care."

I explained what we had to do. I then logged on the NetView web site and bought their WebMonitor3.0 with Chris's Visa, just in case someone was watching the activity on my card or Julie's. The software would record all Raúl's keystrokes, send me his incoming and outgoing e-mails, and tell me the web sites he visited. My next stop was the RemotePCMGR web site where I purchased RemotePCMGR7.0 so I could take over Raúl's laptop from mine.

Before downloading the programs, both sites required I certify that I owned the machine where I would place the software. I lied. They said information obtained through the packages might not be valid in court. That was interesting, but of no consequence to me. I was trying to save my life, not catch a cheating wife. With the software on my hard drive, I drafted an e-mail to Raúl using Gustavo's e-mail address. I asked Raúl to look at the referenced spreadsheet with power generation project analyses. My programs would install on Raúl's hard drive when he opened the attachment. Since there was no Internet intrusion, there were no filters, blockers, or firewalls to warn him. I hit Send, and the message and the attachment were on their way. Time to sit and wait.

55

"Gustavo, Raúl's logged on. Give him a few minutes and then go get him!" I said and hit the phone's Mute button.

"Will do," Gustavo said. He tied me into a three-way conference call and then dialed the U.S. Embassy. "Mr. Denning, are you there?"

"Standing by," Denning answered.

"Thanks. I'll go get Mr. Orellana."

Raúl thought about calling his new drug partners to discuss Blackstone's death, but an encrypted e-mail would be safer. He started to encrypt the note when a Latin American NewsAlert icon popped up on his screen. The lead story was about a terrorist attack on the main runway at the Guayaquil airport. Terrorists threw a half dozen mortar rounds at the runway and came within twenty-five yards of the control tower and twenty yards of two passenger airliners. The damage was minimal, but it terrified the tourists and worried government officials. Raúl clicked off the report. It would not affect his operations.

"Raúl, I've got a call for us in my office," Gustavo said from Raúl's doorway.

"I'm busy," Raúl answered dismissively, not looking up. "Have Carolina take the call for me."

"It's John Denning. I've got him on my speakerphone, and he needs to speak to us about Mr. Blackstone. He couldn't get through on your line."

"I'll be right there." Raúl picked up a notepad, looked at the unsent e-mail and decided to finish it when he got back. He might have more information to pass on after speaking to Denning. He turned on the screen saver and joined Gustavo in his office.

"Okay, Mr. Denning, we're all here," Gustavo said as he sat down at the small conference table.

"Hi, John, how are you?" Raúl opened.

"Doing well. I wanted to bring you both up to speed on Blackstone's death."

I knew that a call from Denning would get Raúl out of his office without turning off his computer. That would allow me to take over his machine while I listened to the conference call, and then release it when he returned to his office. I got to work as soon as Raúl started talking.

My first stop was Outlook Express. I forwarded his entire Inbox and Sent Items to Chris, Denning, Gustavo, and me in separate e-mails. I looked at a few individual messages, but toggled off when I realized I was burning precious time. By the time I opened the Word and PowerPoint files, Gustavo thanked Denning for his time. That was my cue to cut and run. I had been on almost fifteen minutes, though it seemed like thirty seconds.

Raúl opened his screen saver, pulled up his e-mail and hit Send. Denning told him nothing new. He forgot to encrypt the note and cursed. It was gone. No matter, Blackstone was dead. He next sent an e-mail to Steven Price about hiring a search firm to find Blackstone's replacement. Raúl reminded Price he would participate to make sure Phoenix hired the right person this time.

Price read Raúl's e-mail and was irritated that Phoenix had not budgeted the fee a headhunter would charge to find a regional CEO. He made a note to include it in next year's corporate plan. Price was almost done when his secretary buzzed.

"Mr. Price, General Carrasco is on the line, and Colonel Baldonado is here to see you."

"Who is here?" Price asked. Carrasco had given Price a ride to his hotel from the U.S. Embassy dinner party in Bogotá, but he had never heard of the colonel.

"Col. Baldonado works for General Carrasco. The general said it's extremely urgent, and it has to do with your recent trip to Bogotá."

"Show the colonel in and put the general on the line."

Price stood to receive Baldonado, invited him to sit down, and offered him something to drink. Baldonado accepted a glass of water. He opened his briefcase and removed a small tape cassette and a file folder. Price waited for his secretary to close the door before he picked up the phone. Price first met Carrasco when he was the Colombian military attaché in Washington six years earlier. Carrasco was a no-nonsense man, and a personal emissary meant exceptional circumstances.

"General, Col. Baldonado is here with me. My secretary says it's urgent."

"It is. The day after you left we found an audio tape of the attack on your car."

"How the hell did you manage that?"

"One of my investigators found it. Your driver and bodyguards worked for a private protection company here in Bogotá, and they wore throat microphones that recorded everything that happened that night."

"You have my undivided attention, general."

"Steven, Col. Baldonado and I are the only people who know about the tape. Protocol dictates that I turn it over to the CNP and the U.S. Embassy. I'm not going to do that and they don't know it exists. I value our friendship and fear for your safety. This is an extremely delicate matter, and you'll understand in a few minutes. Col. Baldonado has the tape and transcript."

"Tracey, could you please bring in your tape player?"

Price put the tape in the machine, hit Play, and opened the two page transcript. After light banter among Price's bodyguards and driver, there was a cacophony of explosions, small arms fire, screams, and groans. When the shooting stopped, voices appeared on the tape, presumably the attackers'. It was difficult to make out all the words, but Price matched the tape to the transcript. He thanked Carrasco and Baldonado after the tape ended and said he would be in touch. Price locked the tape and transcript in his office safe, and asked his secretary for a cup of coffee. He was shaken. It was not every day you heard the voices of those sent to kill you.

56

I looked through Raúl's electronic files and saw nothing of interest. He encrypted his e-mails and addressed them to ten-digit codes meaningless to me. I was certain I would find something, but found nothing. I started to slam my laptop shut when the system beeped with an activity report from Raúl's computer. I clicked on an unencrypted e-mail from Raúl to Agostini and Burgos. He boasted that he ordered Simpson's death and mine and that their operations were now in the clear. He did not reveal who leaked my meeting with Simpson. I was nevertheless ecstatic. Precursors were incriminating, but an admission of murder would be hard to beat.

"Hey, John," I said excitedly, "did you see Raúl's e-mail I just sent you?"

"Have not. I'm at the crash site and can't log on until late tonight or tomorrow. What does it say?"

"He tells Agostini and Burgos that he ordered the attacks on Simpson and on me. The prick even boasts about it."

"Outstanding! How'd you get it?"

"I took over his laptop remotely while he was talking to you and Gustavo."

"I wondered why Gustavo asked me to call his office instead of Raúl's. Now I know. Does it tell us who the leak was?"

"Zip on that. He encrypts his other e-mails and sends them to random number ten-digit addresses. Maybe your systems guys can figure it out."

"Encryption is tough, but we'll jump on it. With enough time they might get something."

"I'm not sure we have much time. Is the e-mail enough to bring him in?"

"Not by itself."

"What do you mean?" I shouted. "I just told you what it says!"

"Take it easy and listen to me. You know it's not enough to arrest him."

"No, I don't know. Explain it to me."

"A lot of people, including the FBI, have to see that e-mail. We don't have an FBI office here, but the FBI Legal Attaché at the embassy in Santiago covers Bolivia. He's already in La Paz working on Simpson's plane crash. He'll pass it on to the FBI and State in D.C., and they'll develop an action plan. Once that's done, they'll have to talk to the Bolivian government before they actually lay hands on Raúl. This will take a while. I'd love to string him up right now, but this is so big it's out of my control. There is only so much I can do on my own."

"Yeah I know," I said. "How long?"

"Raúl's so high profile, at least a week or two."

"Do you think this might get shut down?"

"No way. He killed a senior U.S. federal law enforcement official and tried to kill you. At the same time, he's well regarded and powerful. We'll get him, but we have to line up our ducks."

"Wonderful. If Raúl and his people find out I'm not dead, they'll come after me again."

"I doubt it. The embassy still considers you officially dead until we resolve this mess. The e-mail is a start, but we have to flush everyone else out. You need to keep your head down a bit longer."

"Yeah, but I wanted to drive a stake through his heart right now."

"Trust me, you're not the only one."

I went to Lucho's refrigerator, grabbed a beer, and sat down at his kitchen table. I was angry and frustrated. Denning was a good guy. He was doing his job, but rules and regulations bound him. Despite understanding that, I was crushed. My job was to protect my family, and I felt as though I had failed. I had given one last good faith effort to get Raúl through the normal channels, and that went nowhere. I stood, stretched, and hoped a shower would make me feel better.

I splashed water on my face and shaved while the shower water got hot. I looked in the mirror and wondered who I saw. After forty your body takes a hit no matter how well you eat, how much you sleep, how far you run, or how many weights you lift. I did all the right things and still felt old. I was tired. It had nothing to do with my body. It was my aging soul. I felt as though everything had been beaten out of me. I had played the corporate game for years. I went to the right schools, joined the right companies, and took the right jobs. Everything was a springboard to the next level. It was a constant game to get "there", and I had no idea where "there" was. I was not sure anyone knew. This had to end.

The hot shower gave me the time and space I needed to think and plot a course of action. It was finally clear. Trusting law enforcement to get Raúl had distracted me, and I finally understood it would never happen. Raúl's power and influence guaranteed that he would never be held accountable. He would come after me and my family until he got us. All the precautions in the world would not protect us against a motivated, resourceful, and patient bad guy. Time was on his side, not mine. Surprise, however, was on my side. Law enforcement wanted to prosecute Raúl. I wanted to kill him. Only I could resolve that fundamental inconsistency.

"Lucho, where are you?" I asked on the sat phone.

"At the Mitsubishi garage in El Alto. I'm getting a part for one of the cars."

"I need you to pick up a few things for me and bring them by your house as soon as you can."

"Of course, Don Richard. Tell me what you need."

"That's all Lucho," I said after I read the list.

"I can get everything near my house. I'll be home in an hour."

I had just taken a large mixing container outside when Lucho pulled into the garage. He came out to the backyard with all the items I asked for. I pulled everything out of two boxes, laid them out on the table, and took an inventory to get organized.

I drew in a deep breath and exhaled slowly. I was not crazy about this stuff, but it was the best option I could think of. The key was to go slowly, pay attention to details, and watch the fumes. I grabbed the eight inch plastic pipe and coated the threads on one end with sealing epoxy, screwed the cap on tight, coated the outside, and waited for it to dry to a watertight seal. My hands were clammy as I drilled a small hole in the top of the other cap, ran a fuse through it, and sealed it in place. Measuring and mixing two parts ammonium nitrate and one part anhydrous hydrazine was next, and I poured the clear liquid from the container into the pipe. I coated the top threads, screwed the cap on, and sealed the outside to make sure the entire vessel was waterproof. Time to go to town.

57

Jay Mansour came up cold after several weeks of trying to track the sale of black market nukes. He knew they were there, he just could not find them. The best sources were Hassan Ali and his son Rahim. Mansour was after them. They disappeared for a couple of weeks, but were returning to Ciudad del Este within the next forty-eight hours. Mansour put together a team of ten contract security specialists who had recently completed private high risk protection work in Latin America. They all knew and trusted each other. There were six former SF operators, three SEALs, and one Force Recon Marine. None was a medic or corpsman, but all had Wilderness EMTs as well as training in edged weapons, gunshot, and explosive blast trauma care. They had been on direct action teams, deployed operationally in Latin America, and spoke Spanish or Portuguese, or both. Seamlessly changing from an Armani suit to fatigues and back to khakis and a blazer was second nature. Each knew his way around the best hotels, the darkest dives, knew how to fit in, and had a real knack for finding bad guys.

Mansour brought seven to Ciudad del Este on a chartered Learjet and the other three on commercial flights. To avoid complications, they traveled without gear or weapons. Mansour had a full load-out kit for each operator—ten thousand dollars cash in expense and bribe money, untraceable credit cards, passports and local IDs for multiple countries, handheld GPS, laptop with integrated GPS, cell phone, sat phone, two-way radio, electronic and video surveillance equipment, soft body armor, ceramic plates and carrier, night vision monocular, binoculars, emergency medical kit, a hand-held radiological detection device, flex cuffs, chem lights, a Beretta 92G 9mm pistol, a Sterling 9mm submachine gun, and ammunition. The specialists loved their M-4s, but the Sterling folded easily into a backpack and used the same ammunition as the pistols. One less detail to worry about.

They checked their gear soon after arrival, reviewed diagrams of Ali's compound, and planned and rehearsed the operation. Mansour and the team raided the complex at 4:05 A.M. the day after Ali's return, but they were a step late. Four bodyguards, two drivers, two cooks, and three maids were dead from multiple gunshot wounds. Hassan and Rahim were slumped in back porch lawn chairs, their throats cut. Mansour was certain that the people who bought the nukes killed them to cover their trail. The team searched Ali's known warehouses and storage facilities over the next three days but found nothing—until they got to a warehouse Mansour thought Ali sold a year before.

At the back of the warehouse they found the outlines of two large rectangular boxes in an area that had been cleared recently. *Trunks*, Mansour thought. Discarded next to the far wall were two plastic tarps that set off their radiological detectors. He packed the tarps, plus a legal pad with Arabic notes found in an office drawer, and sent them to the U.S. for analysis. Mansour then deployed five two-man teams to Argentina, Brazil, and Uruguay to see if they could pick up the trail of the nukes. He e-mailed Roger Harrington, describing the radiological signatures in the warehouse. Harrington was encouraged, but said they needed "more hard data and eyes-on confirmation."

With the Hassan Ali capture option literally dead, Mansour

had to change gears. He needed the reams of analytical data and the sharp minds in the Directorate of Intelligence, but they were not working the nukes. Even if they were, they would never share information with an exile. He thrived being on his own, but wished he could tap that pipeline. The National Counterterrorism Center had been established by intelligence reform legislation, but they could get no active agencies to release any of their good people. The National Counterproliferation Center was a more recent creation to coordinate intelligence analysis on nuclear, biological, and chemical weapons, but the organizations previously working these issues were reluctant to turn over their influence, files, data, and reports to a new entity. The bureaucrats were fighting each other and rearranging the furniture while he was fighting bad guys.

Mansour used the tools he had. With a series of cover usernames and logon IDs, he checked for leads at the Department of State Tip-Off system, the database that converted all-source intelligence about known and suspected terrorists into unclassified watch lists used by consular offices around the world for vetting visa applications. After an hour with no results, he logged off the system disgusted. The people he was looking for were too smart to show up there. Next he looked through the system updates related to Simpson's death. There was little except some guarded speculation that the FARC was involved. He paged through several documents and moved on.

Logging on to CIA's InterSource Registry, Mansour checked to see if there were any human intelligence sources in the region that he did not know. A quick scan of the list revealed that he had already contacted everyone of value. His next stop was the Defense Intelligence Agency J2X system that registered sources the Pentagon uses for military purposes. He gave up after several invalid logon attempts, swearing under his breath that interagency cooperation was not working as envisioned.

Even the CIA Counterterrorist Center gave him no leads. The Center had no overseas stations and relied on the Directorate of Operations' offices. That meant information did not reach headquarters if a country report officer considered it unimportant. Since the Center could not coordinate information or data requirements from the report officers, what came through the system was inconsistent. Mansour found nothing.

The FBI databases were equally useless. They relied on legal attachés for information, and their priorities were different. They tracked lawbreakers, whereas CIA broke laws to find the bad guys. There was no consistent field reporting to give him leads. Everywhere Mansour looked there were gaps he could not bridge, places where fanatics with a grudge against the U.S. could hide and work.

He finally tried the U.S. embassies in the region. It was information not normally available to a NOC, but Mansour had the street-smarts to request full access when he was assigned to Ciudad del Este. Roger Harrington had the foresight to approve it. Mansour logged on to each embassy through a CIA facility tied directly to the State Department computers. He looked at the regional security reports, terror cautions, and any unusual activity reported to the embassy. Working his way down the list of countries from highest to lowest risk, he scrolled through everything from detailed risk analyses to travel cautions about not wearing an expensive watch on the street. His eyes froze on a report filed a week earlier with the embassy in Buenos Aires.

Titled "Colombians at Libyan Embassy," the report was from an unidentified source that saw "out of place" Colombians visiting the Libyan embassy in Buenos Aires early one morning. The American embassy staffer tagged the sighting "low priority/risk" and said it merited no follow-up. Mansour's instinct said otherwise. The reference to an "unidentified source" made him believe a NOC filed the report, and there was only one way to find out. He called Harrington.

"Roger, there's a report from Buenos Aires about some suspicious Colombians at the Libyan embassy. I'd like to talk to whoever called it in."

"I think this is where I say I have no clue what you're talking about," Harrington chuckled.

"And this is where I say it's too important to play games. It has to be another NOC, and you're the only guy who can tell me who it is."

"It's your running buddy Eric Bridges, and he just got back from a trip if you want to call him. It's about time you shared information."

"Thanks."

Eric Bridges was an American expatriate oil and gas executive who lived in Buenos Aires. Mansour was exiled to Latin America as a NOC, but Bridges chose it. A number of years ago, he had asked to meet privately with the U.S. Embassy Political Attaché in Buenos Aires. He offered his services to CIA as a walk in. Expatriate executives around the world often volunteered their services to CIA. Neither cranks nor thrill seekers, they were well traveled, spoke languages fluently, blended in, and wanted to serve their country. Eric Bridges was one of them. His world was a surreal multi-level existence where he dealt daily with legitimate and corrupt business, political, and military leaders, as well as drug dealers, arms traffickers, and money launderers. He was a chameleon who changed colors depending on the circumstance and had the temperament, training, and ability to work alone. Frequently in exceptionally delicate and dangerous situations, he could not count on diplomatic or agency help if things went south.

Bridges had lived in Buenos Aires for nine years and recently bought a 6,500 acre ranch several hours outside of the city. Argentines kept late hours, and Bridges fit right in. Mansour never understood how he managed to eat all that beef, stay up all hours, and still get up early to run. They met for the second time five years ago in Colombia when Bridges worked an oil and gas deal and Mansour was assigned to the Embassy on temporary duty. The first time they met was when Bridges interviewed Mansour during his senior year at Kentucky. Mansour never suspected Bridges was anything other than an oil and gas consultant, but noticed that he seemed to pop up where unusual things happened.

"Eric, it's Jay. How's it going?"

"Well, well," Bridges answered, "I don't suppose you're calling to accept my invitation to get out of that dump of a city you live in to spend some time with good wine and beautiful women in Buenos Aires, are you?"

"Not yet," Mansour laughed. "Thanks for the invite though. I'm still recovering from that weekend at your ranch. I've been swamped, but I'll take you up on it as soon as I break free. Been traveling much?"

"A bit. Was in Colombia and Peru this week and got in this morning from Lima on that damned overnighter. I feel like dog meat. I didn't run all week, so I'll try to make up for it tomorrow."

"I still don't see how you do it. Why not find something fun?"

"Makes me feel good. Anyway, what are you up to these days?"

"Not much, but it's something you've been up to that I want to talk about. You reported some Colombians at the Libyan embassy in Buenos Aires. That's all the log shows. Is there more to the story?"

"Well, my friend," Bridges said slowly, "that's an interesting question to ask. Only one person could have told you to call me."

"I just spoke to Roger Harrington."

"Ha! I guess that means you're doing a lot more in Ciudad del Este than buying and selling washing machines." Bridges laughed. "Why am I not surprised?"

"Just like those oil and gas deals that put you in some strange places."

"Hey, it's not my fault that interesting shit happens in some real garden spots. Anyway, you know the route I run around Belgrano, right?"

"The same one we ran the last time I was there?"

"That's it. I was done around 6:30 A.M., so I walked my normal cool-down by the Libyan embassy. For the first time in years the lights were on, the gate was open, and some Libyans were saying goodbye to a couple of guys on the front porch. It was the usual "glad you came" stuff. I started to blow it off, but these guys weren't diplomats. They looked like they should have web gear on, and their accents were Colombian."

"Keep going."

"I was interested, so I stalled a couple of minutes off to the side to screw around with my shoes. I run that route so much the cop asked if I needed help. I looked up and saw three Colombians piling into an SUV, and another guy was lagging behind. Jay, the last guy was Alberto Maure."

"Alberto Maure of the FARC? Are you sure?"

"Positive."

"What the hell was he doing there?"

"That's what I wanted to know, so I walked around the block to listen a bit more without being too obvious. By the time I got back, the Colombians were gone and the Libyans were loading a van. They were bitching about the heat and humidity in Houston and New Orleans. One guy said he gets seasick and wanted to fly. They're planning a trip to the Gulf Coast soon. It smelled bad to me, so I called it in."

"What did the embassy say?"

"Nothing. I had a plane to catch, so I headed out. My guess is that no one has thought about it since."

"They tagged your report for no follow-up."

"Figures. There are days I wonder why I still keep my eyes and ears open. Does this tie to something you're chasing?"

"I'm not certain, but it might. Are you going to be around for a while?"

"Looks that way. I don't travel for another couple of weeks, so call whenever you want. If you manage to get down here, I've got plenty of cold brews in the fridge."

"Thanks, guy. Later."

Before he turned in, Mansour contacted his teams and told them to concentrate on anything pointing to the Gulf Coast. He hoped Bridges's knack for finding trouble in unusual places would pay off.

58

I returned to Lucho's house by mid afternoon while he stayed at the office for an employee security meeting. He would return home by dinner to get ready for the 10:00 P.M. final game of the La Paz corporate futsal league. Futsal was soccer on a basketball court with a smaller, heavier ball, and six players on a side. The Phoenix team was facing a local law office, and both Gustavo and Lucho would play. Futsal was more than just a game for employees; it was a social affair for families. Unlike U.S. leagues, this was not segregated by socio-economic level. Lawyers and engineers played with waiters, drivers, and shoe shine boys. Even dead, I would not miss it.

Wanting to relax before cleaning up for the game, I grabbed a beer and a bag of chips to watch the tube. Several minutes of Latin American soap operas turned into several hours of channel surfing. I was relieving myself of yet another beer when my phone rang. Since I was supposed to be dead, I hesitated as the screen flashed "unknown caller". It went to Voice Mail, but they left no message. It rang again. I went to the kitchen, opened another beer, hit the Answer button, and hoped the caller would announce himself.

"Richard," Denning said, sounding out of breath, "you there?"

"Yeah John, sorry. I didn't recognize the number, so I didn't pick up."

"Shit, my bad. I'm borrowing a search and rescue guy's phone. I've got some news."

"What's going on?"

"You're not going to believe what happened this afternoon."

"Nothing surprises me any more. Try me."

"Raúl's BMW blew up in the Phoenix garage."

"Outstanding! What happened?"

"Someone tied an Astrolite G pipe bomb into the gas tank and wired it to go off when Raúl started the engine. The force blew the car into the ceiling. This was a professional job. They knew that today was the one day of the week Raúl drives himself to work instead of coming in a company SUV with a driver. He had his car washed in the garage and the crew left it unattended with the alarm off most of the afternoon. Whoever did this knew exactly when to hit him."

"Couldn't happen to a nicer guy." I wanted to shout for joy.

"No kidding. It was almost perfect."

"What do you mean 'almost'?"

"They missed."

"What?" I spit beer onto the kitchen window.

"Yep, Raúl's alive and well."

"How did the prick survive?"

"He installed a remote starter a couple of days ago and cranked the engine from sixty-five feet. Except for that, he'd be toast."

"Damn. Too bad they didn't have better information."

"Yeah, but it was pretty damn good anyway. They managed to slip into the garage when the extra security guard headed out to help one of your drivers tow in a Phoenix SUV that broke down a few blocks from the office."

"Well, now you guys have something else to investigate. No

rest for the weary."

"This is getting ridiculous," Denning said. "I've really got to go. I'll call you later if I hear anything else."

"Thanks for the update, John."

I missed! I threw the beer bottle against the wall and looked for something else to throw. The bastard survived! I wanted to scream. I didn't think about a remote starter. I cursed everything and everyone, my bad luck, and BMW engineers. I tried to think of another plan, but was stuck. I wanted another shot at Raúl, but that would have to wait. I was committed to cheer for the Phoenix team in two hours.

The night was cool, so I zipped my vest closed and pulled my hat over my ears. Lucho dropped me off four blocks from the court and drove on by himself. The court was on the edge of a working class neighborhood near downtown La Paz. The houses were modest, each surrounded by eight foot walls. The entire area was a maze of narrow and poorly lit streets that let me approach unnoticed.

The court was on a small promontory that seemed to float over the city. A twenty foot high chicken wire fence covered its opposite length and the areas behind each goal. The concrete bleachers ran along the near side of the court and adjoined a badly lit partially paved parking lot. There was room for several dozen cars, but I did not expect many as most fans would come in public transportation.

The stands were built into the hill, and the top row put me almost level with the parking lot. My vantage point gave me a good view of the court, the parking lot, and the two narrow side streets that turned into it. I stayed alert, scanning all around every few minutes. Raúl was the least of my worries as he had told me that attending such events was beneath him. His many associates, however, concerned me.

Four hundred spectators filled the bleachers, all of them friends or family of the players. I settled in with Lucho's family, in the middle of the top row, and they pushed coffee my way. It was cold, and I longed for a heavy coat and gloves. The game started inauspiciously as the other team scored on a breakaway when Lucho slipped. They scored again on a dubious penalty, and our fans told everyone in La Paz about the referee's close and extended family, especially his relationship with his mother.

We scored two quick goals to tie the game at the half. The team came to the side for water, a quick talk with the coach, and was back playing in ten minutes. With one minute left, we led four to two, and our fans chanted and shot fireworks.

Despite the noise and flashes, a pair of headlights to my left caught my eye. I turned and saw an SUV back up to the parking lot wall thirty-five yards away. A man came out the driver's side and went to the stairs at the far end of the court. I could not see who it was because of the crowd. He walked onto the court and spoke to Gustavo for less than a minute. They climbed the stairs together, crossed the parking lot, and walked towards the SUV.

My heart pounded, and instinct told me something was wrong. I stood up and fell in behind them. I pressed myself against the wall deep into the shadows and quietly closed the distance. When they were ten feet from the car, a man emerged from the front passenger side pointing a pistol at Gustavo. It was Raúl! He jabbed the pistol into Gustavo's chest, pushed him toward the car, and pistol whipped his face. I had no clue why Raúl would go after Gustavo, but that intellectual exercise was pointless. I had to move.

I reached for my pistol and got a handful of bad grip. The gun was hung up on the inside of my fleece vest, and there was no way to get it free before Raúl shot me. I sprinted forward and shouted at Gustavo to run. Raúl swung the gun away from Gustavo and turned to face me. My hand ran past my pistol and found my folding knife. Even in the dim light, the muzzle of Raúl's pistol seemed enormous. I fought the urge to lock on the gun and forced myself to look at Raúl. My eyes and ears expected a flash and a bang, but nothing happened. Raúl swore. He looked down at his pistol. The safety! The idiot forgot to flip off the safety!

Despite the crowd noise and fireworks, I heard my blade click as it locked in place. I clamped Raúl's gun hand and slammed him against the car. His feet slipped, and I drove the knife straight down into his neck over his left collarbone. I pushed the blade hard out to the right so the serrated edge could cut and tear as much as possible. Blood sprayed me like an over-pressured fire hydrant. He went limp and slumped against the car.

The other man slammed the driver side door, started the engine, and roared off. Raúl was on his back, gurgling and convulsing, blood pouring from the wound. He was still alive, but not for long. I stood over him so he could see the satisfaction on my face. He looked up, tried to say something, and gave me the finger. I spat on him. "No, che, this time it's screw you." The bastard was suffering. Wonderful. Gustavo lay unconscious on the ground several feet away with a deep laceration across his left cheek. I checked his pulse and covered him with my vest.

I called Denning and told him what happened. I wanted to get out of here, but I needed help with Gustavo. Thankfully, no one walked through the parking lot in the twenty minutes Denning took to arrive.

"What happened to you?" Denning asked when he saw blood all over me.

"You might want to ask what happened to Raúl. I left him in a pool of blood over there, deader than a doornail. Did you see a blue SUV when you came in?"

"No. Why?"

"Raúl's partner was driving it. If we find that car, we'll find our leak."

"Did you get a look at him?"

"It was too dark to see his face. Gustavo talked to him, but he's out cold. Probably has a concussion. We need to get him to a doctor."

"Why would Raúl go after Gustavo?"

"I don't have a clue," I said, "but we'll get an answer if we find that driver."

Lucho came over to see if were okay and was impassive when he saw Raúl. We had to decide what to do with the body and whether to report his death. We left him where he was. Someone else could sort it out. Finding Raúl's partner was more important. I left Raúl's gun, but took his cell phone out of his coat pocket. It might give us a lead. We piled into Denning's Explorer and headed off to get medical help for Gustavo. Denning's phone rang, and he hung up in seconds.

"Guys, we're headed to Gordo's. We've got Raúl's partner!"

59

Gordo's Bar & Restaurant, tucked away on downtown side street, was a favorite expatriate community hangout. It was a public place, not the best choice for a discreet meeting, but it was what we had. The embassy doctor said Gustavo would be fine in a day or two. He was still so disoriented he could not recall who spoke to him on the futsal court. We would know soon enough, and we left him in Lucho's care.

Denning parked his Explorer around the corner from the restaurant, and we hustled to get inside. We had no idea if Raúl's partner was already there, so I walked around to the delivery area while Denning went in the front. He found the place mostly empty, and went straight to the rear to let me in through the back door. I locked it behind me and checked the toilets while Denning prepped his pistol and flex cuffs and then sat at a table. He did not have local arrest authority, but that was no longer a concern. We would take Raúl's partner in regardless of the consequences. From my position in the rear hallway, I could see Denning and the front door.

I unholstered my pistol and kept it out. The next few minutes were torture. At first I was bored and could not wait for it to be over. My heart raced as I realized what we were doing, and I wiped my hands on my pants. I took several deep breaths and held them to slow my pulse. My heart still pounded. Sweat ran inside my shirt even though it was 65F and dry. My hands were clammy, and I wiped them on my pants again. A nervous habit. I checked my gun one more time. Another habit. I had to take a leak.

After an eternal five minutes he walked through the front door. I didn't believe Denning when he told me who called, and I still did not believe it when I saw him.

"John, we've got a serious problem with Blackstone," he said, sitting down across from Denning. "He just killed Raúl."

"That's absurd," Denning answered. "Blackstone's dead."

"He's not. He stabbed Raúl an hour ago at a futsal game. I was there."

"Why didn't you do something?"

"We can cover that later. We need to bring Blackstone in."

"Why should we? It's a local police matter. Plus, we don't have the authority to arrest anyone."

"John, do you have any clue the repercussions this will have? Blackstone killed one of the highest placed men in the country."

"So what? Blackstone is a private citizen, and bad things happen to private citizens now and then. Raúl was a civilian too. It's not our problem."

"There will be some very unhappy people, and we'll be toast if we don't do something."

"So be it, Felipe. Look, we'll notify the local authorities, and that's the end of it for us."

"Not for me, John. If you won't help me finish this, I'll do it myself," Torres said as he got up.

I had my pistol raised with a good sight picture on Torres's upper chest, but there was something very wrong about training a weapon on a U.S. federal agent. Killing Raúl was liberating, but this made me nervous. Torres was not supposed to be the bad guy. His shoulder holster bulged underneath his jacket. Would he go after

Denning? No matter how fast he moved, Torres could not pull his pistol before I shot him. Even so, I took no chances. I stepped out and told Torres to put his hands up. He stumbled back against his chair when he saw me.

"Stop, Felipe!" Denning stood up and grabbed Torres's arm. "We know you were with Raúl at the futsal game. It's over."

"No, it's not John. I'm going to take care of this."

"You're not going to do anything. Give me your gun."

"No!" Torres pushed Denning away and reached inside his jacket.

Denning collapsed on top of him as Torres pulled the pistol from his holster. They fought for the gun and Denning pushed Torres across the room and through the plate glass window twenty feet from the table. It was a simple case of a larger mass moving a smaller one. Torres lost and went through the glass on his back. He cranked off a round as he fell fifteen feet to the concrete delivery area below. It was over as quickly as it had started. Torres landed head first and was a mess. I ran down the side exit stairs to the street to make sure he was down and stayed down. I got no pulse and his chest did not move. I waited another couple of minutes before I was convinced he was dead. Denning joined me outside and said that embassy security and DEA guys were on their way. One more bad guy was dead, but we would have to explain this one.

60

With little information and a lot of guesses, Jay Mansour was alone in Ciudad del Este, trying to work one of the toughest problems in the world. He had no illusions that he was Superman, but did have the advantage of being on the ground, knowing the territory, and understanding how the bad guys thought. He also had the advantage of direct contact with what polite society would call "unsavory characters". No software or database could substitute for that experience, since many of those unsavory characters determined whether people woke up to a civilized world each day.

He sent his contract paramilitary teams to ports in Argentina, Brazil, Chile, and Uruguay, looking for leads on the nukes and vessels headed to the U.S. Gulf Coast. They had yet to find anything substantive, but were running hard and turning over every stone. Mansour spoke to them every two hours and relayed pertinent information to Roger Harrington, knowing that old fashioned intelligence gathering would pay off.

His fingers skipped across the keyboard while he drained a Brahma and devoured Twix bars. He brought up databases listing U.S. Gulf Coast population density, manufacturing facilities, refining and chemical plants, tourist attractions, scientific and research facilities, dams, bridges, power stations, sports facilities, airports, and government buildings. An attack could be directed at a single target, but could also go after several in close proximity. He selected a database of vessels scheduled to dock along the Gulf Coast within the next thirty days. He shook his head when he found hundreds, and felt even worse when he realized he had no fix on unscheduled or unknown calls.

Mansour sorted a database of visa applications granted to Latin Americans within the last three years. He searched Argentina first because of its notorious corruption, Paraguay next due to extensive illicit activity, Uruguay because of the ease of through-transit, and then Chile because they got U.S. visas easier than other Latin Americans. He needed to see who might slip through. After several hours, he had a list of forty-one people he considered high risk. He passed the names to contacts that would ensure those on the list received a visit from internal security forces within forty-eight hours.

The number of possible targets was a nightmare. The most probable Gulf Coast targets were Houston and New Orleans. Houston had the Astrodome, the airport, the medical center, Rice University and the University of Houston, the port, the NASA Space Center, and dozens of power plants, bridges, chemical plants, and refineries. New Orleans had the Superdome, the airport, Tulane, the port, and too many bridges, power plants, chemical plants, and refineries to list. Hitting any of them would do extensive damage and cause panic. Mansour got up to stretch and counted four Brahmas and two bags of Twix bars left in the fridge. He knew that would not be enough. He also knew he needed to bounce ideas off someone.

"Eric," Mansour said, "my cheat sheet tells me this is your secure phone."

"Correctomundo guy, just like it was the last time you called," Bridges said as he turned off the television in his Buenos Aires apartment. "If you keep calling me in the middle of the night I'm going to think you like me. We've got to stop meeting like this."

"Thanks, dickhead. I need some help."

"Will this take a minute or an hour? If this is going to be a marathon, I need to get a brew."

"Get it. I'll hang."

"Brew's in hand. Shoot."

"I've been going nuts since we talked about the Libyans at the Colombian embassy and the possibility of nukes. I'm looking at a ton of data on likely Gulf Coast targets, and I'm about to lose my mind."

"Kind of scary, isn't it? That's what it means to be a superpower with an open society. Tell me what you've got."

"That's it," Mansour said after a fifteen minute monologue detailing the reams of data he had, "and I have a lot of theories, none necessarily better than any other."

"Okay. You tell me what you think, and I'll play devil's advocate."

"It's fall," Mansour started, "and we've got football every weekend. It would make a hell of an impact to take out 65,000 people on national TV."

"Yeah, pretty frightening, but I don't think that would be first on the list."

"Why not?"

"First, there's a novel about a nuke attack on a sporting event, and I think they're more creative than that. It would take out a bunch of people at the game and wipe out a chunk of downtown, but it wouldn't have much follow-on effect or economic impact. What's next on your list?"

"The universities—Rice, University of Houston, Tulane."

"That would scare students and parents, but it's not a big deal. Forget it."

"Okay, how about power plants?"

"Now you're talking. The disruption value is decent, but not terminal. The scare factor is pretty good, especially if it's nuclear."

"Why isn't it terminal?"

"The power grids are interconnected so one picks up the slack when another goes down. That's why it's not terminal, but things don't always work the way they're supposed to. The system may crash anyway. That's a pretty good target. Next."

"Airports. Houston and New Orleans have big international airports."

"Even better. First, you kill a bunch of people and freak out millions of road warriors. Second, the follow-on effect is huge. People all over the country will stop flying, and the fear and paranoia would be almost impossible to overcome. Plus, you shut down those airports for at least a year or so. The authorities would lock down every airport in the country for a while. Hell, they sound the alarms if an old lady farts going through security. That one would be high on my list. What else do you have?"

"NASA and the Houston medical center."

"Forget it. One time only, minor disruption, minor scare. Not a big deal. What else?"

"The port facilities in Houston and New Orleans are some of the biggest in the world."

"That one really bothers me," Bridges said. "A lot of people would die. It's not as spectacular as an airport or a football stadium, but the property damage would be immense and the economic impact huge."

"Not to mention locking down other ports, not just on the Gulf Coast."

"You now have two candidates. Keep going."

"There are hundreds of chemical plants in the area."

"Don't waste your time," Bridges answered immediately.

"Why?"

"You answered your own question. There are so many that no single plant has much impact. Even if they took out several, it causes only a local effect. It's not big enough. If they can create a chain effect, though, that's different."

"There are dozens of oil refineries in Houston, New Orleans, and upstream in Baton Rouge."

"Yeah, I know," Bridges said, "I've been to a bunch of them. This one's bad. Refined products drive the economy. An attack on a refinery shuts down not only other ports but also other refineries."

"How about the Strategic Petroleum Reserve?"

"The SPR only helps in small short-term emergencies. This is too big. Forget it."

"Looks like I've got a third target."

"I'd say so. I wouldn't waste my time worrying about crap like bridges, government buildings, or national monuments. With airports, port facilities, and refineries, you have a serious problem."

"You're a master of understatement. This is like a huge black hole."

"You'll also have to figure out how they might get a weapon to the target. Care for a thought?"

"It's late. I'll take all the thoughts I can get."

"They'll want to handle the weapon as little as possible and avoid U.S. Customs completely if they can. That's the path of least resistance."

"That means they'll go after a port. They can handle it on the water and detonate from the vessel. Getting to an airport is tougher."

"Not necessarily. They could fly it in a cargo plane and detonate it in the air or on the ground before customs ever sees it. They may already have the weapons inside the U.S. If so, you're not quite hosed but almost. But don't forget they said they wished they could fly. For my money that tells me they're on the water."

"Damn, they could be just about anywhere. I hope they're still down here dicking around."

"Me too. Anything else you need?"

"Yeah, a crystal ball."

"Do you have enough beer and Twix to keep going?"

"I hope so, but my supply's dwindling fast. Thanks again guy. I'll be in touch."

61

The U.S. and Bolivian authorities determined that Denning's role in Torres's death was self-defense. Torres went for his pistol, and Denning feared for his life. I stayed in La Paz several days while the police interviewed me about the struggle at Gordo's. The legal process was complicated because Torres was born in Santa Cruz of a Bolivian father and a Bolivian-American mother. There was a brief pissing contest over who would handle the case, but the outcome was never in doubt. The mystery was why Torres went bad.

Bolivian authorities found Raúl's body the morning after the futsal game, and police could not explain the circumstances of his death. No one saw him at the game, and his presence in a rough part of town was unusual. Police concluded that Raúl was the victim of a kidnap or robbery attempt by "violent subversives" and was killed where he was found. Authorities still had no idea who bombed his car in the Phoenix garage. Denning had not yet disclosed that I killed Raúl, as he was afraid that doing so would put me in grave danger.

The FBI and DEA analyzed Raúl's e-mails for clues, but came up dry since he encrypted all communications except one. The lone exception to Agostini and Burgos revealed that he headed an illicit drug organization that killed Simpson and ordered the hit on me. It implicated no one else. The photographs of Raúl at the Trinidad airport were not enough to detain Oscar Dávila. Gustavo confirmed that Torres took him from the futsal court and that he was targeted because his initials were on the wire transfer sheets showing payments to Sendero and FARC front organizations. Raúl saw Gustavo as the remaining weak link to be taken out. The FBI arrived in force and picked up the search for a voice tape of Raúl to compare to the NSA tape of the sat phone call that mentioned Simpson's name. They also searched for Raúl's cell phone.

The investigations were in full swing when a phone call to the embassy brought everything to a halt. An anonymous caller said he had information about a large cocaine shipment to the U.S. on a plane owned by Raúl's aviation company. He offered to deliver the entire transaction and details of Raúl's operations if the U.S. government would drop a federal weapons charge against him. What one week earlier would have been considered a crank call turned serious when the caller offered details about Raúl's meeting in Trinidad with Dávila, Agostini, and Burgos.

After a brief negotiation, the ATF director agreed to drop the charges. The source said that within two weeks a Boeing Business Jet would depart La Paz for Atlanta's Hartsfield-Jackson airport carrying five DEA agents and 2,170 pounds of cocaine. The agents on board had no idea they were transporting illegal cargo. Since it was a DEA flight, U.S. Customs would not inspect the contents. Authorities were ecstatic because taking the plane down in Atlanta would establish links in Raúl's operations on both sides of the transaction.

Torres's illicit involvement with drugs threw a dark cloud over the La Paz DEA office. Close examination of his personal effects and records showed an extensive relationship with Raúl. No one understood how the DEA Attaché in Bolivia became so intimately involved in crime. Torres had an impeccable service record. Agents were exposed daily to temptation and quick riches, but why would

Torres take the bait after such a distinguished career? No one knew.

The FBI determined that Raúl's cash payments to Sendero and the FARC were protection money. The laundering was extensive, but analysts were able to see money flowing to narco-terrorist front organizations. Raúl covered his tracks well, but the FBI's financial investigative capabilities were more extensive than he imagined.

The U.S. Embassy tried to secure Raúl's laptop and personal records, but ran into several brick walls. Bolivian authorities did not want to issue an order to search the office and home of such a well-known and powerful man. Intense embassy pressure eventually produced the order, but Raúl's laptop and satellite phone were already long gone.

62

For the last week, the U.S. intercepted Chinese intelligence and private corporate message traffic expressing concern about the vulnerability of the Panama Canal Zone ports and facilities to attack. Jay Mansour was not surprised. Chinese intelligence and corporate interests were essentially one and the same. Even though the information did not point to the nukes, the canal was the transit point from the Pacific to the U.S. Gulf Coast. That was enough to make the information significant.

Mansour worked every contact and mole in his inventory. He could use the stateside databases and satellite photos, but knew that human intelligence would get him most of the way home. With no leads of any consequence in the Southern Cone, Mansour redeployed his contract teams to Peru, Ecuador, Venezuela, and Colombia. Frustrated, he returned to Ciudad del Este after several days of chasing fruitless leads in Asunción. His first stop was his export attorney to see if there were any unusual shipments in the last several days. The attorney did not answer either of his phones and his office was locked. When he could not find him at his golf or tennis clubs, Mansour went to his home.

The man's thirteen year-old son informed Mansour that his father died two days earlier. He left after dinner the night of his death to deliver export papers to the airport for cargo going to Colombia and Ecuador. He did not come back, and the police found his bullet-ridden body in a ditch by the airport fence. The police discovered his abandoned car, presumed it had broken down, and concluded that he was robbed and killed when he walked to get help. Mansour knew that a man who carried two cell phones did not walk deserted roads late at night looking for roadside assistance. He also knew his attorney never made late-night trips to the airport to give clients export documents.

Two hundred dollars persuaded an airport mechanic to tell Mansour he saw the attorney at the airport the night he died, making final arrangements for two planes to leave Ciudad del Este without filing flight plans. For another three hundred dollars he revealed the aircraft were identical Embraer jets owned by a Brazilian leasing company, each carrying two men with light luggage and similar-looking large footlockers. For an extra five hundred, he gave Mansour copies of the fuel operator's log sheets for both planes. The attendant had noted in the margins that the aircraft would stop once before reaching their separate final destinations, Guayaquil, Ecuador, and Coveñas, Colombia. The mechanic also said he fueled the planes simultaneously. The pilots were in a hurry as they had narrow windows to meet their cargo's sailing schedule.

Mansour was certain the nukes went to Ecuador and Colombia to be loaded on vessels destined for refineries in Houston and New Orleans. He was connecting the dots and hoped they were the right ones. He told his teams to forget about Peru and Venezuela. Their objectives were Guayaquil and Coveñas. Mansour then went back and reviewed his database of high-risk travelers and possible transit vessels. Of the forty-one names, various state security services had tracked down and spoken to thirty-five. Of the remaining six unaccounted for, a Uruguayan and a Chilean were believed to be in New York. The other four carried Argentine passports. Mansour froze when he saw that two of the Argentines were chemical engineers with extensive refining backgrounds and the other two worked for a textile company with a joint venture in Ecuador. He sent a message to Roger Harrington to track the Argentine passport holders at once. Even if they could not find them, Mansour's gut told him they were on the water heading to the U.S.

Knowing the nukes left Ciudad del Este two days earlier let Mansour limit his search to ships that had already departed or were to depart Guayaquil or Coveñas for the U.S. in the next ten to fifteen days. He saw that nine vessels had already left and six would do so soon. Of those fifteen, five were bound for Houston and three for Baton Rouge. It was not the final answer, but he was getting closer. He could nail it if he found the four Argentine passport holders. That could take some time, and time was a luxury he did not have. Mansour was frustrated and stumped. His brain was stuck.

He took a break to clear his mind, and that meant ESPN, beer, chips and salsa. Mansour untapped the bottle and stretched out on the couch just as his computer beeped with new e-mail. He tossed the chips aside and got up to see what it was. Within seconds, the latest message traffic intercepts popped up. Mansour cursed, since making sense of the things was like reading Coptic. He got better at it with time, but still needed patience and a modicum of concentration and perseverance. The reports were not designed to be user friendly.

The highest priority intercepts were Chinese, discussing Arabs and possible attacks in the Canal Zone. He moved on. The second highest priority went to a series of messages about drug trafficking in the region. Mansour skipped them. The lowest priority was a series of messages in Arabic originating in Paraguay. The U.S.-based analyst identified the callers as Libyan. Mansour scanned the text and was about to click off when something caught his eye.

One message said "the star has yet to shine" and the other "the eagle is not yet home." The analyst suggested the references were to a son who had not yet graduated and another still not back from a trip. Mansour had seen this before. He brought up his list of ships scheduled to call at Houston and New Orleans. There they were. The *Evening Star* would sail from Guayaquil to Houston in thirty-six hours, the *Flying Eagle* from Coveñas to Baton Rouge in three days—and both would make port at about the same time. Mansour had two calls to make, one to Roger Harrington, the other to his teams in the field. Deciding who to call first was easy.

Mansour gave his teams the ships' names, told them to avoid hostile contact if possible, to get intelligence on the nukes, and to put men on board both vessels. He then called Harrington and brought him up to speed.

"That's good news, Jay," Harrington said excitedly. "There's some shit happening up here too. The data on Hassan Ali plus your warehouse tarps and the Arabic notepad finally got the DDO to move. I swear he's doing it against his will, but he knows he can't block us out any more. They're moving the pieces fast now to chase the nukes. This nails it."

"It's about time, but my men will probably be on board those vessels long before anyone up there gets a tactical plan together."

"Nobody knows about your contractors, and we better keep it that way. They can be our insurance, but they'll disappear in a bureaucratic fight if they get dragged into this. They're more valuable as ghosts right now."

"I've got no problem with that, boss. Later."

63

With my last interview at the embassy over, I headed home to pack. Lucho's hospitality had been wonderful, but I was ready to spend at least one night in my own bed. Almost two weeks had passed since Raúl's death, and I could not wait to see my family. The embassy thought there was no longer a threat, so they quietly told people that I survived the car bomb. They still said nothing about Raúl's death. Julie called, and I told her I would take the American flight to Miami in the morning and spend the night with Chris before heading to Michigan.

"Señor Richard! *Gracias a Dios*, you are safe," Lucy exclaimed when I got home. "Señora Carolina came by the house the other day. I could not reach you."

Raúl's secretary had no reason to be in our home. In a society still ruled by social position and intimidation, Carolina could easily pressure Lucy to get inside.

"It's okay, Lucy. What did she want?"

"She heard you were alive and said the company wanted to talk to you. She insisted, so I let her in."

"What did she do?"

"She looked through your papers, and took a notebook from your bedroom."

I raced upstairs to my bedroom study and found that one of my date books, with the address and phone of our Michigan cottage, was gone. Carolina's visit was no coincidence. She was not worried about me. She was trying to find me or my family, probably for someone else. After everything that had happened, it was stupid to leave that book lying around. My stomach turned as I walked back downstairs. I called Julie to tell her to get out of the cottage, but there was no answer. My mind raced and I realized that Lucy was talking to me.

"Señor Richard, are you listening to me? Señora Carolina made phone calls."

"Which phone did she use?"

"Her cell phone first, but the calls dropped so she used the phone here in the kitchen. Señora Carolina put her phone on the counter and forgot it." Lucy handed me the cell phone.

Carolina's phone log showed three consecutive calls to Oscar Dávila. I pressed Memory Recall on the kitchen phone, and the display flashed one "unknown recipient". The number matched Davila's. That was it. I rang the FBI technician at the embassy and asked if they were still recording my calls. If so, I had Carolina and Dávila on tape. Fountain said they removed the equipment two days after Raúl died. Damn. It was worth a try.

I packed my bags thinking about my alternatives, and it seemed as though I had few. I pulled out one pistol, made sure it was clear, and packed it in my suitcase along with two boxes of ammo. The other pistol was holstered and I had several full mags in case I needed it before getting on the plane. Since most everyone knew I was alive, I decided to travel under my real name. Once packed, I called Denning to tell him what happened.

"Raúl's secretary was in the house while I was away and she took one of my date books. It's got our address in Michigan, and I'm afraid she's passed that on to Raúl's people."

"I admit that's strange, but my secretary said Carolina called the embassy yesterday looking for you. I suspect it's legit since she's a Phoenix employee. It seems a stretch to think she's involved, but we could put someone on her just to be sure."

"That would be great. Maybe she'll lead us somewhere."

"Could be, but I think Dávila's the only one who could be dangerous, and he's lying low. There's no way he'd come after you now, especially once you're the U.S."

"Yeah, I know, but I'm still worried. Is Newman there, or has he gone back to Santiago?" I wanted to speak to the FBI Legat who had camped out in the La Paz embassy since the DEA plane crashed.

"Yeah, right next to me, but he's on the phone."

"Tell him what I told you and ask if they can send someone from one of their field offices to the cottage to see about my family."

Denning put the phone down, then picked back up. "Bad news. He says they can't approve it."

"John, you can't be serious. Even after the attacks on us?"

"That's not the point. Those happened in a foreign country, and there's no verifiable threat against you or your family in the U.S. Without evidence of a threat, they can't give your family protective services. Do you have anything solid?"

"No, I don't, and you know that," I said, dejected and exasperated. "This is bullshit, John."

"He's a good guy, Richard, but he can't do anything unless there's something to go on. Take a deep breath. It'll be okay." Denning hesitated. "I shouldn't tell you this, but the FBI has backed off Raúl and the drug issues for right now."

"You've got to be kidding! What's more important than this?"

"I know only part of it," Denning said quietly. "They're working some high-level terror threat, and they've dropped everything. I know they'll get back to your case soon. I'll let you know."

"Thanks. I'm out of here tomorrow morning. Lucho and I will

eat dinner at my house, so call if something pops up."

"Promise. You'll be with Julie and the kids soon, and they'll be fine. Shout when you get up there to let me know you're okay."

"Will do."

Denning was a great guy, a lifesaver, but I was angry that the rest of the embassy did not share his sense of urgency. I wondered if it took a body bag to establish a verifiable threat. I dialed the cottage, but neither Julie nor the answering machine picked up. I needed to get to her as soon as possible, but still had some unfinished business.

64

Roger Harrington ran with Jay Mansour's intelligence data and bulldozed his way past the obstructionist CIA bureaucracy. Despite their dislike of both Harrington and Mansour, the Deputy Director of Operations (DDO) and the Deputy Director of Central Intelligence (DDCI) got on board once they saw their careers depended on supporting the effort. They tried to hijack the case as their own, but the Director of Central Intelligence (DCI) saw through them and put Harrington and Mansour in charge. The Director of National Intelligence was spending most of his time in congressional hearings explaining intelligence community reform, had no time to be involved with current projects or cases, and told the DCI he would by default concur with any decision he made.

Mansour identified the ships believed to carry the nukes, and the FBI visited the shipping line executives to obtain detailed vessel diagrams. They could not get crew and passenger lists, because both vessels were exempt from providing them to U.S. port and immigration authorities. Mansour's teams in Ecuador and Colombia nonetheless confirmed that men with Argentine passports and oversized footlockers were on the suspect ships. Two of Mansour's specialists boarded the *Evening Star* cargo ship as marine biologists and paid a one hundred dollar passage fee. A separate two-man team boarded the *Flying Eagle* oil tanker disguised as caterers and hid in the ship's mechanical area. Only Harrington and Mansour knew the teams were there.

The vessel schematics suggested that the weapons were within easy reach of the hit teams, either in their quarters or in rooms immediately adjacent. To maintain operational security, the ships' captains would learn of the operation only after the assault teams were aboard and in control of the nukes. As a further security measure, the FBI sequestered the shipping line senior executives for the duration of the mission.

In the White House, the president walked in on a heated debate among the heads of Defense, State, Homeland Security, FBI, CIA, Justice, the Joint Chiefs, the National Security Advisor, and the Director of National Intelligence. They argued about who would take the lead in the operation, with two saying the U.S. should do nothing because there was not enough proof. The president had little patience for argument and said the U.S. would intervene. He also invited anyone who could not support his decision to leave. No one moved. The Director of National Intelligence argued that CIA could deploy a Special Activities Staff team to hunt the nukes, but the president dismissed the suggestion and said the operation would be military.

The president ordered the Special Operations Command (SOCOM) at MacDill Air Force Base in Tampa to plan and execute its own hunt-and-destroy mission. Until recently, SOCOM generally played a secondary role to provide men to fighting commands like the Joint Special Operations Command (JSOC) headquartered at Pope Air Force Base, North Carolina that planned, supervised, and executed attacks. In this case, JSOC would deploy a Special Mission Unit (SMU) and SOCOM would run the mission. SMU covert action teams trained to identify and eliminate terrorist use of weapons of mass destruction. They would take all measures to seize, destroy, render safe, or capture WMDs. The president ordered that CIA would assist with backup covert teams.

The SMUs were made up of the Army's 1st Special Forces Operational Detachment Delta (SFOD-D), the Navy's Special Warfare (NSW) Development Group (DEVGRU), and the Air Force's Special Tactics Squadron 1. The 75th Ranger Regiment and the 160th Special Operations Aviation Regiment (SOAR) were available on an as-needed basis. The Marines were new to SOCOM, and had not yet fully integrated. Because of the transnational threat, the SMUs included Department of Energy Nuclear Emergency Support Team (NEST) technicians and scientists.

The assault teams had two primary objectives. The first was to interdict the ships and either retrieve or destroy the nukes. They preferred retrieval to destruction, so they could follow a technology and hardware trail to the source of the weapons. The second was to take the hit teams alive to find out who planned the attacks.

Because of the maritime environment DEVGRU would run the operation. A Navy Lt. would lead an SMU of eight SEALs, one nuclear weapons expert, and one CIA officer. The weapons expert and the CIA officer were jump, dive, and demolitions qualified. Three of the *Evening Star* SEALs brought Panamanian experience with them from Operation Just Cause in 1989. Five of the *Flying Eagle* operators had substantial Colombian drug interdiction and high-seas piracy experience.

Putting the assault teams aboard and finding the nukes was hard enough, but dealing with the bombs themselves was another matter. SOCOM and CIA knew the devices were small, but they did not know where they were or how they were rigged. The CIA psychological profile did not indicate a suicide attack, so the Libyans likely planned to arm the devices with time to escape. The assault teams wanted to retrieve the nukes, but even more important was to make sure they were never armed.

SOCOM ran out several scenarios. The first was a successful takedown and no active nukes. The second was an armed nuke, but one they could disarm before detonation. The third was an armed nuke they could not disarm before detonation. The SMU would have to determine if they could destroy the device without harming themselves or the crew, and then destroy it without sinking themselves and the vessel. If they could not destroy it, they had to assess if there was time to evacuate everyone and then scuttle the ship. A successful high seas evacuation was unlikely.

The fourth scenario was that the team could neither disarm nor destroy the device. With no further options, the U.S. would sink the vessel then and there. The final scenario was that the insertion failed, the Libyans killed the assault team, and the device was armed. If SOCOM lost communications with the entire team, the mission would be deemed a failure and the president would order the vessel sunk. There would be no time for a second attempt.

Under no circumstances would the U.S. let a nuclear device explode on the surface. The only acceptable alternative to interdiction and recovery was to sink the ships and let the nukes explode underwater. People would die, but the U.S. would do everything possible to minimize the loss.

The mission clock would start to run when the SMU teams advised SOCOM they were on the ships. Planners estimated the SMUs needed eight minutes from the time of insertion to breach the hit team's quarters. They calculated five minutes to capture or kill the Libyans, assess, and secure the nuke. With a margin of another two minutes, the teams should call in at the fifteen minute mark.

From evidence found in Ali's warehouse, CIA technical experts estimated that the hit teams could arm the devices in under ten minutes and they could detonate twenty-five minutes later. If the Libyans somehow became aware of the SMU and armed the device immediately, that could put detonation between thirty-three and thirty-five minutes after team insertion. In the event of lost communications the president would order a strike at twenty-six minutes, weapons release at twenty-eight minutes, and would expect the vessel to be underwater by the thirty-two minute mark.

Virginia or Seawolf class attack submarines were first slotted to destroy the surface vessels, though planners did not know how much time the subs would need to locate the ships or to retarget if they got the wrong ones. Ultimately, the logistical and time constraints eliminated the subs as the primary means to take out the surface vessels. Regardless, three SSNs were directed to the Gulf to hunt the ships and serve as backup.

The primary task for sinking the nuke delivery vessels fell to the Navy's F/A-18 Hornet equipped with two Boeing AGM-84D Harpoon missiles. The Harpoon's active radar guidance, low-level sea-skimming capability, and sixty-two mile range, made it a unique all-weather over-the-horizon anti-ship missile system. Harpoons excelled at destroying ships in the open ocean. The missile did not need a launching platform, and could be fired 180 degrees away from its target position. The Harpoon could turn around and find its correct objective, then deliver its 490 pound high-explosive penetration blast with deadly accuracy.

65

I put my gear in the front passenger seat of Lucho's van and made one last check of the gas, lights, and tires. This was not a good night for mechanical problems. Lucho lent me his work van since I needed one with no passenger seats. I lined the compartment floor with heavy plastic, taped it down, attached bogus license plates from the junkyard, put my gloves on, and checked my maps. Lucho stood in the driveway staring at me mournfully, waiting for me to ask him to come along. I could use his help, but would not ask him to risk his life. He wished me luck and said he would call Denning if I was not back by 1:00 A.M. With the El Alto streets dark, I cranked the engine and headed down to La Paz.

I slowed three blocks from the house as two women walked through the front gate. They looked like domestic help going home for the night and I hoped they would not come back. I rolled the van to a stop directly in front of the house, thirty feet from two bodyguards who stared straight at me. I cut the lights, but left the engine running in case I needed to bolt. Both men walked over to the passenger window to talk to me. I said I was lost and asked for directions, shoving a La Paz map in their faces. They noticed my hand move, but could do nothing before I put a suppressed .45 round into each man.

Before getting out, I changed magazines and stowed my pistol in my vest. I put both men inside the back of the van, checked pulses to make sure they were dead, took their gate and house keys, turned off their radios, and covered them with a blanket. From what I knew, the last serious obstacle should be the driver who doubled as a bodyguard. I was once more amazed at how small the La Paz community was when Lucho told me his cousin delivered bottled water to the residences in the area. He gave Lucho enough information about the house and who was in it that I figured I had a pretty good chance of success.

Rather than go through the front door, I eased quickly down the driveway along the right side of the property. I slowed when I heard noise coming from the back of the house. My plan had not considered domestic help making dinner at this time of night. I stood against a tree near the garage at the rear and saw the driver reading a newspaper over a worktable twenty feet away. He reacted slowly as he heard me approach, and I put a round through his left temple from less than five feet. He slumped onto the table, and I dragged him off and dumped him behind the hedge. I topped off my magazine with a spare round, put the spent brass casing in my pocket, and moved to the service entrance.

There was a maid with her back to me, cutting meat on the kitchen counter. The shadows near the screen door concealed me while she rocked to Shakira. I pulled three strips of duct tape from my pocket and stuck them to my leg. As soon as she put the butcher knife down, I blew through the door and went straight to her. With my arm around her throat and a hand on her mouth, I said I would not hurt her. I taped her mouth and eyes, and flex-cuffed her hands behind her back. My rule of thumb was that ninety-nine percent of maids scream even when you say you will not hurt them. I had to tie her up.

I told her to kneel in the pantry and taped her ankles together. The poor woman shook from fright, but I would take no chances. I repeated that I would not hurt her and asked her to nod if her *patrón* was in the house. She nodded yes. Was he alone? He was. Were the two women who left gone for the night? They were. Was there anyone else in the house? She shook her head, no. I patted her on the shoulder, told her not to worry or move until I came back, and closed the door.

The kitchen led to the house in two different directions, so I went straight to the sound of Maná and Latin MTV. I held the pistol out slightly as I scanned and walked cautiously through the living room and the dining room. I saw him. He sat against the far wall of a media room packed with dozens of high-tech toys. I pointed my muzzle at his head, and told him to turn the sound down. I liked Maná, but it was so loud my heart vibrated. He sat comfortably in a black leather chair, sipping red wine. I settled into a similar chair ten feet across from him. His surprise at seeing me matched his disdain.

"How did you get in here, gringo?"

"Walked right through the door. You really should find better help, Oscar."

"Go to hell, Blackstone."

"Oh, you know my name. That's interesting, I didn't introduce myself."

"You didn't have to. What do you want?"

"This is very simple. I want to know who Raúl worked with."

"No one. You imagine things."

"No, you imagine things if you think I'm that stupid. Carolina was in my house. She went through my things. She made phone calls—to you."

"That proves nothing. Don Raúl was my friend."

"Please, you can do better than that."

Dávila did not respond. He drank his wine and tried to look disinterested. I leaned forward slightly and depressed the 1911 safety. Cool as he was, Dávila noticed. He was, however, unfazed. I had the feeling we would be in a standoff forever.

"You don't have the *cojones* to shoot me, Blackstone, and you know it."

"I have plenty of cojones, but all I need to shoot you is bullets."

Dávila sat up slightly in the chair, but left his bare feet and legs on the black leather ottoman in front of him. I was done fencing. I squeezed off a round through his left foot. The top of his foot blew out, spraying him with blood, and the round imbedded in his left side. Dávila howled and lifted his foot to his chest.

"You're crazy!"

"No, not crazy. Just motivated. You can make this easy, or you can make it hard. I'll be here all night until I get what I want."

He spat at me, cursed me, my mother, and my entire extended family. I moved the muzzle slightly to the left and shot him in the right leg. He let out another scream as the round shattered the shin and left exposed bone protruding through the skin. He seemed to forget the pain from the first wound.

"*La concha de tu madre!*"

I did not like the reference to my mother's private parts, so I shot his right hand. The round went clean through the palm, and he pulled his hand into his stomach.

"Oscar, you better tell me what I want to know, or this is going to be a long night. I've got more bullets than you have body parts. So, now it's your turn. Try again. You shit on me or I don't like your answer, and I shoot you. That's how it works. There's a message here, and we've already established a pattern. Let's try it again." I shot his left knee without waiting for an answer.

"Please, no more! It's Price and Whitworth, damn it! Both of them!"

"Anyone else?"

"No! No! That's it."

Dávila bled some, but the wounds would not kill him. It was time to send him to a better place. I stood up and shot him through the right eye. His head recoiled slightly and rested on the back of the chair. I shot him twice more through the head for good measure, changed magazines, and picked up the spent brass. I felt no remorse for this piece of garbage. He and Raúl tried to kill me and my family. Pricks like him needed shooting.

Dávila's information was interesting, but I was not sure how reliable it was. Being shot was painful. People said almost anything to stop pain, so I had to test what he told me. I had a hunch. I flipped open Raúl's cell phone and pulled the first e-mail address from his contact list. Dávila had a PC booted up and was logged on. I brought up his instant message software and threw the dice. I was in luck. AguilaDeamon1 was online.

"The embassy reports that Blackstone is alive," I typed.

"I understand the same. Bad break for us," AguilaDeamon1 wrote back.

"I am concerned. Have you taken precautions?"

"We have Blackstone's family as insurance."

"In a secure place, I hope."

"Yes, at their cottage in the U.S."

"Good." I could barely type, my fingers almost crushing the keys. "Need to talk. Can you call my home phone?"

"Yes. Give me two minutes."

It seemed like an eternity, but Dávila's phone finally rang. I picked up on the third ring and pressed the receiver to my ear.

"Price here. What do you want to talk about?"

My heart stopped and I thought I would choke. I wanted to scream. I wanted to strangle the bastard. I said nothing.

"Dávila? Are you there?"

I hung up and jumped back on the computer to type an IM.

"Can barely hear you, very garbled. Will try you tonight or tomorrow. When can I call?"

"Three tomorrow afternoon."

"Talk to you then if I can get through." I signed off.

I was done and looked around to make sure there was nothing else I needed to take with me. I picked up my brass, went to the kitchen to let the maid out of the closet, cut the flex cuffs, and thanked her. I told her she was safe and to count to a hundred before she removed the duct tape. I went out the back and jogged to the van, stuffed the house keys back in the bodyguards' pockets, dragged them to the front yard, and shoved them behind the shrubbery. All I had left was to burn the plastic liner, collect the brass casings from the van, and change the tags. I would do that later and would return Lucho's van as promised. Five minutes from my house, I called Chris.

"Chris, this has gone to shit." I gave him the Reader's Digest version of what I feared might happen to Julie. The silence was deafening. "I'm not staying with you tomorrow. I need to go straight to Michigan. Can you pull some stuff together for me?"

"Sure. What do you need?"

I brought my pistols and a shotgun to Bolivia and left all my other gear with Chris. What I had with me would not be enough if it got ugly, and I knew in my gut it was going to get nasty. I also knew that sound carried like mad on our lake, and I would have to be as quiet as possible.

"Bring my short suppressed carbine, a bunch of magazines, and three hundred rounds of 240 grain subsonic. Pack my 1911 thigh rig, two boxes of .45 ball, armor, and new batteries for everything."

"Is that all?" Chris laughed. "Sounds like you're going hunting, bro. You can't do this alone, you know."

"Chris, I need help."

"I thought you'd never ask. Book me on your flight, and I'll have all the gear checked through."

"Thanks. Listen, check it only to Chicago."

"Got it."

I already knew that the flight from La Paz would not get me

through Miami to Chicago in time to catch a commercial connection to Northern Michigan. That meant a charter, and there was a service that could put us into Pellston at a quarter of ten. That was great, since it was an hour closer to the cottage than Traverse City. I booked two one-way passengers with a hundred pounds of luggage. We would drive back to Chicago from Pellston, since I did not want a suspicious pilot calling the police if something looked odd on the back end. The charter operator confirmed a rental car would be waiting for us by the plane when we arrived. I went over my list of things to do and wondered what I might have missed. Lucho would be fine while I was gone, and Denning said he would keep an eye on Gustavo. As far as I could see, I was done here.

66

The *Evening Star* Special Mission Unit flew to the Colón International Airport on the northern coast of Panama, and then went directly to their staging area on the outskirts of the city. As the team prepared, the *Evening Star* cargo ship passed the Canal Zone southern port of Balboa and sailed north through the Miraflores and Pedro Miguel locks on its way to Colón. Accompanying the SMU on the mission were two HH-60H Seahawk helicopters. The Seahawk was similar to the Army Blackhawk, specially modified to carry ten fully equipped operators instead of eight. The aircraft had an impeccable service record inserting and extracting special operators.

The team reviewed its assault plans while the *Star* crossed Gatún Lake on its way north. Although there were multiple opportunities to board the ship before it reached the locks, tactical planners chose the northern exit point in case the Libyans armed the nuclear device and the vessel had to be sunk. The U.S. preferred to sink the vessel offshore rather than damage the locks with a high-order explosion or block the passageway with a dead ship.

The *Flying Eagle* SMU reached Coveñas on the Colombian coast as the *Star* operators flew into Colón. The *Eagle* team expected to catch their vessel still in port, but the ship unexpectedly put out to sea before they were in place. SOCOM considered asking the Colombians to detain the vessel, but feared a security leak would compromise the operation. Providence smiled when mechanical trouble slowed the *Eagle* significantly several hours after it got underway. As the Seahawk cleared the heliport, turned, and roared offshore, the team joined the hunt for a nuclear device less than a hundred miles off the Colombian coast. If all went as planned, the *Eagle* would be taken down immediately after the *Star.*

Shortly before 3:00 A.M. Lt. John Tucker's SMU waited at the Gatún locks to board the *Evening Star.* A CIA Military Special Projects team had already incapacitated over a dozen local security personnel, five of them Chinese, so the SMU could board the vessel unimpeded. Suddenly, Tucker called the team off. As the *Star* moved slowly through the locks in the dead of night and heavy rain, something did not look right. He called SOCOM.

"Tucker here, sir. A ship is clearing the locks, but it's not the right one."

"Come again, Lieutenant?" Jay Mansour asked from the SOCOM operations center.

"Sir, the name on the ship is the *Eternal Star.* It has a big hole in the middle, and it doesn't look like a cargo ship. We've got another several minutes to board before she's out of reach. Please advise."

"Lieutenant, to confirm. You have eyes on, your vessel is called the *Eternal Star*, and it has a hole in the middle?" Mansour asked as he watched the analysts furiously typing on their computer keyboards.

"That's correct, sir."

"Stand by Lieutenant," Col. Sanderson said, signaling urgently to Mansour to find out what was going on.

"Yes, sir."

Mansour felt the blood drain from his face when he saw the

analyst's printout. He handed it to Sanderson without a word. It was a colossal mistake. The ship in the locks was indeed the *Eternal Star*, not the *Evening Star*. Tucker and his team were looking at an oil and gas drill ship sailing from Peru. The printout revealed that the mission planning analyst had typed *E. Star* when searching for the transit time. There were two *E. Stars* passing back-to-back, listed alphabetically instead of chronologically. Simply scrolling to the next record would have revealed the correct passage times and avoided a huge error. The *Evening Star*, the Libyans, and the nuke had cleared the locks hours earlier and were on the high seas.

"Lieutenant, you are in fact looking at the wrong vessel," Sanderson said. "It appears we had an intelligence breakdown. Your *Evening Star* is already through the locks. You need to move your collective asses out of there right now. We're on the horn, and your helo is three minutes from the parking lot behind the locks administration building."

"I understand, sir. That will make quite a racket at this time of the morning," Tucker observed.

"That's not a concern, Lieutenant. Just get on the bird."

"Yes, sir."

With Tucker in pursuit of the *Evening Star*, Col. Sanderson hailed Lt. Mark Roberts as his team chased the *Flying Eagle* off the Colombian coast. Roberts was told to refuel with a U.S. Navy vessel and hold for orders, since that was the only way both teams could board simultaneously. The newer operators breathed a quiet sigh of relief. The experienced assaulters were pissed. They wanted to lock and load, and they knew that it was draining to be called off and then cycle back up in a short time.

Tucker and his team checked their gear one last time as the Seahawk slowed and the pilot held up two fingers and shouted "*Two Minutes!*" They could see the *Evening Star*. The snafu at the Gatún locks meant a change in plans, but they were prepared for any contingency. They had come to Panama with parachutes, rappel, and fastrope gear. Seas were calm and there was only a light breeze. Boarding on the open ocean meant fastroping to the deck of the ship.

Three hundred yards from the *Star*, Tucker extended his fingers, and then made a fist with each hand to make sure his fastrope gloves were snug. He hated it when they bunched up. The gloves were all that would support him down the rope. Tucker reminded his men to "wring out the towel" to slow their descent. A hundred yards out, the copilot said no one was topside.

The Seahawk flared amidships, and the team tossed out the ropes. Each operator released the rope once on deck, shouldered his MP5, and established a perimeter. When the entire team was on board, the Seahawk was gone into the night. Tucker called their status and location in to SOCOM, and the clock started to run. The operators moved quickly down the ship's port side, past the crew quarters, through the mechanical area, and cleared the internal stairs down one level to the stern of the ship. The team had only one objective to take down, so they did not have to clear and secure the entire vessel or hold rear security. Still, the last man continuously checked behind him to be sure.

The team was forty-five feet from the quarters believed to house the Libyans. They checked their waterproof ship diagrams in the low-level passageway light and confirmed that their objective was the second door on the left. They ignored the first closed door, an electrical box. They held when Tucker signaled them to stack up four feet short of the second door.

The Libyans were in two adjoining rooms beyond the door. The first room was a thirty-four by twenty-eight foot storage space. Toward the back of that space, a door on the right rear led to a twenty by eighteen foot bunk room where the Libyans slept. Since the team's final and only objective was in those two rooms, no one would stay outside to secure the passageway. The team wanted to concentrate all its force on the targets.

Seven SEALs, the CIA officer, and the nuclear weapons expert formed a foot behind each other to the left of the door on the hinge side. Tucker signaled the eighth SEAL, the breacher, to post alone to the right on the knob side.

The nuke expert, the last man in the stack, silently checked his firearms and gear. Each operator did the same. He released the grip on his MP5 and touched his hand to his thigh holstered SIG 226 pistol, patted himself down and took an inventory of his gear; pistol mags, MP5 mags, flash bangs, frag grenade, chem lights, flex cuffs, flashlight, gas mask. It was all there. He felt to make sure nothing hung from him that would catch on anything and that his subgun sling was not caught on a pouch on his vest. Reacquiring his MP5 grip, the nuke expert was ready. It took six seconds.

The nuke specialist stepped forward, pressed his body in tight and squeezed the left bicep hard of the man in front of him. That clear non-verbal communication told each operator that the man behind him was ready to go. Each assaulter repeated the squeeze until it reached the front. Tucker felt the squeeze, held his thumb up to signal a door breach, and the team immediately acknowledged with thumb squeezes up and down the stack. Each man stacked up even tighter. They were not nine individuals. They were one unit.

Tucker pulled his MP5 tight into his shoulder and pointed the muzzle at the door. He started to nod to his teammate across from him to initiate the breach when he noticed there was no light coming from the room. Probably no one was in the storage space, and the Libyans were asleep in the bunk room. There was no reason to give advance warning, so Tucker lifted his hand and waved off the breach.

"Dave, see if you can pick the lock."

Dave Johansen let his breacher's shotgun hang and touched the door handle. "I don't think I want to pick this lock, John," he whispered.

"Why the hell not?"

"Because the door's open," Johansen smiled.

Having waived off the breach, Tucker signaled to the team to confirm the stack again. Each assaulter had every muscle primed, like racehorses in the gate. Tucker nodded to his breacher that it was time.

His MP5 in his right hand, Johansen pushed the door open with his left, and the team poured by him into the room as rapidly and fluidly as cells splitting. Tucker turned on his MP5-mounted light and flipped the safety off as he buttonhooked left into the room and dug his corner looking for targets. His number two went to the right, and the rest flooded in, each going opposite the man before him. Johansen was the last man in and took a position in the center of the room, empty except for stacks of boxes and crates at the back. The team split to pursue separate objectives. No one said a word or made a sound.

The first six operators and the CIA officer went straight to the open doorway, while the nuke expert and two assaulters moved directly to the crates and boxes. Five assaulters and the CIA man stacked up left of the door and another stood on the right. Tucker led on the left and lit the room with his weapon-mounted light. He saw nothing but the edges of a bunk bed and heard nothing. The Libyans were likely asleep, but they could be waiting with weapons drawn. Never knowing what was in a dark room, the team always banged when moving from room to room. The lone assaulter to the right of the door pulled a flash bang from his thigh pouch and turned it upside down so the spoon fit into the palm of his left hand. He pulled the pin and held the active flash bang up to show those across the doorway he was ready to deploy the device.

Tucker nodded and turned off his weapon-mounted light. With one fluid motion, the operator on the right snapped his left wrist and tossed the flash bang into the room. The tell-tale clanking of the metal body on the floor was followed by a fierce detonation. Tucker turned his light back on and was in the room a microsecond later, followed by the entire stack, rousting the Libyans from their beds before the room filled with smoke. The terrorists were face down on the deck and flex cuffed within seconds. The operators illuminated them and checked for weapons and explosives. The CIA officer spoke in Arabic, but they answered in Spanish.

"*Hablamos español, nada más*," they said in unison

"Where's the nuke?" the CIA assaulter insisted in Arabic. "We want the nuke, and we want it now."

"*Jodéte, hijo de puta*!"

"What did he say?" Johansen asked.

"Screw you, son of a bitch.'"

"I don't think so." Johansen kicked the Libyan in the groin. The man cried out in pain and made no further smart-ass remarks.

"We are Argentine passengers on our way to Houston," one said in English.

"Bullshit!"

"No! Please! Look at our passports!"

"Found it!" shouted the nuke specialist from the next room. "It's not armed! We're in good shape, guys. We just need to secure it and get it home with us."

Tucker called in at the thirteen minute mark that they had found and secured the package, had two Libyans in tow, and were ready for recovery. SOCOM called the *Star's* security officer on shore and told him to inform the captain that he had been boarded and should cooperate with the assault team. SOCOM recalled the two F/A-18 Hornets and their four Harpoon missiles. A U.S. Navy ship was twenty minutes away and the two Seahawks were several minutes out. The SMU operators and the CIA officer went through the crates, boxes, lockers, and storage units to be sure there were no booby traps and that they left nothing of value behind.

Repeated questions to the Libyans yielded nothing. They swore they were innocent and had no idea how or why a nuclear device was in a hold next to their bunks. They said they had been set up. In several hours, both would have the chance to tell their story to a lot of new friends at a remote stateside location.

67

Less than three hundred yards from the *Flying Eagle*, Lt. Mark Roberts reminded his team to get down the fastropes quickly and move away from the lines as soon as they hit the deck. Approaching the *Eagle*, the Seahawk pilot advised Roberts of two civilians on the port side of the vessel. *That's all we need*, Roberts thought.

The Seahawk flared, they threw out the fastropes, and the first man was on the deck in seconds. All went smoothly until the ninth man, the nuke specialist, was on the fastrope. He slowed his descent by braking with his feet rather than cinching his hands, and he slowed too fast. The CIA officer behind narrowly averted a disaster by hanging on hard to avoid a pile up. The operators were on board with a perimeter secured in under a minute. The two civilians were sound asleep with an empty Jack Daniels bottle between them. The team taped their mouths, cuffed them, and moved on.

Roberts advised SOCOM the insertion was a success, and Col. Sanderson started the timer. The team moved quickly below decks where bright ceiling lights whited out their night optical devices. They advanced, cursing silently while shedding their NODs, and formed at the corner of the next passageway. Around the corner, the first door on the right opened into the ship's gym. Forty feet beyond that, the Libyans were behind another closed door. The operators moved slowly around the corner and heard what sounded like someone working out on weight machines. Roberts signaled to the team to clear the gym while he held the passageway. He stepped a couple of feet to his left, his muzzle pointed straight ahead, while his teammates stacked up and filled the gap beside him to his right. They flooded the room and found nothing. Someone had left a treadmill running. They turned it off. Roberts hugged the left side of the hallway and moved forward as the team exited the gym and fell in behind him.

The SMU was outside the Libyans' door within seconds. Seven SEALs, the CIA officer, and the nuke expert stacked up on the far side of the door. Don Stuart, the breacher was on the near doorknob side. They saw light under the door and guessed someone was awake. Roberts looked through the keyhole and saw nothing. He put his head to the door and swore he heard "I'm a Virgin" playing. The team passed bicep squeezes forward. Roberts took a deep breath and touched his left index finger to the infrared American flag velcroed to the front of his assault vest.

Stuart readied his breaching shotgun while Roberts pulled a flash bang from his pouch. Roberts signaled to the team, and they acknowledged with squeezes, that he would bang the room as soon as they breached the door. He showed the flash bang to Stuart who nodded. Stuart stepped forward, lowered the barrel to less than an inch from the doorknob at a slightly offset forty-five degree angle, and pulled the trigger. The breaching round sheared the bolt off and Stuart kicked the door open. Roberts tossed the flash bang through the doorway. The instant it detonated, the team flooded the room. The Libyans were in the back, near a large footlocker. The flash bang rattled them, but they recovered. The Libyan closest to the door raised a knife and sprinted towards Roberts, while the other lunged at the footlocker. Both shouted in Arabic.

Roberts collapsed his field of fire into the room as soon as he saw his corner was clear and took down the knife wielder with a burst to the chest. The Libyan fell straight to the deck. Another SEAL hit the man at the footlocker with several MP5 bursts to the neck and side of the head. The nuke specialist ran to the device. After a quick check, he gave Roberts a thumbs-up. The weapon was not armed, and there was no danger. The assaulters checked the terrorists for pulses and patted them down for booby traps and weapons. They searched the area for explosives, took the Libyans' documents and personal effects, and found a satellite phone under a bunk. Within minutes, they had secured the entire area. Time to call SOCOM.

Roberts got no response when he pressed his radio transmit button. He pressed it again. Nothing. He asked the CIA officer to hail SOCOM. His system was dead too. Roberts's chronometer told him that their operational run time was fourteen minutes. In unison, the rest of the team checked their radios and found them inoperative. The nuke specialist wondered half facetiously if the batteries were dead. Roberts barked that they broke out brand new batteries before the assault and they worked when he called in. No one, however, checked charge levels before boarding the Seahawk. No one had any spares either.

All the batteries were dead, and there was no way to contact the operations center. A different clock was running now, and their survival depended on how well they resolved their new problem. SOCOM would soon move the pieces to sink the ship. His mind raced. *The Libyan's satellite phone!*

"Bob, throw me that sat phone," Roberts shouted.

"Good idea, skipper," Bob Morgan said, "but it's too late for that."

"No battery?" The sat phone flew across the room.

"Worse. Take a look."

"No, I don't believe this shit!" The phone was scorched, the

LCD screen was cracked, the antenna was broken off, and half the buttons were gone. The flash bang had detonated right next to it.

Roberts knew the bridge and the ship's captain had communications gear. He left two operators, the weapons man, and the CIA officer with the nuke and took the other five with him. He would use the bridge radio to call SOCOM at MacDill and the captain's satellite phone to call JSOC at Pope.

The operators stormed the bridge and identified themselves as SEALs to the *Eagle's* First Officer. Roberts told him why they were on the ship, and asked him to establish a ship-to-shore communication so he could make a phone call. He also told him to advise the captain that SEALs were about to visit his quarters.

The first officer did not cooperate. "Nobody advised me about your team. How do I know you're not terrorists?"

"Look, you idiot, I'm advising you now. I'm not trying to take over your damned ship. I just want to make a phone call. If I don't, two Hornets and four Harpoon missiles will blow us out of the water. Make the call now or I will. Five seconds." Roberts raised his MP5 to the first officer's head from less than six feet and clicked the safety through to full auto.

"I'm calling, I'm calling!" He picked up the handset, dialed the operator, and told a crewman to raise the captain.

The next sixty seconds were an eternity as Roberts waited for the ship-to-shore operator. When she answered, he gave her the SOCOM number at MacDill. His chronometer showed nineteen minutes. The order to sink was seven minutes away.

"Sir," came the operator's business-like voice, "the lines are congested. It will take seven to eight minutes to connect your call. Please stand by."

"Ma'am, this is a matter of national security. Please put me through now."

"They're always matters of national security," was the taciturn reply. "Please wait."

"We're going to get smoked because we can't get a damned phone connection!" Roberts shouted.

General Yarbrough paced the SOCOM operations center faster than ever. Roberts had not called in since he confirmed the insertion. "We're at twenty-one minutes," he said. "Try them again."

"Yes, sir." Mansour pressed the switch on his microphone. His hail went unanswered. He tried again. Silence. Mansour hesitated. He knew what was about to go into motion.

"And?" the general asked.

"You heard what I did, general. Nothing. All comms were up and running when they hit the deck. They're all down now. It's your call, sir."

"I have to advise the president." Yarbrough picked up the telephone. "Mr. President," he said, "I regret to inform you that we've had no contact with the *Eagle* SMU since they confirmed a successful insertion. Repeated attempts to contact them have failed. They're more than six minutes overdue, and they're fast approaching our window for a possible panic detonation by the terrorists."

"Have you tried contacting the ship directly?" the president asked. "If you think the team has been compromised, there's no risk in a direct link."

"As we speak, sir. We can't get through to the bridge. A direct hail raises no one, the lines are full, and the captain's satellite phone does not respond. We are flat out of options, sir."

"I understand, general, but wait as long as possible. I won't order the strike a moment before I have to. Keep this line open."

"Yes, Mr. President."

As Roberts waited for the operator to put him through, the bridge intercom squelched. It was one of his SEALs. "Lieutenant? We've got a problem down here with the captain. He's out, snoring like a fiend, and we can't find his sat phone."

"On my way," Roberts said as he looked at his senior SEAL. "Ed, you handle this if a line opens up. You know what to say. Pull this place apart and see if you can find a sat phone or some batteries. If you do, call SOCOM or JSOC first and advise me later."

Roberts flew to the captain's quarters and found his three SEALs tearing the room apart, looking for the phone. The captain snored. One of the operators pointed to an empty Don Julio tequila bottle on the nightstand.

"We tried to wake him, but he's out for a while. His phone has to be here somewhere."

"At least he got drunk on the good stuff. Unbelievable," spat Roberts.

Roberts looked at his chronometer. Three minutes from the order to sink. In one, the SEALs located the phone. Roberts hit the Power button, and the screen jumped to life. He ran topside to get a signal, praying the satellite would recognize the phone. Once on deck, his heart stopped when the screen blinked and asked for a four digit ID code. His chronometer told him he was out of time, but he would keep trying until he saw tail flames from the Harpoons.

"Mr. President, the SMU is still out of contact," Yarbrough said. "We are now overdue at twenty six minutes, sir."

"Order the strike, general."

Yarbrough instructed the Hornets to deliver their missiles. At 1,300 mph, they would launch the Harpoons in two minutes. When he heard the order, Mansour tried to raise the SMU one more time, but got no response. There was little time left. His contractors, posing as caterers, had placed listening devices throughout the *Eagle.* Mansour knew the *Eagle* team had killed the Libyans, secured the nuke, and that their comms were out because of dead batteries. His specialists were listening and transmitting everything to his cell phone via satellite text message, including that Roberts was topside on a sat phone trying to get through to MacDill. Mansour could call the strike off, but doing so would reveal his own team's presence. He watched the text line on his cell phone and waited.

Roberts knew he was cooked without the ID code. There was no time to search the cabin, and guessing was futile. Almost everyone wrote their ID numbers somewhere. He flipped the phone over and saw a piece of tape on the underside: 0149. That had to be it. He punched furiously at the keypad, but his tactical gloves caused him to enter multiple numbers at once. The phone beeped an error message. He had ninety seconds left.

He stripped off his gloves with his teeth and tried again. The connection icon beeped that he was on-line. The first call to SOCOM dropped. He dialed again and got a busy signal. He had fifty-five seconds. Roberts pulled a piece of tape from inside his kneepad that listed emergency phone numbers. He gambled and entered Jay Mansour's cell phone. With fewer than forty seconds to weapons release, it finally rang.

"Shit!" Mansour muttered, as his cell phone flashed "unknown caller," repeatedly. "Can you believe my cell phone is ringing at a time like this?"

"Oh hell," General Yarbrough said, "answer the damn thing. You never know who it might be. This will play out regardless."

Taking the call would mean he could not receive messages from his contract team. The screen continued to flash "unknown caller". Mansour ran his finger over the Power button to disconnect the line. Few people had his number. Mansour saw thirty seconds flash up on the digital timer and started to tell General Yarbrough to call off the strike as he pressed the Answer button. Before he could open his mouth, Roberts screamed at the top of his lungs. "Jay, Roberts! We're alive, our comms went down! We secured the package, and the Libyans are dead! Call off the

Hornets! Call them off!"

"General," Mansour shouted, "it's Roberts. He says their comms went down and he's got two dead Libyans and a secure package. He's screaming to call off the Hornets."

"Are you sure it's Roberts?"

"Sir, we have less than thirty seconds. It's his voice. Nobody else would know about the missiles. They're dead if we hesitate, sir."

"Abort general, now!" the president shouted into the open phone line.

"Done, sir."

Yarbrough issued the abort order at twenty seconds, and at fourteen the Hornets acknowledged and asked for reconfirmation. They got it at nine seconds, locked their weapons, peeled off, and headed for home. America's best had improvised and overcome. By the time Roberts detailed the take-down and the president congratulated him, their ride was within earshot.

Jay Mansour sat down and finally relaxed when the communication was cut. He was wrung out, had nothing left, and could finally disconnect. He wanted a beer, but had to settle for the Gatorade next to his laptop. Everything had come together. While his own contribution was likely to be acknowledged, perhaps even rewarded, few would ever know of the determining role that ten ghost warriors played in the overall mission success. In a secret world, he and Roger Harrington had their own secrets. It was time to go home.

68

"Where are you coming from, sir?" the U.S. Customs officer in Miami asked me as I handed him a stamped immigrations form.

"La Paz, Bolivia."

"Business or pleasure?"

"A bit of both. I have something to declare."

"Line 15, please."

Line 15 was for declaration of goods or anybody customs thought looked suspicious. The line was long, but it moved. Evidently, coming in from Latin America automatically put most everyone on the "we think you've done something wrong" list. When my turn came, I said I needed to declare a firearm.

"Do you have the ATF form?" the officer asked.

"No, I have this." I handed her a piece of paper.

The Personal Effects Taken Abroad Form showed the model, the serial number, and the caliber of the firearm in my checked luggage. It was signed, dated, and stamped by customs in Miami when I took it out of the country months before. U.S. law required no other form.

"This won't work," she rejoined. "You need ATF and State Department permission to import that weapon."

"I'm not importing it. I'm just bringing it back. The form has the U.S. Customs stamp and signature on it. State and ATF told me before I got on the plane that the procedure was still the same."

"You're not listening," she almost shouted. "You can't bring this in. It's illegal. We'll have to confiscate it."

Another officer came over to see what sort of trouble I was causing. She told him I was trying to import a firearm illegally, and that I did not understand the rules and regulations. He looked at the form and told her I had exactly what I needed.

"What do you use this for, hunting?" she asked sharply.

"No. As you can see, it's a 1911, full-size Government Model, in .45 ACP."

"Which government? The U.S. government or a foreign government?" She squinted at the form. "Why do you need it?" she asked, hands on her hips. "Do you think you need this for personal defense or something?"

"Something like that." I smiled.

She tossed the form on the table and told me to put my things on the belt to be X-rayed. As I walked by the machine, I asked the officer watching the monitor if he wanted to compare the serial number of the gun to my paperwork. No need, he waved me on. I picked up my bags and was headed out when I heard, "Sir, could you please come here?"

I looked around. Another officer motioned me back.

"Yes?"

"Your firearm is supposed to be unloaded when you travel. Make sure that's the case next time."

"Yes, sir, I'm sorry. It won't happen again."

Several feet short of the sliding glass door leading out of customs, I stopped and turned around. After years of traveling with firearms, I was meticulous about packing my bags. I walked back to the officers, opened my suitcase, and asked them to show me the loaded gun. The officer had trouble racking the slide to check the chamber, so I suggested she cock the hammer. Her Glock, she noted, did not have a hammer. Imagine that. I asked them to check all the magazines in the gun case.

"Empty?"

"All empty, have a nice day."

I was tired from the flight and wondered if this was a dream. Once through customs, TSA inspected my bags, gave them to the American Airlines baggage attendant, and I took the escalator up to the main terminal for my Concourse B connecting flight.

"Man, I thought you'd never make it," Chris said as I arrived at the gate.

"I wasn't sure I would either. I had a stupidity attack and told customs I was bringing a firearm back. I'll just walk through next time."

"Everything's checked to Chicago. I looked at the weather a couple of hours ago, and there's not much of a moon. Plus, a storm blew in that's hanging over the entire area."

"No wonder Julie doesn't answer. Storms up there always knock the phones out. I can't get a message to her. Damn."

"We'll be there soon. They'll be okay."

"Man, I hope so."

69

The charter pulled up within a hundred feet of the Pellston Regional Airport terminal at 9:40 P.M., and the rental car was waiting as promised. I thanked the pilots for the ride, and we walked down the stairs into a crisp Michigan fall evening. Chris and I pulled our gear from the baggage compartment and loaded it into the car. I dialed the cottage as soon as we pulled onto the highway.

"Julie, am I glad you picked up, sweetheart. Are you okay?"

"We're fine." She was calm. "Some bad weather blew in yesterday and will be here for six days. Sean and Kathy are already restless. Where are you?"

"I just got to Traverse City, and I still have to get my bag and the car. I should be there in about two hours. See you then, love. Bye."

"Man, don't you even know what airport we flew into?" Chris asked.

"Yeah, I know exactly where we landed. If someone's listening, I want them to think we're farther away than we are. Julie's in trouble."

"How do you know?"

"Well, for starters, Price told me so when he thought he was messaging Dávila. Julie confirmed it. Our code for trouble is 'bad weather.' Six bad guys came in yesterday."

"Hey, great odds for us. Two against six."

"We're thirty to forty minutes from the cottage. We know they're waiting for me, but they don't know you're coming along. All we need is a lot of luck."

I drove southeast on U.S. 31 to Petoskey while we reviewed our plans. Pike Lake was five miles from Petoskey, and the extension from the tip of the west arm near Lake Michigan to the south arm was almost six miles. Hundreds of cottages dotted the shoreline. Ours perched thirty feet above the shoreline with a panoramic view of the lake. Winding stone steps led to a forty foot long dock.

Chris and I went over the layout as we drove. A packed gravel driveway descended 125 yards to the house, almost perfectly bisecting our six acres. Dense trees surrounded the driveway. We would expose ourselves walking down to the cottage, and someone would hear us if we walked through the woods. The best option was a footpath from the neighbor's property that would conceal us up to twenty feet from the east side of the house. From there, we could see the lake on the left and the driveway on the right.

The cottage lay east to west with three bedrooms near the footpath, then the living room, kitchen, dining room, sun room, and the master bedroom with a wood deck facing the lake. We guessed my family was in the living room, the most logical place to hold a group of people. If so, we would come at them from two directions. Chris would go right and come in through the front, straight into the living room. I would go left and come in through the master bedroom.

We pulled into a Lake Michigan beach access a few miles from the cottage to get ready. I threw soft body armor on over my shirt, and then pulled on a sweater and a light jacket. The armor would stop handgun rounds, but would not even slow long guns down. I hoped they didn't have any long guns or body armor. I hated better odds for the bad guys.

We opened new packs of batteries for the long gun light mounts, the red dot scopes, and our hand-held flashlights. We tested the batteries to make sure they were charged. I clicked the carbine-mounted light on and off several times and adjusted the red dot scope to find the right brightness setting.

I prepped my 1911, loaded several pistol magazines, and charged my carbine magazines with 240 grain subsonic rounds. The suppressor would not eliminate the supersonic crack with normal ammo, but suppressed subsonic would sound no louder than an air gun. Perfect for sentries and inside the house. I inserted the magazine in my carbine and heard it click in place, tugged to make sure it was seated, hit the bolt release, checked that I chambered a round, and made sure it was on safe. Even with four pistol mags and five carbine mags, I wondered if I had enough. I pulled, tugged, and squatted a few times to make sure everything was snug but not too tight. The last thing I needed was my legs to go numb on a cold night. I cleaned off my shooting glasses, pulled my hat on tight, and gave Chris a thumbs up that I was ready.

Chris strapped on his SIG 226 pistol, and loaded his suppressed MP5-SD. He would make no noise tonight beyond brass falling. He had three subgun magazines in a drop leg pouch and three more on his vest. He chamber checked his SIG and his MP5. He pulled, tugged, and squatted. Ready.

We put our long guns in the back seat, squeezed into the front, and pulled out of the beach access. We turned onto West Shore Road at 10:35 P.M. and drove along the left side of the lake. It was cold, very quiet, with no lights anywhere. A quarter of a mile from the cottage, the road twisted and turned every twenty to thirty yards. Trees hid most of the driveways, including mine, so we kept our eyes open to make sure we would not drive right past it. I had done that at night too many times before.

We rolled to a stop less than a hundred yards from the house, pulled into a dirt parking area on the left side of the road, and got out of the car. We pulled the long guns out of the back, turned on the scopes, chamber-checked pistols, and checked mags. We tugged on everything one more time.

After Raúl's attempt on my family, I was past worrying about the implications of what we were going to do. It was a question of survival. My family and I would survive. The bad guys would not.

70

We moved slowly through the trees along West Grove, opposite the cottage, stepping carefully to avoid branches or twigs. I took short steps as the rain had left the ground soft and slippery. We would move to contact. After several minutes we were near our property and still saw and heard nothing. I wondered if they had bothered to post a lookout when we heard a cough in front of us. Someone cleared his throat. We took advantage of the racket and bounded towards him. He was forty-five feet away, smoking and leaning against a tree almost directly across from my driveway.

When he took a second drag, we saw he had a cigarette in his right hand and a radio in his left. He turned in our direction when we were thirty feet from him. We froze. It was so dark he would not pick up movement if he looked directly at us. If he looked slightly away, he would notice even the smallest twitch. Funny how the human eye worked. His radio squelched after a few seconds, he turned away, and reported there was no activity.

We had a clear line to the guy and moved while he continued to talk. Ten feet away, Chris rushed forward and was on him before he could react. He wrapped a bandana around the lookout's neck and rode him straight to the ground. The guy hit face first with Chris's knee in his back. Holding the bandana tight, Chris twisted the guy's head to one side and asked how many of his people were in the house.

"I don't know what you're talking about," he replied, spitting dirt.

"Wrong answer. Let's try this one more time. How many of you are there?" Chris tightened the bandana.

"Five," came the labored reply. "I can't breathe man. I'm choking."

"That's the point. Any other lookouts? Weapons?"

"One guy on the lake side of the house on the deck and one walking around the front," he gasped. "Only pistols and one shotgun. Nothing else."

"Where's the shotgun?" I asked.

"In the living room, closest to the front door."

"That's good," Chris said. "See how easy this is when you cooperate?"

"Vehicles?" I asked.

"One Suburban. In the driveway."

"Where are the rest of your people, and where's my family?" I knelt beside him and pulled his hair back so I could see his face.

"Two more guys in the living room with your family."

"What were you planning to do?"

"We were supposed to wait three days. If you showed, we'd kill all of you. If you didn't, we'd kill the family and leave them for you to find."

I drew my hand across my throat as I got to my feet, and Chris cranked hard to the left. The resounding crack announced a bad guy gone. Chris dead-checked him with two MP5 rounds to the head. We pulled his body back into the bushes, left his pistol holstered, and turned his radio off. We crossed the road to walk down the neighbor's driveway and hung a right onto the footpath. Chris scanned the woods around us with his night vision monocular and saw nothing. At the edge of our property, we crouched in the dense growth less than twenty feet from the cottage.

The lake was to our left, the sloping driveway and circular turnaround was to our right. Julie's Tahoe was parked headed uphill at the far end of the turnaround, and our uninvited guests' Suburban was right behind it. The bedrooms directly in front of us were dark. A little light came from the front of the house to our right and a lot shone from the living room on the lake side to our left. That meant the curtains were open.

There was a man on the deck at the far end of the lake side of the house about thirty yards in front of me. He was almost entirely in the shadows, but lit himself up every couple of minutes when he moved enough to activate the motion light on the edge of the deck.

Less than a minute later a second bad guy came around the house from the driveway to our right, walking slowly and cradling an Uzi with both hands. Our friend up the hill conveniently neglected to mention the Uzi. The man stopped less than a yard to Chris's right at the edge of the lawn, put the Uzi under his arm, and unzipped to relieve himself. Thankfully, he was out of the line of sight of the guy on the deck. As soon as he turned around to walk away, Chris was on him with a good grip on his hair, jerked his head back, and ripped the blade across his throat so hard it nearly decapitated him. Just like killing sheep. We pulled our second score back into the bushes. It was my turn. I stretched out and relaxed to make my shooting position as natural as possible.

I wanted to hit the guy on the deck in the head, but I didn't think I could make the shot with his upper body in the shadows. Without a night vision scope on my carbine, I was going to have to get him the old fashioned way. The deck was almost a foot off the grass, so he was slightly elevated. He paced back and forth. I needed him to stop moving. He finally stood still and faced slightly towards me looking at the lake. The light projecting from the living room silhouetted his entire body.

I took two deep breaths and centered my sight on his upper chest. Tonight I was especially glad that the red dot was an internal aiming device and not a laser that painted the target. No need to announce what was about to happen. I slid the safety off and placed my right index finger on the trigger. One more breath and exhale, and I pressed the trigger. I heard a *pfft* from the suppressor and a *thwack* as the 240 grain round hit his upper chest. He dropped to his knees and slumped upright against the post on the edge of the deck. The motion light lit him up like a sunburst.

With his head fully illuminated, I took another breath and steadied my sight below his forehead on the soft spot near his eyes. *Pfft. Thwack.* The impact was softer and wetter. His head turned into a pink mist that swirled in the light breeze. He pitched forward and fell face first into the grass. I put my safety on as Chris headed to the driveway to create our distraction.

Running to the deck, I saw Julie and the children in the living room to my right. Two men sat directly across from Julie, both mid-thirties, one blond and the other with jet-black hair. They were dressed casually without coats or ties, and each sported a shoulder rig. The good news was their pistols were holstered. The bad news was the blond guy talked into a cell phone. To the far right, a skinny guy sat with a shotgun on his lap about twenty feet from where Chris would come through the front door. As I drew even with the living room, the blond fellow stood up, slapped Julie, and shouted at her. He would get a few extra bullets for that.

I jumped onto the deck, slipped in the sentry's blood and brain matter, and landed hard on my back. Scrambling up hoping no one heard the *thud* of my fall, I went through the master bedroom and sunroom, and held to the left of the open doorway that led to the living room. Without exposing myself, I could see my family and one of the bad guys. Chris started Julie's car and the skinny guy with the shotgun got up to check on the noise. As he disappeared around the corner to the front hall, I leaned slightly to the right and cleared my muzzle of the wall. I could now see both bad guys sitting next to Julie. Chris drilled the skinny guy with several bursts to the chest when he opened the front door. The instant I heard his suppressed rounds, I nailed the blond guy next to Julie with a handful in the chest and shot his buddy as he stood up to go to the front door.

We had killed a bunch of bad guys, but I was worried there might be more. I put my family in the master bedroom, armed them, and told Julie and Sean to shoot anyone who came in before we returned. Back in the living room, Chris and I checked for pulses. We did not recognize the first two goons, but the skinny guy seemed familiar.

Chris and I headed down to the lake and walked the grounds to satisfy ourselves that nobody was left. I checked the cell phone. It was turned off and there was no record of calls in or out. Crap, I thought we might have a lead. While I cursed, Chris reminded me that we had to clean up and get downtown Chicago to visit Whitworth and Price at their lunch meeting tomorrow.

71

I was elated as I looked at the mess around us, and felt neither remorse nor sorrow. I was glad the bastards were dead, and could not wait to get the rest of them. Julie was shaken, but adrenalin and the maternal instinct kicked in. She was more worried about the children than about herself. Kathy's eyes were wide and fixed, and her mouth trembled as tears streamed down her cheeks. She had the look of a child about to shut down and held on to Julie for dear life. Julie rocked her gently and stroked her hair. I hugged and kissed them. I told Kathy I was sorry she had to see this happen, but the bad guys were dead and we were safe. She burst into tears and said she was afraid something would happen to me. She was definitely Julie's daughter. Sean was frightened, but masked it by pacing around the room and swearing.

The logistics of cleaning up were upon us as we had six bodies and a lot of blood to deal with. Sean and Chris started with the lookout across the road, and I went out back. Part of the guy's head was on the deck, and I had to hose everything down to keep him from becoming the neighbor's dog's breakfast the next day. We threw the bodies into their Suburban, cleaned up as much blood as we could, and policed all our brass. We decided to drive the hit team's car to a Lake Michigan rest stop and leave it there.

Before we loaded the cars, I phoned Denning and Newman in La Paz. They wanted to know we were safe, so I owed them a call. It was late, but I knew they would be up.

"Richard," Newman answered, "I'm pulling duty alone tonight. John got called away for a day or so. Is the family okay?"

"That's why I'm calling. Everyone's fine. Just wanted you to know."

"Glad to hear it. Are you going to stay up there for a while?"

"Probably. I'd like to get some rest. I'm beat from these past couple weeks, and this is a great place to recharge the batteries."

"Sounds good to me. Listen, a couple of things have happened that you might want to know about."

"Such as?"

"Well, first, Dávila's dead. He and several of his bodyguards were shot to shit."

"Fabulous. Maybe they're taking each other out now that Raúl's gone."

"That's what we figured. There's something else too. Our guys discovered that Raúl's company doesn't own the Boeing outright that's running the DEA guys and the cocaine to Atlanta. He bought it through one of his companies and then did a sale-leaseback with a Phoenix subsidiary. That allows us to see through Raúl to Phoenix. Based on that connection, we got warrants to raid Phoenix's headquarters and impound files and computers. We're starting to think that someone at Phoenix might be tied to these deals. We couldn't get arrest warrants, but we'll seize a ton of data."

"Great. When does all that happen?"

"Faster than we thought. The flight was supposed to be next week, but we found out an hour ago it's been moved up to tomorrow. The customers are nervous since Raúl's dead, and they want delivery now. The plane lands in Atlanta at 2:55 P.M. eastern time, and we'll nail it as soon as it taxis to the hangar."

"What does that mean for a raid on Phoenix's offices?"

"They'll go in as soon as the Atlanta bust goes down. I'd guess somewhere around 2:00 P.M. central time."

"I sure hope they find something," I said, biting my tongue. "As soon as you get the chance, bring Denning up to speed and let him know we're safe, okay?"

"Will do, Richard."

"Thanks. Good luck tomorrow."

"Chose not to come clean did we?" Chris smiled.

"No way. I'm glad we killed those jerks, and if we're lucky we might just get away with it. Denning and Newman have been helpful, but they're federal agents and they don't need to know what we did. Denning had a reason to keep quiet about Raúl, but this is entirely different. Besides, I'm having a damn good time."

"I noticed. That's the scary part."

"We've got a problem, though."

"What's that?"

"They're going to seize Raúl's plane in Atlanta tomorrow afternoon and raid the Phoenix corporate offices in Chicago at the same time, around 2:00 P.M. central."

"Damn! That doesn't give us much time to get in and out."

"Tell me about it."

We threw suitcases and duffle bags into Julie's SUV and locked up the house. Chris and I took the hit team's Suburban up to West Shore with Julie and the children close behind in her car. I jumped out down the road and got the rental car. Chris took the lead to Lake Michigan in the Suburban, with Julie next, and I brought up the rear. We left the Suburban in a picnic area on Highway 31. With Kathy sound asleep in the back seat, Julie and I pulled back onto the highway and headed for Chicago. I had my 1911 in a concealment holster and the carbine between us. Sean rode with Chris in the rental. For good measure, Chris's MP5 was loaded and Sean had the shotgun.

Shortly after midnight, the phone rang in the study of Steven Price's Barrington Hills home northwest of Chicago. He savored his brandy and ignored the phone until the number flashed on the screen.

"We have a serious problem with Blackstone," the voice said over the crackling line.

"What kind of problem, Zimmerman? Hasn't he shown up yet?"

"Worse. He's already been there, and our people didn't get him."

"What?" Price put the brandy down and got up to close the study door. "Don't tell me he survived."

"Not only is he alive, he's on the move."

"You were supposed to get this over with once and for all."

"Steven, these guys were good. We used them before, and they always did the job. This is the first time they failed."

"Were good? What does that mean?"

"Precisely that. They're all dead."

"You said this would be a piece of cake. Now you're telling me Blackstone single-handedly took out six armed professionals?"

"He had help."

"How do you know that?"

"The bugs we planted in the house picked it up."

"You're holding out," Price said. "Start over."

"I talked to the team leader about 10:00 P.M. Blackstone had just spoken to his wife, was on his way from Traverse City, and they expected him in two hours. They were going to call me after they killed him."

"I'm listening."

"I was hungry and grabbed a burger down the road. I came

back and waited for the call."

"You didn't listen to the bugs while you waited?"

"Hell no. I muted the sound and ran them through the tape recorder so I could listen later. Our men were there anyway. I ate my burger, took a nap, and called them at midnight my time. No one picked up, so I flipped on the tapes. Blackstone showed up an hour early. He must have flown into Pellston instead of Traverse City. He knew something was going on."

"No shit, Sherlock. Your people should have known better, Zimmerman."

"We're short on time, and I think you'll want to hear the rest of what I have to say. Now, do you want to listen, or are we going to sling shit at each other?"

"Keep talking."

"Shortly after eleven one of my men went out to check on some car engine noise. There was shouting, shooting, and then it was quiet."

"What a time to eat and take a nap, you idiot."

"Last warning. One more editorial comment and I hang up. Anyway, it sounded like Blackstone and a buddy took our team out. They cleaned the place up and moved out ten minutes ago."

"Did you go by the cottage?"

"No way. This deal is dead and we're out of here. There's nothing anyone can trace to us, not even the bugs. We're wheels up in five minutes."

"Where's Blackstone now?"

"Headed to Chicago to take you and Whitworth out tomorrow during lunch."

"Damn it, Zimmerman, we have to get him before he gets here," Price insisted.

"Wake up, man! What do you think this is? Just pick up the phone and dial 1-800-HIT-TEAM? Delivery in thirty minutes or your hit's free? They're already on their way! There's no time to get another team together, and you're on your own. You screwed with the wrong guy. He was awfully cool on tape, and only regretted there weren't more people to shoot. He's looking forward to seeing you and Whitworth tomorrow, so you better have a plan. We can go after him again, but not any time soon. We're going to lie low on the West Coast for a while. I'll be in touch."

"You do that," was all Price said as he put the handset in the cradle and then "asshole" once the connection was cut.

"Blackstone, you prick," Price said to the empty study. "All that work, the perfect plan, and you turned it upside down on us."

Price knew every enterprise had a life cycle, but was angry to see this one close so quickly. What started as a chance meeting with Raúl many years ago became the most efficient drug business in the world, but Blackstone knew too much and this part of the operation would phase out quickly. Still, despite what he knew, Blackstone had no idea it was only an isolated piece of a much larger, richer landscape. Price could live with this loss.

He refilled his brandy, booted up his laptop, and eased himself into the chair behind the desk. Curious how Blackstone knew where to find him, Price logged on the Phoenix system and went directly to his on-line calendar. Only selected senior executives could view his calendar, and Blackstone was one of them. "Damn," he muttered as the access log came up, cursing the systems group for not canceling Blackstone's authorization.

Blackstone knew when and where he and Whitworth would eat lunch. It was time for Price to go into overdrive to protect himself and cut his losses. There was no time to lament the lost operation or what could have been. Steven Price knew he was the ultimate survivor and would always come out on top.

72

I woke Julie up an hour out of Chicago so I could find her aunt and uncle's house. She had called them an hour earlier to say we were making an impromptu visit. We pulled into their driveway in the northern suburbs at 9:00 A.M., and her aunt had breakfast ready. After a meal, a shower, and a change of clothes, Chris and I were back upstairs in the guest bedroom trying to figure out what was next. I wanted to sleep, but our window of opportunity was narrowing.

Federal agents would descend on the Phoenix headquarters as the Atlanta bust went down, and we had to get to the Loop and be gone before they arrived. I knew they would do nothing more than seize some computers and files. So what? For my longevity and my family's safety, Steven Price and Geoff Whitworth needed permanent ballistic counseling. How we would accomplish that was not entirely obvious.

"Man, I'm really tired of this," I said to Chris while I looked over my gear. "We have no clue how to get these guys, and we're making this up as we go along. Again."

"Yeah, I know. They're not stupid enough to let computer files nail them. That's a waste of time. Are you sure they're eating together today?"

"As of yesterday I was, but I'll check again."

I logged on the Phoenix system, hoping no one would notice the brief incursion. They were still on for 1:00 P.M.

We had few alternatives. Our first option was to walk into the building and go straight up to their offices. We nixed the idea since it was unlikely we could get past the ground floor reception desk. Even if we did, the card key system, the security cameras, or the executive suite secretaries would pick us up. We would be cuffed in short order. Dumb plan.

The second option was to take the executive elevator from the underground garage straight to Whitworth's office, but the video cameras would probably pick us up. Even if the security group had not cancelled my garage access, my card would generate an exception report and set their screens on fire. I had already tempted fate several times by going into the computer system, and I did not want to push my luck any more. We needed direct, fast, and undetected access and escape from the building. We were stumped.

"I've got it!" Chris jumped out of his chair. "We'll parachute to the top of the building in broad daylight, rappel over the side, crash into Whitworth's office, and shoot the shit out of everybody. Then we'll parachute to the street and catch a plane to live the good life in Tahiti."

"Awesome plan!"

We were having a good laugh when Julie's uncle knocked on the door. "What's going on, guys?" he asked as he sat down in a chair across from us.

"Not much," I said dryly as I kicked the top of my duffle bag shut.

"I don't think so," he said with a smile. "You blow into town with no warning, have blood on you, have a bunch of gear up here, and Julie is downstairs being evasive. So what gives?"

I had known Riley since Julie and I started dating over twenty years before. He was a retired helicopter gunship pilot and not much escaped him. He was family. We gave him the five minute drill to bring him up to speed. His reaction was immediate.

"I'm in."

"Forget it, Riley. This is serious. Tell you what though, do you have any ideas?"

"Yeah, but only if I'm in. You need to get in and out fast. Right?"

"Yep."

"Get a helicopter," Riley beamed, "and I'm your man."

"What are you talking about?" Chris asked.

"Does the building have a helipad?"

"Yeah, it does," I said slowly, "but they rarely use it."

"Okay, now we're getting somewhere," Riley said, slapping his hands together. "Who has access to the pad, and how do you get into the building from there?"

"Whitworth's really the only one, and the rooftop elevator opens directly to his executive suite."

"There's your answer, and I'm the man who can put you there."

"I like the idea, but I'm not going to drag you into this."

"Forget the 'drag you into it' crap. I'm pushing. Look, I still fly a hundred hours a year. We can grab a helo from Palwaukee Field, I'll take you directly to the Phoenix helipad, you do your business, and we blow out of there. Are you sure no one uses it except Phoenix?"

"Positive. Phoenix owns the entire building. Access is via electronic keypad, and unless they've changed the code, Whitworth's birthday unlocks the door."

"How on earth do you know that?" Riley asked.

"I used the helipad when I interviewed with Phoenix, and Whitworth bragged that the code was his birthday. Oh, plus, there are no security cameras up there."

"Even if they've changed the code," Chris said, "we can get

past it."

"Riley, look . . .," I started.

"Richard, do you guys have a better alternative?"

"No."

"Okay, then. Let's get moving. I'll make a couple of calls to get the bird ready. Can you be ready in an hour?"

"Done."

73

"Gail, tell Steven I'm waiting," Geoff Whitworth said into the speakerphone from his Phoenix Tower dining room.

"I'm sorry, Mr. Whitworth. He just called and said he can't make it."

"Call him, please," Whitworth said ringing off, only to stab the Talk button almost immediately.

"Steven, what's going on?"

"You won't believe this," Price said over a background of people talking and shouting. "The power in my study cut out last night, so I left a lit candle while I went to flip the breaker. The room was in flames when I got back. The fire destroyed both my computers, and all my files are toast. The insurance guys are here right now, so I won't be in until later today."

"What a way to start the day. Any news on Blackstone?"

"Zimmerman said Blackstone showed up last night around 11:00 P.M. and everyone's dead."

"Excellent. Did he get the package?"

"I'm waiting for a confirmation. I'll call you as soon as I hear."

Riley floated the JetRanger to a dead center landing on the Phoenix oval at 1:05 P.M. I pulled my leather gloves on tight, and we made a beeline to the rooftop door that led into the building. I entered the code, the pad beeped, the green light flashed, and the electronic lock released. The Phoenix security group had not integrated rooftop access into the overall system because the accountants refused to release $85,000 for the project. They believed no one would be on the helipad unless they belonged there. The stairwell had no cameras and the elevator was right in front of us. Easy.

I got on the elevator and pressed the button for the 47th floor while Chris stayed topside. The disembodied female computer voice announced my arrival at Whitworth's executive suite almost immediately. My heart pounded as the door opened to an immense office—an empty one. I breathed a bit easier since I still had the tactical advantage. A large sitting and reception area with a television and a bar was to the left, Whitworth's desk and work area was to the right. The window behind the desk was one continuous expanse of floor-to-ceiling glass overlooking Lake Michigan.

Two sets of closed doors on the far side led out of the office. The double doors directly across from me led out to Whitworth's secretary, and the single door ten feet to its right led to his private dining room. I locked the door to the secretary's area and then disconnected the panic alarm under his desk. Whitworth had boasted during my hire interview that shutting off his panic alarm would alert security in thirty minutes. I set my watch chronometer for twenty eight minutes, attached my pistol suppressor, and then opened the private dining room door.

"Hello Geoff," I said as the door swung open and Whitworth came into view. His open mouth froze, and he dropped his fork. My jaw dropped more than his when I saw Price was not there. "Where the hell is Price?"

"As you can see, he's not here," Whitworth's guest, facing away from me, said, "but if he were, he'd be as amazed as we are that you're still alive. You are one persistent bastard, Richard."

My surprise at Price's absence paled compared to the shock that rolled over me. The broad back was unmistakable and the booming voice even more so. I was stunned. The last couple of months flashed before me.

"Denning, you son of a bitch! You played me the whole time!"

"I did, and you were more than willing," he said as he turned to face me. "You really made it so easy."

"You prick," I said, fighting the urge to shoot him on the spot. "I trusted you with my life, my family's lives!"

"Hey, whose fault was that? You of all people should have known better."

I took a deep breath and told them to get up slowly and come into Whitworth's office. I locked the door behind them with one hand and trained the pistol on them with the other. Whitworth sat at his desk while Denning leaned against its right front corner and lit a cigar.

"You know you wouldn't get away with taking us out of here," Whitworth said. "Steven would have a team on you in no time."

"Better than the one you sent last night, I hope."

"You surprised even me," Denning said. "We thought they'd finish you off once and for all. It looks like you have some competent friends."

"At least some friends I can still count on."

"Oh, a little hurt are we?"

"No, just disappointed. I thought more of you. Planning on early retirement in Rio?"

"Richard, get a grip. The drug business is a license to print cash, and we can thank the U.S. government for that. We've spent twenty-five billion dollars in overseas drug enforcement in the last two decades and guess what? It's done nothing! The interdiction work breaks my balls, but it doesn't keep drugs off the street. It just keeps prices high for the drug lords. Thanks to Geoff and Steven, I've finally been able to tap into that income stream."

"I'm glad for you, John. Now you can put drug lord lackey on your résumé. Very nice."

"Hey, you do what you gotta do. So, where do we go from here?"

"Straight to hell for both you assholes," I said pointing my pistol at Denning.

"Oh, come on, Richard," Denning shot back. "Don't be so melodramatic. You're not going to kill us here. You'd spend the rest of your life in jail. How does that look for the man who would do anything to protect his family?"

"I trusted you with their safety, John. You were in on this all along. No wonder. You knew all of my movements, that my phones were tapped, who I called, who I suspected, when and how I did things."

"Of course I did," he laughed. "Why do you think this worked so seamlessly?"

"I don't understand. Raúl tapped my phones, killed Simpson, and tried to kill me. Indulge me. Where were you in this?"

"Raúl didn't tap your phones. I did. When you saw my man climbing the pole, I made Raúl the fall guy. You suspected him instantly, so he was a natural. I thought you would drop this or turn it over to me, but you were on a mission to save the world."

"No, just to do the right thing. Seems to be a foreign concept to you."

"Be that as it may, you sealed your fate when you met with Simpson. You sealed his as well. You killed Simpson, not Raúl."

"Man, you're beyond broken. If you knew where this was going, why did you let me meet with Simpson?"

"I was astounded by the amount of information you brought me, but it was too late to keep you from the DEA or anyone else. No matter how hard I tried to cover it up, you would have kept it alive. You and Raúl were going to do what you wanted, regardless of what I did. My only option was to back away and watch it play out."

"Are you saying Raúl acted completely on his own?"

"Hell, no," Whitworth answered. "Steven ran all of this and approved the hits on you and Simpson."

"You got Simpson, but I don't think you missed me intentionally."

"You're right, we didn't," Whitworth said. "Our man set the explosives to trigger when the car was put in gear, even though we specifically told him to detonate it remotely only when he saw you and your family in the vehicle. We wanted a visual confirmation, but he decided to improvise. He knew you didn't have your driver, but didn't anticipate John would send someone to drive you home. If he'd done what we told him, you would've been killed. Driver or no driver."

"You sent Jefferson knowing he was going to die?"

"Absolutely," Denning said matter-of-factly. "This deal was a lot bigger than one stupid MILGROUP guy."

"But why didn't you try again, and why didn't you rein me in before I killed Raúl?"

"You didn't want to be reined in. You wanted to kill Raúl, and we knew it. We didn't try to kill you again because after you survived the attack we realized you were much more valuable alive than dead."

"What the hell are you talking about?"

"Your hatred of Raúl suited us," Whitworth replied, pushing away from the desk. "Raúl was pissed off that he wasn't president of the region. He lost face, hated you, and was furious because he believed we no longer supported him. Raúl was volatile, but he always came back around. This time it didn't go away—it got worse. He controlled the drug infrastructure and thought he could run the business without us."

"Are you saying you needed Raúl out of the picture and let me kill him so you wouldn't have to?"

"In a word, yes," Whitworth said. "Raúl drove four nails into his own coffin. We suspected him of straying, and you conveniently brought us most of the proof. First, he cut us out of lucrative deals by manipulating share ownership in our chemical company joint ventures. Your information from Citibank and Grant & Co. confirmed that. He negotiated alliances with other drug dealers on his own behalf, and your photographs of Raúl in Trinidad with Agostini and Burgos proved it."

"It sounds like you were having a little trouble controlling your employees."

"Raúl's emotions were running away with him," Whitworth said. "They clouded his judgment to the point that he ordered a hit on Steven in Bogotá."

"That's absurd. How did you find that out?"

"Pure luck," Whitworth said. "Steven's driver and bodyguards wore headsets that recorded everything they said, and a Colombian general sent him the tape. The hit team leader cursed that the car was empty despite the fact that Raúl had promised Steven would be inside. We could have worked with Raúl on the share manipulation or the side deals, but the attack on Steven was the point of no return. That was his death sentence, and you willingly carried it out for us. The hit on you was real. When you survived, we knew you would do anything to get Raúl—including killing him. We just had to wait. You missed with your own bomb. Quite ingenious by the way. We knew you'd get him eventually, and you did."

"But why did you kill Torres?"

"He panicked when you killed Raúl, and he might have compromised us. John had to keep him quiet and had to keep playing his good guy role for you."

"So I was your instrument to clean up the operation."

"You were," Denning smiled. "By the way, that was a very nice job on Dávila, if a bit messy. We still haven't figured out who to blame for that one. Anyway, my guess is he pointed you to us."

"Let's just say he got talkative towards the end. Funny thing, he pointed me to Price and Whitworth. He had no idea you were part of this. Had you stayed away today, I wouldn't either. Regardless, I'm here and he's not."

"You're still here," Denning spat, "because you and your friend managed to take out our team. Make no mistake though, you left Bolivia alive only because you have something we need."

"What you need are morals and ethics."

"Spare me," Denning said as he relit his cigar. "Raúl kept a record of our correspondence and transactions history. If he went down, we all went down. That was the last nail in the coffin, and was why we needed you. Raúl burned a CD before the futsal game and was going to hide it after he killed Gustavo. You weren't the only one, by the way, who had spyware on Raúl's laptop. The problem is that we had no idea where he hid them, but we thought an actual CD might give us a lead. Anyway, he had it when you killed him, but I found nothing on his body or in any of Torres's things. Then I remembered you reached into Raúl's pocket and pulled something out before you got into my car. It must have been the disc. We figured the best way to the CD was through your family. You frustrated that plan last night. So, the final pitch is ours, not yours."

"Fat chance. I'm the one with the gun."

"We want the CD," Whitworth said, cutting Denning off before he could respond. "We'll put twenty-five million in any offshore bank, and you keep your mouth shut forever. You walk away wealthy, and we go right on doing business as usual."

My heart pounded so hard I could hardly breathe. If Denning only knew that all I pulled from Raúl's pocket was his cell phone. Regardless, he thought I had something worth twenty-five million dollars and I was not about to disappoint him. I was out of options. If I shot them here, I would probably never see another sunrise outside the U.S. penitentiary system. If I tried to take them on, my family would have to run forever. My heart and stomach hurt, but I had to deal with the bastards. I had no choice.

"No way. You get off cheap, you get the data, and you kill me. Without the CD, I have no insurance. Here's the deal. I keep the CD, you pay me fifty million, and you never hear from me or the data again. You hurt me or my family, and the CD and its contents are on every web page and in every newspaper. Take it or leave it."

"Done," Whitworth answered immediately, and then moved his hands to reach under the desk.

"Don't bother Geoff. There's nothing there."

Whitworth called his bank and arranged for an immediate wire transfer to my account in Montevideo, Uruguay. I called my Montevideo banker to alert him that a substantial deposit was on its way. Though most Latin American financial institutions were generally risky, Uruguay was known as the Switzerland of Latin America due to its discrete, efficient, and trustworthy banks. Within minutes, my banker and I held fax confirmations of the transaction. Seeing how fast it all happened, I was angry that I probably left money on the table.

My watch beeped, and I put the pistol inside my vest. It was time to go. We walked to the elevator and they told me I would leave the building unescorted. We would go our separate ways, never to meet again. Whitworth told me smugly that I made a wise choice. They had me, and they knew it. They both flashed the self-satisfied grin Raúl threw at me so often. I hated them. They stood on either side of me as the keypad beeped and the elevator arrived. I could not stand to be around them any more. As the doors opened, I took a step back, put an arm around each, and pushed forward as hard as I could. I launched them into the black void of the elevator shaft, and they fell to the oily concrete floor forty-seven stories below.

"Adios, assholes." I spat after them and waited for the door to close. Ten seconds later, it opened and Chris smiled at me.

"Like my rapid descent special?" he asked with a grin.

Chris had stayed behind to rig the elevator so Whitworth and Denning stepped into space. He set the relays to activate the elevator light in Whitworth's office and open the outer doors while he held the elevator on forty-eight.

"Very nice, Chris, but guess what? We got two out of three. Price wasn't there."

"Damn. Then who was the other person I heard?"

"You won't believe this. Denning."

"Whoa! Tell me later. We've gotta go."

I told him to wait a minute while I put the office back in order. I unlocked the dining room and office doors and jumped into the elevator. In under a minute, we piled into Riley's helicopter and buckled out seatbelts. We were off the pad by 1:37 P.M., almost twenty minutes before the Atlanta drug bust.

The Phoenix security team got an alert exactly thirty minutes after I disconnected Whitworth's panic alarm. They sealed off all exits from the building and rallied at the garage sublevel in front of Whitworth's private elevator. It did not respond to calls, and there was an "out of service" message on their handhelds. As they turned to the stairwell, the last man thought he heard a *whoosh* and two virtually simultaneous thuds from inside the shaft. He waited a second, thinking the elevator was back in service, but ran up the stairs when nothing happened.

The takedown of the Boeing Business Jet in Atlanta happened as expected, and the DEA came away with 2,170 pounds of cocaine. The senior agent took the pilot into custody and escorted him from the airfield. He said nothing until they were inside the Black Crown Victoria.

"Mr. Payton, it has been a pleasure to work with you," the agent said. "I can't thank you enough for delivering this operation to us. We prepaid your round-trip ticket to Cape Town and your thirty day hotel stay. Plus, there's $700,000 in cash in the briefcase. You might want to open a bank account at some point as you know how we feel about cash transactions. Good luck."

"Thanks. I'm looking forward to a vacation."

August Payton shook the agent's hand and accepted the briefcase. Although it was a great deal of money, nothing would bring Dave Anderson back. Payton sucked it up and controlled his rage that morning in Dávila's garden when Anderson's fate became crystal clear. He tried to kill Dávila several times shortly thereafter, but was not able to get close enough to him. That left Payton with no alternative but to finger an operation to the authorities. The satisfaction of revenge was short-lived when he discovered that Dávila was found shot in his home. His mind drifted to South Africa and the beautiful women. The lovely lilt in their voices did wonderful things for him. He would soon toast his buddy, as well as the man who sent Dávila on to another place.

74

Five weeks after the activities in Michigan and Chicago, I met in Washington with senior FBI, DEA, and CIA officials for the better part of a day to discuss recent events. Their desire to debrief me was at least in part professional courtesy because of my association with Phoenix. I suspected they also wanted to see if I could help them tie up any loose ends. A high-ranking official from each agency was at the table, as was FBI Legat Newman who flew in from Santiago, the FBI Assistant Director for the Counterterrorism Division, the DCI for the CIA Counterterrorist Center, and the Undersecretary of the Treasury, responsible for the Office of Terrorism and Financial Intelligence. Also at the meeting was Jay Mansour, a two star, and one colonel. No one from the National Counterterrorism Center or the National Security Service was able to attend.

Federal agents seized Whitworth's laptop after the Atlanta bust, but their eagerness to extract data proved fatal. The agents tried to boot up the machine on the scene rather than send it to the Bureau's systems experts. Sophisticated security measures deleted all data files and destroyed the hard drive after two invalid log-on attempts. The e-mails that I had lifted from Raúl's computer revealed little because they were encrypted, and the FBI could not reconstruct the algorithm that translated the random ten digit codes to e-mail addresses.

Authorities interviewed Steven Price and found him extremely cooperative. He turned over his laptop computer as well as all the files in his fireproof safe. The FBI report noted that Price's office laptop had the standard corporate security package and not the extremely sophisticated measures found on Whitworth's computer. The report further observed that the laptop and all the fireproof safe files contained nothing but official Phoenix corporate business. The insurance company fire report listed the complete destruction of one personal laptop and a desktop computer plus dozens of computer diskettes and CDs. Price was not a suspect, and all fingers pointed to Raúl and Whitworth as the architects of various illegal schemes.

Law enforcement knew that several deaths were directly related to the illicit drug operation Raúl ran under the cover of his own companies and Phoenix's subsidiaries. He ordered both me and DEA Chief of Operations Simpson killed to protect that scheme. The NSA compared the sat call mentioning Simpson to a recorded speech Raúl gave in La Paz and determined that one of the voices on the phone was Raúl's. The other voice on the line was unrecognizable. The two-star noted how convenient it was that the satellite provider was a Phoenix subsidiary.

Neither the FBI nor the DEA could explain Raúl's or Dávila's deaths, guessing it was drug barons settling accounts. My part in both murders accompanied Denning and Whitworth to their graves. The authorities could, however, explain Felipe Torres. The DEA Attaché did not go bad; he was bad from the start. A DEA agent had killed his brother in a Santa Cruz bar fight. He and his Bolivian-American mother moved to the U.S., and she raised him under her maiden name in Tucson. Torres joined the DEA to return to Bolivia to destroy the agency from within and to enrich himself—and get revenge.

Michigan police found six bodies in a black Suburban at a Lake Michigan picnic area a few miles from my cottage. They estimated the men died about the time I rented a car in Pellston the day before the FBI raided the Phoenix offices in Chicago. Five of the deceased were known "security consultants" from the Southwest who worked as a high-powered hit team. The sixth was Ilidio "Nacho" Quevedo, employed by Raúl and Dávila, a man with substantial weapons and explosives experience. A raid on his La Paz house revealed that he planted the Semtex in my Mitsubishi. The FBI man said a couple of the victims had been strangled or cut, and multiple 240 grain carbine rounds and 9mm pistol rounds killed the rest. The Army colonel said two men appeared to have been dead-checked, which they found unusual in a non-war zone. The wounds implied that the shooters meant to kill, not wound.

Within hours of discovering Whitworth's body, the FBI identified John Denning's. Initially they suspected Denning was in Chicago to discuss the attempt on my life and security measures to prevent future attacks on expatriate executives. That theory did not last long. Shortly before he died, Whitworth's secretary placed a call to Steven Price, inadvertently hit the Record button on her tape recorder, and then went to lunch. Price hung up when they were done, but Whitworth neglected to hit the Off button on his speaker phone. The result was a revealing eight minute tape of Whitworth's and Denning's lunch conversation.

Whitworth was the Phoenix point man covering for Raúl at the corporate level. Denning monitored operations in Latin America on the ground, though neither Raúl nor Torres knew he was Phoenix's insurance of last resort. His role explained his tenure in Bolivia. Diplomatic postings were normally two years with a possible third year before a mandatory move. The State Department had already confirmed Denning for a third year. Extraordinarily, they slotted him for a fourth year and had him on track to be the next Deputy Chief of Mission—a move unheard of for an RSO. His long tenure derived from Phoenix's involvement in eradication and Whitworth's convincing State that he was critical to the program's long-term success. All of that ensured Denning's privileged status, long postings, and promotions in La Paz.

The tape revealed that Denning was fed up with working for a quarter of his private sector salary and having his living allowance cut every year to support "career diplomatic morons." He was ecstatic when Whitworth told him his current annual bonus would be almost two million dollars. The tape ended as a visitor interrupted their lunch, but the FBI found no record of anyone in the office suite except the secretaries. If that were not strange enough, no one knew how Whitworth and Denning fell to their deaths. The elevator technicians said it was a freak accident, one in a million.

Steven Price, who enjoyed high esteem before the debacle, came out smelling like a rose. He took over as interim CEO after Whitworth died and coordinated the search for Whitworth's replacement as well as his own, since he would soon retire to spend more time with his family. He would, however, retain his ownership position in Phoenix and stay on five years as the senior board member to oversee the transition process and exercise oversight. No scandal touched Price, and the press was genuinely sorry for him. They marveled at how he held up so well under the stress. Raúl's activity using Phoenix to run a drug operation was major news in the world press, and Price turned an untenable situation to his advantage. Though he was not a suspect, some expected such a whirlwind of corporate scandal to taint him. It did not.

Price was in form when he spoke to Capitol Hill legislators on live television a week before my meeting in D.C. He thanked his Washington friends for letting him discuss the issues in front of the American people. The FBI concluded that Raúl abused his position to enrich himself, skimming millions from a legitimate Phoenix service contract and running a drug operation worth hundreds of millions. He conned his closest friends and took advantage of U.S. laws and regulations to hide his activity with creative deal structuring and accounting.

The active role of Barry Leiffer, Phoenix's audit partner, appalled Price. Under Whitworth's supervision, Leiffer worked with Phoenix and its banks to structure and account for investments, acquisitions, financings, and joint ventures out of the public and regulatory purview. It was no coincidence, Price speculated, that Whitworth paid Leiffer over a million dollars a year from his discretionary fund. Finally, Price was shocked by the lengths to which Whitworth and Leiffer went to hide questionable activity from him. He extended his heartfelt condolences to Leiffer's family on his unfortunate death in a car accident on a skiing vacation, only three days before federal authorities were to question him.

Price said he was deeply hurt that an old friend, Raúl, and a colleague of long standing, Whitworth, betrayed his trust. More than one observer noticed Price's artful pause to take a deep breath at that point. The sympathy was palpable, almost overwhelming. As much as it hurt him, Price said Raúl's behavior was a personal character flaw neither he nor the government could correct. Government could, however, punish people who engaged in political and financial abuses. He spent the next half hour making "humble suggestions" for legislation to prevent similar corporate transgressions in the future. He understood the senators were busy with affairs of state, but asked them to consider his recommendations. He closed saying it sliced him to the core that evil people like Whitworth and Raúl not only ran drugs but also deceived Phoenix management and employees, the U.S. government, and the American people. It was a perfectly amazing performance.

Raúl's and Whitworth's ability to create a new model of the drug trade under the cover of legitimate activities impressed everyone in the room. Even more intriguing were the additional variables they introduced. They knew Latin American governments could not simultaneously fight terrorists and the drug trade. Whitworth tipped the balance in his favor by funding Latin American terrorists to divert resources from the war on drugs.

The intelligence agencies estimated Raúl and Whitworth channeled thirty to forty million dollars a year to terrorist groups throughout South America, as well as some incipient subversive and drug gang activity in Central America. They also suspected Raúl had a number of intelligence agencies, politicians, and military officers on his payroll. That, however, would be much harder to prove. He covered money movements well, but the U.S. Treasury discovered that he used a U.S. organization called GEM as a conduit for some transfers. GEM was held blameless, but was more than ever on law enforcement's watch list. The Treasury undersecretary said the activity would have been hard to detect, even if they had looked for it. His group had learned lessons, and would use them to develop procedures to detect similar operations.

Following the cash, U.S. authorities suspected Raúl in a series of attacks. Money funneled to Sendero bought the attack on the Excelsior Palace Hotel, strikes against airports in Ecuador and Peru, and destruction of several bridges in the countryside. The MST blew up the Bolivia-to-Brazil gas pipeline, several small power generation facilities in Recife, and two auto manufacturing plants in São Paulo. The Bolivian COB funded country-wide strikes, built a training facility with the FARC, and armed an indigenous paramilitary insurgency. FARC money catalyzed a Libyan connection that attempted a nuclear attack on the U.S. No one thought Raúl or Whitworth masterminded the attack—it was an unintended consequence.

Although getting lost in the details was easy, authorities found three issues particularly disturbing. The first was that a duplicitous U.S. corporation inserted itself so successfully into U.S. government affairs, the illicit drug business, and narco-terrorist campaigns. Phoenix was one of the most respected and well-run companies in the world. If that happened with the best America had to offer, what was to prevent it from happening again with lesser outfits?

Second was the extent to which terror organizations no longer let borders, differences in culture, religion, ideology, or even language get in their way. A dedicated cadre of terrorists wanted attention, acknowledgement, and recognition. Others wanted political power, control, and money. Some just liked to blow things up. They were cults of terror with smart leaders manipulating misguided and faithful followers. Regardless of motives, objectives, or dedication, they were all businesses that needed income and funding to survive and thrive. Terror organizations would consider any joint venture, partnership, or merger to further their objectives. Even groups like the violent Islamic leagues that once preferred to work in isolation would join with others. They were not suicidal maniacs, but instead people bent on achieving their goals.

The third and most obvious concern was that North Korea built and sold sophisticated low-yield nuclear devices. I asked how they acquired the capability to produce such weapons. Before proceeding, the FBI reminded me that I signed an ironclad non-disclosure agreement before the meeting and that nothing discussed today would ever leave the room. I acknowledged the fact, and stated that I understood my obligation.

The North Korean devices were slightly modified but improved versions of U.S. models, built almost exactly from U.S. plans. The U.S. deployed the device until 1986, then took it out of service. The FBI believed a senior scientist, fired from his U.S. government weapons job, sold detailed Medium Atomic Demolition Munition plans to the Chinese in 1987 or 1988 and that China in turn sold the plans and matériel to North Korea. CIA knew Hassan Ali bought and sold the nukes, but they could not establish a direct North Korean link. The captured Libyans, after considerable encouragement, fingered their handlers. A CIA paramilitary team found them dead in Guatemala City. There were no other leads.

The FBI asked me several follow-up questions about my dealings with Raúl, Whitworth, Torres, Denning, and Price. I added a few minor details about Raúl, but nothing substantial.

"Richard, is there anything else that you want to add to this?" the FBI asked.

I saw this as my last chance to come clean and tell all. I suspected that the people around the table knew more than they were letting on. If they wanted me to tell all, they would have broached the subject earlier with handcuffs, an arrest warrant, and an interrogation room. I decided to let sleeping dogs lie. Just as I helped Price, Whitworth, and Denning, perhaps I also helped the good guys. Who knows? Maybe I was wrong. In any event, I was not in the mood to trouble the waters. I felt no remorse for anything. I was done with coming clean, my family had been through enough, I did more than my share to get some bad guys, and the bad guys got what they deserved. All but one.

"Not much to say, except that a terrorist doesn't always dress or act the way your hard wiring might think. Corporations are the same way. I think notions of respectability die hard in our society. That's why sharp dressers who speak well get away with so much. The fact is that many corporations and those who run them lack morals or ethics. It's all just one big game to them, and they play to win no matter what. Just like terrorists, they believe they're above and beyond the law. The other thing is that all the laws, rules, regulations, and controls in the world won't keep evil people from doing bad things. They will always find a way, and you'll find yourself doing nothing but reacting to their next move. No matter how much you want it, you can't guarantee a crime-free or a terror-free society. You can't protect every single asset or person. We have to accept that and deal with it as adults. Americans say that the world changed on September 11th. The world didn't change; we just became more aware of it. There are people who hate us, and we have to understand that in order to deal with it. The world's a dangerous place."

"So, what will you do now Mr. Blackstone?" the CIA representative asked.

"Well, I don't have a job with Phoenix, but they readily agreed to a generous separation package," I said, thinking of the three million dollar severance payment I declared to the U.S. Treasury, and the fifty million dollars in my Uruguayan account that the IRS would never know about. Small reward for what my family had been through. "I won't have to work for a while, so we'll probably travel a bit. We've got an invitation from an American friend to visit a ranch he recently purchased in Argentina. I think we'll take him up on his offer."

It was a shame that America would never know how good these professionals were. Only the SMU teams and a handful of civilian and military authorities knew that the U.S. had intercepted two vessels carrying nuclear weapons targeting the U.S. The rest of America was enthralled by the continuous news broadcasts describing how American commandos intercepted terrorists with small arms and conventional explosives only days before they were to attack Gulf Coast oil refineries and chemical plants.

We got up, shook hands, and everyone thanked me for my time and assistance. I would miss these exceptional people, but I knew I would see some of them again. Legat Newman and I agreed to get together when I returned to Latin America. The senior CIA rep asked me to say hello to Chris. Small world. Mansour gave me a business card and asked that I look him up in Ciudad del Este. He hoped I could get to my friend's ranch as he was familiar with that part of the Argentine *campo* and thought I would enjoy it. Even smaller world.

I looked forward to seeing my family and getting some rest. I was going to miss being in the hunt, and there was still some hunting to do. Steven Price was still out there. The problem was, I had nothing on him. Not yet.

My cab driver to the airport was a Guatemalan who had been in D.C. for twelve years and loved the U.S. He could not understand why people would want to harm this country. I told him I could not understand it either. The radio news brief ended ten minutes from the airport, and he tuned in the classical jazz hour. I heard a familiar song and asked him to turn up the volume. The sweet melody of Moonlight Serenade filled the car. I took a deep breath and saw the smile on Julie's face and her open arms that would greet me in several hours. We would have a candlelight dinner and soft music tonight. I would pull her close, kiss her gently, and whisper that I loved her. I would tell her she was safe, that I was there to protect her. I am coming home my lovely Julie. I am coming home.

75

4 Months Later

It was a brilliant blue sky Washington day with radiant sun and a cool light breeze. An unusually large number of administration and government officials, high-ranking military, invited guests, the press corps, and an exceptionally heavy contingent of security packed the Rose Garden. Everyone was waiting for the president. He arrived as scheduled and took the podium quietly and comfortably.

"Ladies and gentlemen, I would like to thank all of you for coming today. I guess it's not easy to turn down an invitation from the president to come to the Rose Garden, is it?" He flashed a smile. "America has endured some trying times recently. We are challenged each day by those who want to harm us. I would like to thank our national, state, and local leaders as well as law enforcement officers for their efforts to keep our citizens safe and secure. I would especially like to express my gratitude to our men and women in uniform, as they have all distinguished themselves. My thanks finally to all Americans who understand that we require certain sacrifices of them in times like these.

"My responsibility as president involves many duties to ensure our citizens' safety, and that obligation has become increasingly urgent in the last several years. One of my duties is to create and oversee an organization that enables us to efficiently and effectively detect, assess, and interdict terrorist activity worldwide before it affects American citizens. For many years, the business world has understood the need to view their affairs from a global perspective. The United States is about as global as they come."

The comment generated some laughter, and the president looked as though he might ad lib. He stayed on course.

"For many years, our intelligence and law enforcement capabilities were confined to narrow and separate domestic and international silos. Each organization functioned well within those constraints, but we could no longer afford to operate that way with American lives at risk. We will take all necessary measures to make sure our people feel safe. Part of that effort includes restructuring and streamlining our intelligence systems, our anti-terror capabilities, and our national security apparatus whenever we believe it is necessary.

"The first step in that process took place several years ago when we created the Department of Homeland Security. DHS's charge was to coordinate the security and intelligence efforts to safeguard U.S. citizen's right here at home. The second step was the passage of the intelligence reform legislation and the creation of the cabinet level post of Director of National Intelligence. The director has full budget, administrative, and operational responsibility for all of the nation's intelligence agencies. The third step was the implementation of the vast majority of the White House WMD commission recommendations to further strengthen our intelligence capabilities. Among the measures adopted, we endorsed the creation of a National Counterproliferation Center, a National Security Service within the FBI, and the reorganization of the management of human intelligence at CIA. We have made great progress in a short period of time, but I believe that our results have been limited because our structural changes have focused narrowly and exclusively on the coordination of intelligence collection and analysis. To derive the maximum benefit from our integrated intelligence efforts, we need to take the next step to centralize the operational control of our national security apparatus. Only then will we see the results we expect to make America safe. Towards that end, today I am announcing the creation of a new position and a new office.

"The new position of Secretary of National Security will be responsible for crafting and implementing all aspects of U.S. national security policy. This position will have the full budget, legal, administrative, strategic, and operational responsibility for all U.S. law enforcement, intelligence, and security agencies. The directors and heads of these individual agencies—the Attorney General, the Director of National Intelligence, as well as all others—will report on direct line to the Secretary of National Security. The Secretaries of State and Defense and the Chairman of the Joint Chiefs will report directly to the secretary on any and all security matters. The current National Security Council and its members will no longer report to me, but will instead report to the secretary in an advisory capacity only and will serve at the secretary's pleasure. Finally, the secretary will be the point of contact for the heads of any and all congressional law enforcement, intelligence, security, and military committees.

"The Vice President and I, along with the Secretary of National Security, will form the Office of the President Security Council. OPSC will serve as the lightening rod to move efficiently, expeditiously, and decisively to act on any and all matters of national security. By centralizing control and reducing the number of decision-makers, we will more effectively respond to, confront, and overcome the threats facing America today.

"Understanding the extremely urgent need for this new position, key members of Congress assure me of a fast-track confirmation. I would particularly like to thank Senators Carlson of New York and Foster of California for their assistance and their pledges of support.

"This position requires someone with broad experience and a keen intellect, as well as great courage, dedication, foresight, and integrity. It calls for a person with the private sector experience to structure organizations to achieve complex goals and objectives. This person must also have the public sector experience to understand the role of government in today's world. We are fortunate to have such a person to take on this challenge and responsibility. Those who have worked with him know how capable he is, and those who have not will soon discover he is unique. I would like to introduce the Secretary Designate of National Security, Steven Price."

The president stepped away from the podium and shook Price's hand. The applause from the Capitol Hill contingent was particularly strong. Price strode confidently to the podium, and it was apparent he would not speak from prepared notes. He was in his element.

"Mr. President, Mr. Vice President, members of Congress, our military chiefs, other invited guests, and of course my very good friends in the press corps: I am honored to be here and privileged to be the recipient of the trust and confidence that the president has invested in me. I would like to share with you several things that . . ."

Price was a master speaker and held his audience close as he described his plans for his new position. He finished in slightly less than five minutes and thanked the president. As he stepped back and listened to the president's concluding remarks, Price marveled at how well everything was going. He was almost where he deserved to be, where he wanted to be. Almost.

76

One Month Later

Rafik Hamza flipped through the final pages of *The Economist Intelligence Unit Angola Country Report* as the TAP Air Portugal stewardess brought him a second glass of champagne. It was the early morning after an all-night flight from Lisbon, but he preferred bubbly to orange juice. He smiled and drained half the glass with one gulp as he closed the report and tossed it into the open briefcase at his feet. It fell on top of the EIU reports on Angola, Chad, Mozambique, Namibia, and Nigeria. He had read enough harsh statistical reality about Africa for now. Within an hour, he would touch down in his new home of Luanda, Angola. The civil war in the former Portuguese colony had been over for several years, and Hamza saw a brave new frontier of economic opportunity. He also saw a new safe-haven from which to conduct terror campaigns. Adventurers, risk-takers, and investors of all kinds were coming to Angola. Hamza would fit right in.

As he gazed at the dark blue Atlantic waters along the West African coastline below, he wondered what went wrong with his perfectly planned nuclear attack on the United States. His team planned and executed the operation to the last detail and covered their tracks by eliminating everyone in the information chain. He knew there had been no leaks. Hamza never before lamented killing anyone, but he regretted ordering the death of Hassan Ali and his son. The Americans were closing in on Ali, and it was only a matter of time before they got him. Hamza's informants confirmed that the Americans stormed Ali's compound only hours after his own hit team had left. That was too close for comfort.

Hamza knew someone made a mistake or committed an indiscretion to give them away. There was no other explanation, but he had no idea who or what. The Americans were smart, but not that smart. Hamza's sources told him the *Evening Star* hit team revealed the names of their handlers after two weeks of interrogation. No matter. Hamza killed the handlers the day the *Evening Star* and *Flying Eagle* set sail. Hamza did not know if the Americans had found the North Korean general, or if they had even established that link. He should have killed the general, but had no idea where he was.

The Americans probably knew that Ali sold two nukes, and not just the one on the *Evening Star*. Hamza was glad he held insurance by deploying only one real nuke and putting an inert device on the *Flying Eagle*. His Argentine team on the *Eagle* did not know they had a fake; only Hamza knew the complete plan. The other nuclear device was safe in a location known only to Hamza. He reflected on recent operations and recalled his grandfather's teachings to never forget, to always remember the past, and to take it forward. Wise words and Hamza would compartmentalize future operations even more than previously. He would keep his past in front of him.

Hamza's route from Ciudad del Este to Manaus, to Lisbon, and finally to Luanda was circuitous. He avoided calling attention to himself and would settle comfortably in his new African home to run a continental restaurant and a development company. His team members would also establish themselves in new locations until it was time to restart operations. Ahmad was in Canada, Faysal in Costa Rica, and Mohammed in Hungary. They would contact each other in six months and then only via encrypted e-mail. Although he looked forward to getting back into the game, there was no sense pushing the envelope when the Americans were chasing the nuke trail hard. They were bothersome, but they had no idea who they were looking for. There was no rush. Rafik Hamza was a patient man and he had plenty of time.

About the Author

Thomas Graves is an American and has lived and worked in Africa, Europe, and Latin America. He received his undergraduate and graduate degrees in the United States, and has experience as an executive in several multinational corporations in the international oil and gas, engineering and construction, and project development fields. He has also worked as an independent consultant and entrepreneur in these same fields as well as in providing security services and solutions to high risk clients and governments around the world. Mr. Graves currently resides in South Africa.